DIAGRAMMING THE BIG IDEA

As a beginning design student, you need to learn to think like a designer, to visualize ideas and concepts, as well as objects. In *Diagramming the Big Idea,* Jeffrey Balmer and Michael T. Swisher illustrate how you can create and use diagrams to clarify your understanding of both particular projects and organizing principles and ideas. With accessible, step-by-step exercises that interweave diagrams, drawings and virtual models, the authors clearly show you how to compose meaningful and useful diagrams.

As you follow the development of the four project groups drawn from the authors' teaching, you will become familiar with architectural composition concepts such as proportion, site, form, hierarchy and spatial construction. In addition, description and demonstration essays extend concepts to show you more examples of the methods used in the projects. Whether preparing for a desk critique, or any time when a fundamental insight can help to resolve a design problem, this book is your essential studio resource.

Jeffrey Balmer is an assistant professor of architecture at the University of North Carolina at Charlotte.

Michael T. Swisher is an associate professor of architecture at the University of North Carolina at Charlotte.

DIAGRAMMING THE BIG IDEA
Methods for Architectural Composition

Jeffrey Balmer
&
Michael T. Swisher

Routledge
Taylor & Francis Group

NEW YORK AND LONDON

First published 2012
by Routledge
711 Third Avenue, New York, NY 10017

Simultaneously published in the UK
by Routledge
2 Park Square, Milton Park, Abingdon, Oxon OX14 4RN

Routledge is an imprint of the Taylor & Francis Group, an informa business

Library of Congress Cataloging in Publication Data
Balmer, Jeffrey.
Diagramming the big idea : methods for architectural composition / Jeffrey Balmer and
Michael T. Swisher.
pages cm
Includes index.
1. Architectural design. 2. Architecture--Composition, proportion, etc. I. Swisher,
Michael T. II. Title.
NA2750.B3225 2012
720.28'4--dc23
2012004984

ISBN: 978-0-415-89408-1 (hbk)
ISBN: 978-0-415-89409-8 (pbk)
ISBN: 978-0-203-10359-3 (ebk)

Typeset in Adobe Chaparral Pro and Myriad Pro
by Jeffrey D. Balmer and Michael T. Swisher

Printed and bound in India by Replika Press Pvt. Ltd.

for Jean and for Harper
                    J.B.
for Leslie Laskey
                    M.T.S.

DIAGRAMMING THE BIG IDEA
Contents

FOREWORD

Architects don't make buildings

Architects make diagrams not buildings. Most of these diagrams organize
the details of how someone else will make the building and architects refer to
them as *drawings*. Even as we drift toward the virtual, designers refer to the
building's documents – its 'blueprints' – as contract *drawings*. However, if we
wish to be accurate we would deem even these as *diagrams* – defined in the
Oxford English Dictionary as 'Figures composed of lines, serving to illustrate a
definition or statement, or to aid in the proof of a proposition.'

Architects draw lines to define a proposition. The proposition is architecture.

History

Most books have a story behind their writing. Ours begins four years ago with
an epiphany – a realization that, in the absence of any specific instruction,
schools expect architecture students to know how to diagram. Given its fundamental role in design, Jeff discovered – much to his surprise – the absence
of useful texts on diagramming. He suggested to Michael that such a book
needed writing.

Michael meanwhile completed *What We Do Now*, a treatise on our first-
semester curriculum. As a painter, he believed that a primer on diagramming
must also include the fundamentals of visual composition. Together, we realized that the issue went further than that of diagrams. Our entire system of
education values text over image – it neither celebrates nor cultivates visual
aptitude. As a result, novice architecture students confront enormous challenges, faced as they are with an entirely unfamiliar mode of knowledge –
what we call *design thinking*.

Beyond the immediate purview of problem solving, design comprises a
search for possibilities. As described throughout this book, design thinking
defines a method for engaging the world through observation and analysis.
For designers, observation is necessarily extra-verbal, even when we stress the
requirement to articulate our findings. Design analysis, though methodical, is
seldom linear. It requires the synthesis of deductive *and* imaginative reasoning, both shrewd scrutiny *and* fevered speculation.

The result of our discussions led us to focus on diagramming – making visible the abstractions that order and support the phenomena of the built environment. Moreover, as the diagram shares conceptual space with the PARTI,
we adopt the 'Big Idea' as a foil and as a suitcase to package student learning. Above all, our goal is to make explicit to students what they are learning,
why they are learning it and how to internalize such lessons for their lifelong
development as designers.

The structure

Our first-year program uses a project structure that follows an intentional skills-based sequence. We articulate design projects as daily tasks that teach specific skills, with a reasoned sequence of design strategies and tactics as context. Skills are thus central to method. The context of strategies and tactics represents an unabashed entreaty for order. We teach our students how to make things through order and pattern. Moreover, we teach them in a transparent, illustrative manner, responsive to feedback. That order, in turn, defines the architecture of our learning outcomes.

On a practical level, the assignments embody several broad concepts or procedural themes. We organize them through recursive development. The lessons build an increasingly complex matrix of design experience. The basic structure of the first semester follows three procedural themes and moves from figure-ground, to plan and proportion, and thence to structure and volume. In the second semester, we turn to the study and use of precedent and companion issues of site and landscape.

Educational intent

The structure of both our teaching and this book also reflects our audience – students beginning the study of architecture. This leads to three important considerations.

- Where do the students come from?
- Where do they need to go?
- What skills and capacities do they need to construct a suitcase for the trip?

Because students do not arrive uniformly equipped for the study of architecture, it is of paramount importance that their first course of study furnishes a consistent preparation. Those familiar with the language of instructional design will recognize this as a request for probable outcomes. After all, if we must judge students on how well they accomplish tasks, we ought to define those tasks clearly. In the studio and this book, tasks – as practices – commingle with defined skills.

The first skills discussed in our narrative address higher-order concept skills. With roots in the literature of visual psychology, they focus on the perception and implementation of order. Order leads to pattern and ideas of pattern. Thus, our first discussions confront recognizing patterns and pattern systems, identifying useful strategies and tactics, and diagramming patterns with particular intent.

Mastery of design thinking takes more time than any single course can provide. However, the capacity for judging order in a constructed environment builds from simple cognitive steps using diagrams. In this book, those steps include: inferring structure from formal order, recognizing scale within structure and imagining space through visualizing order – all of which lead to an understanding of architecture.

The role of examples

One of the tools present throughout our first-year program is the deliberate and extensive use of images and models as exemplars for the project sequence. Models and drawings – digital and hand-made – form a particular background for the daily assignment and lectures. Together with photographs, they provide a consistent visual reference for study. After nearly seven years there are a lot of them – at last count over six thousand. This profusion led us to begin the process of outlining this book. It also brought with it our most difficult task: translating an overabundance of images from lectures and assignments into a more compact form.

Although we base this narrative on our teaching, this book remains an independent discussion. It draws from but does not replicate our classes. The book describes diagramming as an intellectual method of analysis and action in service of architectural study in general. We have attempted to address a general audience and diverse reasons for study by describing an analytical method that has broad utility and relevance.

Much of architectural learning occurs in reaction to individual work. In studio discussion, the creative output of the students serves as the cause of important commentary. Student questions also create important learning opportunities and sponsor rich dialogue wherein everyone – including the instructor – finds inspiration.

In addition, when showing drawings, models and photographs, we routinely point, zoom in on and explain various features, supplemented by improvised drawings on chalkboard or paper. Digital technology expands these actions to include on-the-fly animation and live sections. In contrast, a book remains a fixed resource. It follows a predetermined path. It manifests an idealized if not ideal discourse.

In response to that challenge, we integrate into our text, thematic asides – DISCUSSIONS – and allied materials – DEMONSTRATIONS. These represent some of our more fruitful extemporaneous moments. To adopt the lesson structure to the book, we found it necessary not only to edit the lessons, but also to reformulate and reinvent most of the illustrations for the book.

Figure 1: Teaching is an interactive exercise.

Making the images serve

As teachers, we use our images in both printed handouts and digital presentations. In response, we have developed particular techniques and practices for developing and using images, relying on Adobe® *Creative Suite*® and *Vector Magic*, a clever autotrace program. We have developed most of our diagrams as layered *Illustrator*® files, allowing for rapid conversion from color to grayscale, and to various sizes. We adapted and processed photographs using *Photoshop*®, *Vector Magic* and *Illustrator*® in order to reduce their visual complexity in accordance with their captions. This process served for hand drawings, maps and engravings as well.

We used two applications to create digital models. The first, *Strata Design 3D*, served to develop the majority of our virtual model renderings. Some we subsequently exported to the second program, *Google SketchUp Pro*, to render as vector images. *SketchUp* was also instrumental in preparing the three-dimensional diagrams shown in CHAPTER 9. For layout in preparation for publication, we used Adobe® *InDesign*.

Last words

We have one clear hope for this book: to improve and expand the discourse of design. Adapting our methods to a new format – from the classroom to a book – sharpened our understanding of the material. By sending it out into a wider realm, we aim to prompt further discussion and feedback. We encourage readers from a wide range of places and perspectives to share their impressions. Remaining open to that possibility leaves us with an intoxicating sense of potential.

ACKNOWLEDGEMENTS

This book reflects the efforts of a host of good people. They deserve public recognition.

First, we wish to thank Wendy Fuller, our editor at Routledge. We thank Wendy for her expertise and her wisdom. Most of all, we give thanks for her belief in this project, and for providing the possibility of its very existence. We thank our managing editor, Laura Williamson, for her professionalism and enduring patience, as we struggled toward the timely completion of the manuscript while maintaining a busy teaching schedule. Proof-reader, Kate Manson, provided a keen and careful review that helped hone the look and feel of the book's text and visual material, making them both clearer. We also wish to express our sincere appreciation to Joanna Endell-Cooper, our production editor, for her constant wisdom and encouragement while readying the text and images for publication.

Among our colleagues at the College of Arts + Architecture at UNC Charlotte, we wish to thank Dean Kenneth Lambla for his endorsement of excellence in first year teaching, first as a colleague, then chair and continuing into his current position. We thank Associate Dean Lee Gray for his good advice and good cheer. Special appreciation also goes to Chris Jarrett, Director of the School of Architecture. Without his encouragement and support, the first-year teaching program would simply not be what it is.

During the past eight years, a group of faculty worked together to define and construct an integrated pedagogy of particular clarity and organization. The structure continues to refine and change, however, there is recognition due for their contributions.

The first-year program's teaching structure is straightforward. Each semester, two permanent faculty members teach in studio and one in the visual studies class – a.k.a. skills. In addition, two adjuncts teach studio sections in both semesters. The four studio sections share assignments, teaching materials, lectures, critiques and other activities. There is much to coordinate and abundant opportunity to collaborate.

We are two of the permanent faculty members in the first semester studio. Past visiting colleagues have included Jason Slatinsky, Jeremy Fisher, Christine Abbott, Nora Wendl and Kristina Luce. They all helped to make the College, the School and the first-year richer, better and more effective. They left their mark on the program. Acknowledgement of our debt to them is too little, even if it is all we have to give here.

Our current adjuncts are Landon Robinson and Christopher Campbell. Aside from teaching studio, they have improved the visual studies component of the program beyond measure. They also participated substantively in our examination of Kahn's *Exeter Library*. Our undergraduate assistant, Ryan

Miller, developed an obsession with researching and drawing that building, making everything that followed more precise. Anastasia Krasnoslobodtseva assisted with our modeling of *Unity Temple.*

In earlier iterations of the program, Peter Wong played the role of lead in the second semester. He is an exceptional teacher, colleague and friend. His contribution to our dialogue remains generous and noteworthy.

Greg Snyder, for five years a chief collaborator in both studio and skills classes deserves special recognition and praise. He is a gifted and careful teacher and a principled colleague who radiates poised energy. His inspired participation in the development of the projects presented herein was steadfast and vital. His support, counsel and insights are everywhere in what we continue. We thank him warmly.

Apart from colleagues at our school, several others inspired us and provided encouragement. Simon Unwin has been both an inspiration and a boon. During his memorable visit to our Beginning Design conference, he took time out to share his experience as teacher turned author. Moreover, he generously reviewed the materials that led to this book.

As a final note, Michael once more acknowledges his secret weapon, Mary Lou Albano, PHD, his touchstone in all things pedagogical. She vets his intuitions about teaching and keeps him grounded and on task, all the while remaining charmed and magical.

Jeff Balmer and Michael T. Swisher
Charlotte, February, 2012

CHAPTER 1
Introduction

Read me first!

Approaching the study of architecture can be a daunting prospect. Though we spend the majority of our lives inside and among buildings, the processes that underlie their design remain impenetrable to most, even to those who profess a keen interest in the built environment.

We might ask why these processes remain obscure, even while the products of architectural design appear all around us. Three common answers to that question suggest themselves. First, the criteria for realizing buildings are intrinsically complex, comprising the aspirations of client and designer, the utility and comfort of intended occupants, and compliance with myriad legal and life-safety regulations. Second, the process of designing and building engages the technical expertise of a wide range of specialists, including designers, engineers, builders, financiers and public officials, and this network of expertise lies beyond the direct experience of the rest of us. Third, architects indulge in bewildering jargon that renders their discourse largely unintelligible to others.

All of the suggestions above have merit. However, the primary reason that design thinking remains inscrutable to most is, in our opinion, the same reason that it provides such a perplexing challenge to students beginning the study of architecture: the fundamental alpha-numeric bias of our education system. Reading, writing and arithmetic alone do not and cannot provide the means for evaluating form and space. Despite living in a culture commonly described as 'visually oriented', few learn to analyze what, and how, we see. At the same time, each of us shares in an innate understanding of order in the perception and comprehension of the world around us. This native sensibility can, and should, form the basis for engaging the fundamental principles that underpin architectural composition.

This book is the product of almost fifty years of combined experience teaching architecture. The essential challenge faced by beginning students – learning to think as a designer – shaped our efforts. We have come to believe that the most effective way to introduce DESIGN THINKING is to study and practice one of the primary means by which experienced designers analyze and generate architecture: through the use of diagrams. Architects create diagrams in order to clarify their understanding of both particular projects and general principles. Diagrams can form the basis for analyzing existing precedents, or they may generate entirely new works of architecture.

We have written this book with the beginning design student in mind. At the same time, this work aims at a broader audience, one with a general interest in architecture. Using diagrams, drawings and virtual models, we aim to illustrate the broad reciprocity between geometric composition and order in

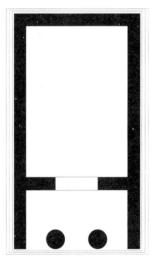

Figure 1: To the uninitiated this image may read as a stylized 'A' with a reversed *umlaut*. Someone familiar with plan conventions might recognize it as a simplified antique temple plan, in this case the *Sycyonian Treasury,* Olympia.

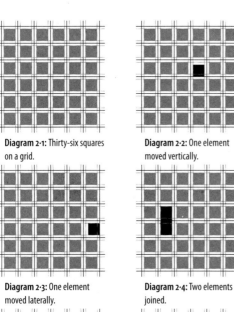

Diagram 2·1: Thirty-six squares on a grid.

Diagram 2·2: One element moved vertically.

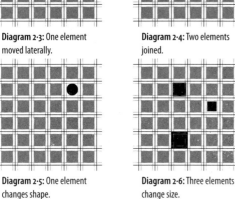

Diagram 2·3: One element moved laterally.

Diagram 2·4: Two elements joined.

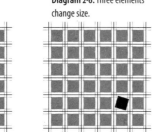

Diagram 2·5: One element changes shape.

Diagram 2·6: Three elements change size.

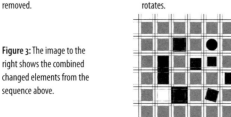

Diagram 2·7: One element removed.

Diagram 2·8: One element rotates.

Figure 3: The image to the right shows the combined changed elements from the sequence above.

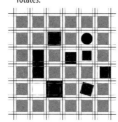

Figure 4: This image shows the changed elements alone in the context of the grid.

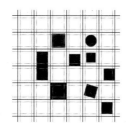

Figure 2: To the left, a figure-ground demonstration in dynamic spatial ordering: identical squares on a grid demonstrate principles of movement, combination, shape, size, removal and rotation.

architecture. The text also lays out a road map for design thinking, illustrating processes by way of exercises that begin with simple figure-ground organization and progress toward more complex spatial investigations. These exercises proceed in a manner that encourages the reader to test and to explore their premises. The book thus invites a high degree of participation – we have designed it to be engaged with as readily as we mean it to be read.

Learning to think like a designer is no small task. It calls upon faculties and patterns of thought seldom exercised by the modalities of alphanumeric education. It obliges us to perceive and to interact with our environment in unaccustomed ways, even as it requires us to recover an innate sense of order and orientation. It compels us to question all our assumptions and expectations, yet also asks that we draw deeply from hard-won experience. Perhaps most paradoxically, design thinking directs us to assess dispassionately all that surrounds us, all the while admonishing us to experience the world in a state of wonderment.

As design instructors, we confront these same challenges. In determining what – and how – to teach novice students, we feel compelled to question the way that we ourselves discovered architecture. In doing so, we have cause to interrogate any and all assumptions about best practices in beginning design pedagogy. A simple question guides our research: What is design thinking, and how do we teach it best? The degree to which our students acquire these concepts and skills leads us to another simple question: Have they acquired the ability to decide and to describe what is important in their work? Underpinning these questions is another that we ask of ourselves and bring to our students, a question so fundamental that it usually remains hidden in plain sight: What is architecture?

What is architecture?

Defining what architecture is proves to be more difficult to do than one might first imagine. Despite centuries of debate concerning architecture, its definition remains unsettled. Moreover, because other disciplines borrow the term 'architecture', its parameters inevitably vary by CONTEXT. When asked on their first day, our students offer a range of definitions, usually including the design of buildings.

The definition that we share with them on that first day is as follows: *architecture is organization toward a purpose.*

'What about buildings?' they ask. This is an excellent question. Our response goes something like this: While it is possible and desirable to build toward a purpose, it is not a foregone conclusion. Sadly, examples of buildings without clear organization or clear purpose surround us.

The alternative to these ill-conceived constructions enriches our definition. First and necessarily, architecture is a conceptual organization, an intellectual structuring. It is the means by which we give order to what is knowable. It is in this larger sense that other disciplines borrow the term architecture. Invariably, architecture denotes a system of organization, of order.

When it engages with the physical world, we say that architecture organizes environment toward a purpose. By environment, we mean the tangible, four-dimensional world that surrounds us and through which our bodies play their part. In this more tangible definition, architecture is how we make sense of the world by establishing our place within it. When we rest beneath a solitary tree in a large field, our relative spatial proximity – what Simon Unwin calls 'circles of presence' – help us make sense of our environment, whether we are conscious of doing so or not.

In this same sense, architecture can also involve the physical arrangement of environment. It is this re-ordering of the physical world that we may define further, in terms of MEASURE and MATTER. Measure comprises the dimensional attributes of form and space. Matter is the 'stuff' of the world, its materials and their intrinsic properties. Form is subject to the presence of visible matter, while space is contingent upon its absence.

The diagram, as an agent of analysis, serves to make sense of the physical environment by revealing or proposing its underlying conceptual organization. As such, a diagram may not only act to represent architecture, it constitutes architecture in the sense that it demonstrates or embodies an intellectual structuring.

The proof of architecture resides in its diagram.

Organization, order, composition

If in fact architecture is organization toward a purpose, how do we define organization? We begin to answer this by asking another question. What it is that we do when we design? In large part, design thinking constitutes generating, then evaluating, choices. The number of individual decisions that an architect makes during the design and construction of a building can easily number in the tens of thousands. Decisions made in one small part of a project will inevitably affect cascades of inter-dependent conditions. Design thinking becomes further complicated as we factor in the competing agendas of clients, contractors, and building codes. The entire enterprise may seem to risk going off the rails by virtue of its intrinsic increasing complexities.

Fortunately, help is at hand. Design thinking distinguishes architecture from haphazard, indiscriminate choice by way of ANALYSIS. An analytic structure helps to guide those myriad decisions by conceptually organizing them, allowing them to coalesce, and culminate in the creation of architecture. In turn, the agency of the diagram helps conduct analysis. Formulating diagrams provides the method by which architects analyze and organize priorities.

In a simple narrative, one might imagine a client who required a sleeping space, a living space and a kitchen, with a stipulation for two differentiated entrances and a minimal use of space. Sorting that simple list might conceiv-

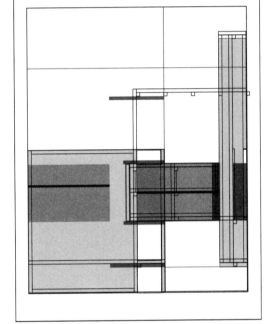

Figure 5: Diagrammatic images such as this one help the designer visualize the implied motion – the grain – within an architectural scheme.

Figure 6: Figure-ground diagrams such as the three simple courtyard schemes on the left can make initial form strategies for a design vivid to the designer. They help order compositional thinking as to overall spatial intent.

ably involve a bubble diagram, a spatial diagram, a flow diagram and others, to generate and evaluate options. Common uses also include determining and refining interactive functions prior to determining form. It starts with ORDER – the hierarchical heart of organization. Order in architecture is a FORMAL idea. Order begets COMPOSITION, and composition organizes both form and space.

The how or why of any particular organization or formal composition is the idea, literally the picture, that drives both the architecture and our judgment of it. This is what we call the BIG IDEA. There are other possible names for it.* In all cases, we recognize that form and purpose can be intertwined conceptually. Louis Sullivan coined the phrase 'form ever follows function.' The term applies to a building when that building's order facilitates human objectives. Order refers to, or directs, the form and space of a building by way of composition.

Utility, function, purpose

As architecture manifests organization toward a purpose, how might we define PURPOSE in architecture? First, purpose is a statement of ends. It reflects our sense of final state or goals. For educated Greeks, the ultimate goal was to understand and live a good life. The debate was about what was good. Modern secular architecture re-embraces this moral imperative. In either instance, we recognize that purpose makes clarity an essential part of the good, particularly good form. The further extension into the civic and moral realms is beyond the concern of beginning design.

Toward the end of the first century BCE, the Roman architect Vitruvius defined the discipline of architecture as combining *firmitas, utilitas* and *venustas* – stability, utility and beauty. Ever since, the notion of utility in architecture has been contested: it is either the essential premise for architecture, or as its proverbial fly-in-the-ointment. The question of usefulness in architecture provokes another – use to what end? Or, to quote another Roman, *cui bono?* To whose benefit? Along with beauty, *venustas*, utility is in the eye of the beholder.

Purpose allows us to avoid linking problematic associations with function, thus disabusing students of the notion that architecture is necessarily utilitarian. Purpose implies using with meaning. It denotes resolution, determination, intent. It primarily requires clarity of form and composition. Clarity defines the Big Idea.

Measure, matter, method

We have defined measure and matter as composing the physical environment, where measure comprises form and space, and matter constitutes the 'stuff' of the world. As we suggest above, order and composition shape the elements of measure. Matter, having form, follows suit. At the same time, the physical properties of matter impose their own will upon measure. Within this matrix of reciprocities, we begin to grasp the inherent complexity of design thinking, while we marvel anew at the richness of architecture.

In addition to being subject to order and composition, matter's physical properties must satisfy an additional pair of covalent criteria, what we might categorize as the performative and the palpable. The performance of any given material allows it to fulfill two fundamental roles in architecture – as structure and as skin. As structure, a material's strength is brought to bear in a number of ways: its resistance to being pushed and pulled – compression and tension – and its ability to withstand bending and breaking, its moment

* BY ANY OTHER NAME

By tradition in the ÉCOLE DES BEAUX-ARTS, the PARTI identifies the Big Idea, assumed to derive from the French *prendre parti*, literally 'to make a decision.'

Other critics suggest the term 'commanding form' as a description of the visible expression of the Big Idea. Both refer to the principal organizing aspect of an architect's design presented in the form of a basic diagram or statement of intent.

and shear. Use as skin reveals a material's ability to cover and protect its color and translucence, its malleability and permeability. The palpable qualities of a material appeal to our senses: the fragrant folds of full-grain leather, the soothing chill of polished stone, the scintillating perfection of chromed steel, and the mottled patina of hand-hewn timber, worn smooth with age.

Design & method

Architecture is also complex in the sense that it composes many parts. These may include the studs, shingle, and sheathing of a simple shed. They might comprise the mechanical, electrical and life-safety systems of an office tower. At every scale, designers select and arrange materials that fulfill the myriad components required of a building. What we call construction is the ordered assembly of these parts; their selection and arrangement form part of the broader process of design thinking.

On any given project, designers face innumerable individual decisions. Methodology, having a method of thinking, assists the designer in making choices. It may be possible to act without thought or deliberation, but it is not desirable. It may also be possible to make choices in a vacuum, as if no one had ever made a building before. However, a real architect begins by sorting through the methods of her discipline. She chooses strategies and tactics by virtue of method and in response to goals.

Any architect practicing for a length of time acquires an arsenal of design thinking and sequences of design development – a transparent method and a pattern of thought. The sum of her design thinking comprises a diagrammatic overlap to her method. This is not a means for architects to copy or repeat themselves blindly. In the best of cases, it allows the architect to analyze the connecting ideas across the range of her portfolio.

This idea of the portfolio, with its roots in the École des Beaux-Arts, still has relevance, particularly for the beginning student. It organizes projects across scales and aids in developing an approach to design and architecture. Its features should include: theme and variation, evolution from the simple to the complex, a process of aggregation and a sense of purposeful choice, a methodology.

Method & methodology

Method leads from basic root insights about any practice. A design methodology is, therefore, a description of the basic insights and procedures of design thinking. It proposes and uses particular sets of cause-and-effect as essential concerns regarding design.

Along the way, a methodology develops and articulates a framework or theory, for going about something particular – in this case, design – in pursuit of a goal for the practice. In general, we can describe the collective goals as STRATEGIES – actions focused on an overall objective – and the individual actions as TACTICS – actions limited to a specific procedure.

The specific methodology underlying the principles outlined in this book proceeds from a basic observation about architectural design: with architecture, form and space are distinct and separate facets of the same object. The relationship between form and space is, therefore, open to analysis and interpretation. Appreciating or resolving the dynamics of that relationship, as well as describing it, is analytic, imaginative and problematic. This, in turn, generates a method, a guiding speculation and set of criteria for judgment. In this

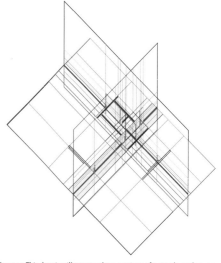

Figure 7: This drawing illustrates three sections of a simple enclosure as intersecting planes. Schematic axonometric diagrams such as these help the beginning designer visualize the relationship between orthographic representations and the formal structuring of form in space.

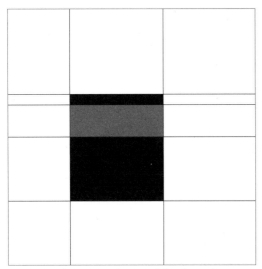

Figure 8: Two figures positioned on a ground plane shown with connecting field and bounding lines, as discussed in CHAPTER 4.

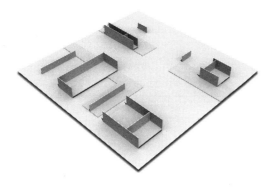

Figure 9: Model of the group composition in its mid-stage of development as explored in CHAPTER 5.

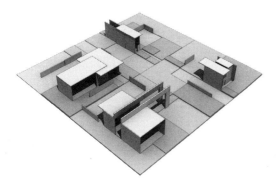

Figure 10: The final model of the same group composition as described in CHAPTER 6.

way, design thinking defines a process of analysis, visualizing possibilities and a path towards judging the potential result.

Our method and approach toward a methodology also addresses the observation that while form is a composite whole, a composition, the possibilities of space within any form is both aggregate and multi-stable. Form, while open to interpretation, exists as finite objects occupying defined space or a determined set of spaces within its composition. In contrast, the aggregate of space includes defined and implied – negotiable and multivalent – occupations within the form. Form is corporeal and solid even if it is movable or malleable. Space is correspondingly ethereal and fluid. Consequently, or in response to these observations, one goal of architectural design is to be clear about how form brings order and clarity to the mutability of space.

Visualizing the complexity of space and form begins the process of making clear sense of distinct and relevant qualities of both. In addition, when approached systematically, the cumulative tools for description begin to form a basis for future observations and judgments. They start to build a method. This process of making a system of thought about design clarifies both analysis and judgment. It empowers the designer to make better decisions. It builds an arsenal.

How this book works

There are a number of ways to build an arsenal, just as there are a number of ways to learn any discipline that embodies both thought and practice. Giving form to an introductory sequence inevitably reflects certain preferences. It gives privilege to one idea over another by virtue of the order of presentation and its abstraction from the fuller practice.

We began this introduction with a working definition of architecture, our description of the diagram, the Big Idea and design thinking. These ideas underwrite our teaching of beginning design. In addition, the results of that teaching, its method and content illustrate our overall thesis.

In the following chapters, we proceed through a series of examples, descriptions and demonstrations to illustrate this beginning. Though the examples aspire to arrive at general conclusions, they are not a formula for design. Instead, we use them to make fundamental design concepts clearer.

The examples illustrate five groups or theme sets. Each group addresses the same basic formal learning goal: observing and analyzing design to better understand design method. The overall prejudice in this text appears with the first theme: we represent analyzing architecture as engaging the fundamental language of GESTALT. This does not align our ideas with either the phenomenological or formalist commentaries prevalent today. Gestalt instead simply offers the clearest language for describing form and formal perception.

Beginning from the notion that drawing is a route to visualizing design, our first theme set, starting in the following chapter, introduces the idea of diagramming that underwrites our theme sets. From there, we add a brief discourse on order that leads to the three project groups that organize the rest of the book

The procedure that occupies CHAPTER 4 takes the reader through an elementary project premised on basic visual judgment of figures within a GROUND. It also introduces complementary methods of analyzing figures and fields and differentiating between form and space (8). The chapter also introduces important formal vocabulary for diagramming positive and negative space in plan.

Building on that sequence, the second procedure group moves toward a greater complexity of figure and ground, and treats the evolution of three-dimensional spatial objects on that basis. Adding to the previous discussion of diagrammatic analysis, CHAPTER 5 extends the method to more deliberate engagement with figures that represent enclosed space. In addition, the project articulates the ground as composed of multiple fields. The model also develops into a three-dimensional reality (9).

Moving on to CHAPTER 6, the complexity of the model – figures and fields – grows in response to further refinement through analytical drawings (10). Each of these steps reflects both descriptive illustration and diagrammatic analysis. The concluding model and drawings of this thematic group depict a robust expression of architectural order among forms and across space, setting the stage for the procedures that follow.

The third procedural theme – featured in CHAPTER 7 – adds to the mix of ideas of order explicit notions of physical matter. The use and examination of three-dimensional models moves to the fore both as a subject of analysis and as a means of exploring the difference between structural form and envelope. In the process, we discover and discuss other forms of internal measure and proportion. By building on the method established earlier, this thematic set balances the role of drawing and three-dimensional modeling as both representation and analysis (11–12).

Throughout the first three procedures, the text provides a developing narrative concerning the relationship between two-dimensional expressions of form and three-dimensional representations. In the final group, the discussion focuses on two sets of precedent analysis – CHAPTERS 8 and 9.

Two roles for precedents

Systems of order embedded within works of design are not readily evident to the novice student. To nurture this, we engage beginning designers in the close visual analysis of exemplary building projects – what architects refer to as PRECEDENTS. Asking our students to diagram precedents has proven to be highly effective in enabling them to discover how patterns of order are intrinsic to the design process.

In the book, we employ architectural precedents in two ways. First, within each chapter, a DESCRIPTION introduces one or more precedents that demonstrate the principles of visual order discussed in that chapter. These essays aim to reveal principles in action, allowing the reader to discover systems of visual order embedded within iconic works of architecture. Second, in the final two chapters, we utilize precedents to outline essential categories of diagrams in two and three dimensions. These chapters not only summarize the role of diagrams in the design process, they also emphasize the significant role that precedents play in the practice of architecture.

Students generally begin the study of architecture with a firmly held notion that originality is paramount, and that inspiration is necessarily autonomous and unfettered. They resist the idea that architecture works within an enduring discourse of theme and variation that serves as a source for informed inspiration. The analysis of precedents not only provides evidence for the presence of recurrent systems of visual order in iconic works of architecture, it also establishes the abiding presence of precedent among the works of exemplary architects.

CHAPTER 8 begins with the methods embodied in the analysis of two-dimensional logic as manifested in two architecture precedents. Ludwig Mies

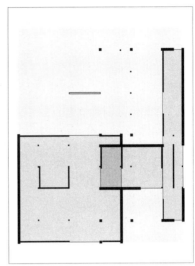

Figure 11: This analytic plan for the model below is part of a set of drawings exploring formal tectonic expression – CHAPTER 7.

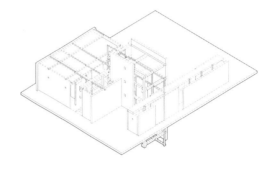

Figure 12: This model reflects the analysis in two dimensions of a composition proposed in model form – CHAPTER 7.

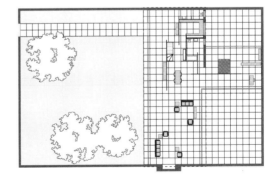

Figure 13: Mies's *House with Three Courts* – shown here in plan – is the subject of the first precedent analysis in CHAPTER 8.

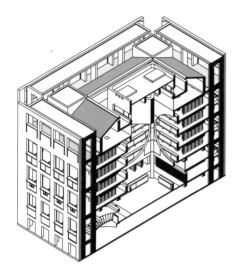

Figure 14: Kahn's *Exeter Library* – shown in isometric section – receives a full three-dimensional analysis in CHAPTER 9.

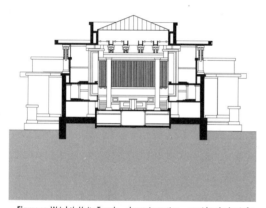

Figure 15: Wright's *Unity Temple* – shown in section – provides the basis for a comparable three-dimensional investigation also in CHAPTER 9.

van der Rohe's *House with Three Courts* and Giuseppe Terragni's *Danteum* both utilize two-dimensional geometries central to their architectural logic. However, while Mies' project (13) remains uniform in section, the *Danteum* embodies a helix of spatial movement and serves as a complement for analysis of three-dimensional form through two-dimensional means.

The two precedents in CHAPTER 9 – not surprisingly – continue to develop the investigation of three-dimensional design thinking, adding analysis of material tectonics and volumetric strategies. Louis Kahn's *Exeter Library* and Frank Lloyd Wright's *Unity Temple* serve as companionable subjects, each embodying a manifestation of resolutely volumetric architecture (14–15).

Certain ideas weave their way through this chapter sequence. Relational measure plays against the universal grid. Two-dimensional analysis and diagrams contrast with three-dimensional counterparts, extending a growing vocabulary to introduce and then develop fundamental architectural terminology and organizational principles.

The illustrations throughout the majority of the text – as in this introductory chapter – render examples as LINE and tone, the dominant form of traditional architectural representation. In the first year design studio at our institution, we use physical media to accomplish the exercises for both drawing and making models. In contrast, our examples make full use of digital construction and processing to create a consistent palette for reproduction.

Our final essay, CHAPTER 10, takes full advantage of digital flexibility to present color variations of the project images as a basis for discussing the effective use of color and material palettes to enhance presentation. The intent is to use simple variations to suggest alternatives in media and presentation for the analysis detailed throughout the book.

The form of the argument

This book holds three parallel narratives, intertwined and juxtaposed: chapters, illustrations and supplements. Chapter texts – like the one you are reading now – present an ongoing account of learning about design through diagrams. The images and captions that accompany the text also stand on their own as a sequence of illustrations with commentary. Continuing the pattern of words and pictures, following the chapters the reader will find the third episodic narrative also in three parts: glossary, thematic essay and visual supplement. The glossary of terms accrues key vocabulary found in each chapter. The 'Descriptions' – mentioned earlier – present fundamental architectural precedents relevant to CHAPTERS 1–6. In addition, 'Demonstrations' augment the examples and procedures encountered within the primary narrative. These appear following the chapters where the need exists more profoundly. This reflects our experience teaching this material.

A quick glance at the table of contents will help guide the reader through this structure.

GLOSSARY OF TERMS

ANALYSIS: A detailed examination of the parts or structure of something, the process of separating something into its constituent elements. Derived from the Greek for 'unbundling', it is often contrasted with synthesis.

ARCHETYPE: An ideal form that existing things approach but never duplicate.

BIG IDEA: The primary idea or conceit governing the development of a particular design. Architects often call this the PARTI or main concept of a project.

COMPOSITION: The elements that comprise any intentional arrangement, form or shape. The formal configuration of parts within a whole.

DESIGN THINKING: A practice for discerning, analyzing and composing systems of order, wherein critical assessment is balanced with generative and iterative creation.

ÉCOLE DES BEAUX-ARTS: Generally considered the first 'school' of architecture, it developed many of the formal rituals and terminology of architectural education. Responsible for a corresponding 'style' of public works of architecture, which held sway in Northern Europe and America throughout much of the nineteenth and early twentieth centuries.

FORMAL: Of and relating to form and composition.

MATTER: The 'stuff' of the physical world, material.

MEASURE: Comprises the dimensional attributes of form and space.

ORDER: The organizational principle of any composition.

PURPOSE: The identification of ends reflecting a sense of final state or goals.

STRATEGY: A plan of action designed to achieve a major or overall end.

TACTIC: An action or strategy carefully planned to achieve a specific end, a component of an overall STRATEGY.

DESCRIPTION 1
Order & measure

From the divine to the secular

As we initially describe it, order may seem an abstract notion, disconnected from the earthy reality of the built environment. Nothing could be further from the truth. The deceptively simple, physical act of measurement binds architecture to the concepts of order that we discuss at length in this book. This is true not only of contemporary building practices; order and measure are intrinsic to the earliest traces of human occupation throughout the world.

Ancient Egyptian mythology credited the goddess Seshat, 'she who scribe', with the invention of surveying. They also identified her as the goddess of architecture, astronomy, mathematics, record keeping and writing. The commingling of these forms of knowledge in one divinity is instructive. For the Egyptians, two pressing necessities prompted the invention of surveying: water, and religious observance. The development of intensive agriculture along the Nile valley relied upon an irrigation network of channels and chases. In turn, this intricate system required accurate measurement of distance and area, as well as minute changes in elevation. These practices also aided in re-establishing, or scribing, property lines following the annual floods.

Equally significant, surveying enabled the Egyptians to transcribe the divine order of the universe onto, and into, the natural world. Instruments designed to map the movement of the heavens also found use in charting the surface of the earth. Sacred texts contained mathematical formulae and their resultant proportional systems, their secrets guarded closely by a caste of architect-priests and their attendant surveyors – *harpedonaptae*, or 'rope-stretchers'. Scholars believe that the Pharaohs themselves symbolically assumed this role: Egyptian mythology describes Seshat assisting pharaohs in 'stretching the rope', the ritual related to laying out the foundations of temples and other sacred structures in order to establish dimensional precision, thereby assuring celestial alignments. Murals and reliefs throughout Egypt depict various pharaohs wielding ropes associated with the literal act of *ruling*: knotted cords one-hundred royal cubits in length measured distance, while shorter cords twelve knots long form a right angle when arrayed as a triangle with sides three, four and five knots in length respectively (1).

Stonehenge provides another vivid example of measure in the service of order. Inhabitants repeatedly altered the site over the course of more than fifteen hundred years, and theories about its use and significance vary widely in past decades' scholarship. Nevertheless, several self-evident attributes of the archeological evidence suggest one pre-eminent role: that of celestial observatory. From the center of its iterative rings of post-holes, trenching and *trilithons*, the so-called Heel Stone – a monolith to the northeast – marks the

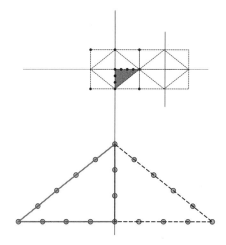

Figure 1: Egyptian surveyors formed ropes of 12 equally-spaced knots into triangles with sides 3, 4 and 5 knots long to ensure accurate right angles.

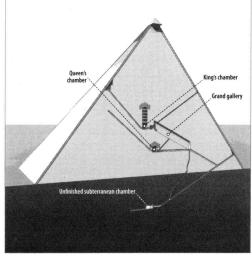

Figure 2: Egyptian builders achieved great precision. The square footprint of the Great Pyramid at Giza is accurate to within two inches on each side.

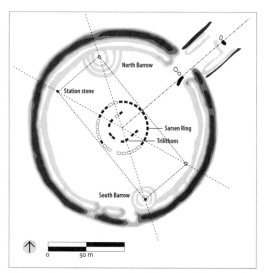

Figure 3: Stonehenge was, among other things, a celestial observatory: its stones align to mark the positions of both sun and moon at summer solstice.

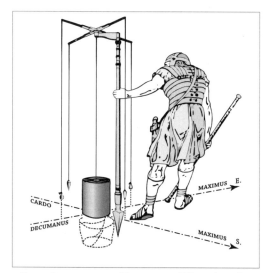

Figure 4: Roman surveyors used the *groma* to establish an orthogonal intersection aligned with the cardinal axes (after P. Figerio, 1933).

position of the summer solstice sunrise. An arranged quartet of lesser stones indicates major and minor solstice moonrise and moonset positions (3).

Archeologists with the Stonehenge Riverside project contend that the monument was part of a ritual landscape that extended upstream along the River Avon. Their theory suggests that the area surrounding nearby Durrington, Walls Henge, was a place of the living, while Stonehenge was a domain of the dead. A journey along the Avon to reach Stonehenge was part of a ritual passage between this world and the underworld, to celebrate past ancestors and the recently deceased. Whatever its specific role, Stonehenge, like the pharaonic projects along the banks of the Nile built during the same period, demonstrates the practice of using geometry to both measure and replicate received notions of divine order within the earthly abode of humanity.

The groma

The Romans, those most tenacious surveyors of the ancient world, laid out their empire with the aid of the *groma* (4). Composed of a cruciform arrangement of plumb lines, it established perpendicular avenues aligned with the cardinal axes – *cardo* and *decumanus*. This intersection determined the center of military camps, and subsequently the center of urban settlements established throughout Roman territories.

The *groma* was the principal tool of the *agrimensores* – literally 'field-measurers' – who settled property disputes and supervised the re-distribution of lands acquired by conquest. Together with the *chorobates* – water-level – and *dioptra* – sighting tube – the Empire employed the *groma* in all aspects of imperial and civic infrastructure: military surveyors used it to lay out the vast network of consular roads, as well as the far-flung encampments and defensive works maintained by Roman legionaries. These same tools helped to arrange the remarkable system of aqueducts that supplied the fountains, baths and privileged residences of urban centers. Architectural surveyors, in turn, laid out the streets, public spaces and buildings of cities and towns throughout the Empire.

As with their Bronze Age predecessors, these practical manifestations of Roman surveying traced their origin to sacred rituals that superimposed patterns of cosmic order on the apparent chaos of the natural world. The cruciform intersection prescribed by the *groma* derived from the *inauguratio*, the ancient ceremony that sanctified the founding of a city. Presiding over the ceremony was an *augur*, a priest trained in the art of divining the heavens. He began by scrutinizing the full sweep of the horizon and naming all that he saw. Simultaneously, he drew a circle on the ground with his staff, representing the totality of the cosmos. The *augur* then divided the circle into quadrants by inscribing the cruciform lines of the *templum*, the term for both the newly consecrated site, and the simple sketch on the ground. This single diagram aligned the site with the divine order of the universe, and delineated the essential form of their cities. For the Romans, it reified the power of order.

DEMONSTRATION 1·1
Organizational figures

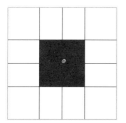

Diagram 1·1: The square.

Diagram 1·2: The circle.

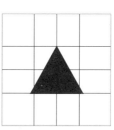

Diagram 1·3: The triangle.

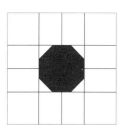

Diagram 1·4: The octagon.

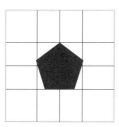

Diagram 1·5: The pentagon.

Diagram 1·6: The hexagon.

Diagram 1·7: A cruciform.

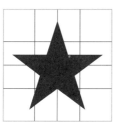

Diagram 1·8: The pentagram.

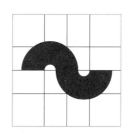

Diagram 1·9: A serpentine figure.

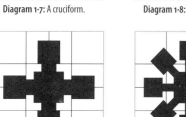

Diagram 1·10: Cruciform satellites.

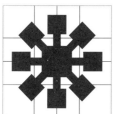

Diagram 1·11: Radial satellites.

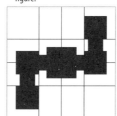

Diagram 1·12: Serpentine satellites.

Diagram 1·13: Perimeter satellites.

Diagram 1·14: Pentagon satellites.

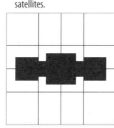

Diagram 1·15: Wing satellites.

SIMPLE ORGANIZATION

The images to the left illustrate three columns of related formal organizational figures in sequence. Each row proceeds from a basic conceptual premise. Correspondence along the columns exists as well.

· The first row shows three figures often associated with ideal geometries because of their regular form (1·1–3). In this context, there is little difference between the square and most rectangles – they both have four sides, parallel and perpendicular. The same is true for the circle and other elliptical forms as well as most forms of the triangle.

· The second row shows three regular polygons related to the solids immediately above (1·4–6).

· In the third row, we encounter three archetypical shapes sometimes found in architectural compositions – the pentagram and other star forms being the rarer (1·7–9).

· The fourth and fifth rows demonstrate related satellite organizations rendering a hierarchy of shapes and path forms (1·10–15).

Figure 1: Diagrams of organization figures (left).

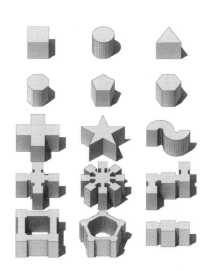

Figure 2: The same figures illustrated as solid extrusions .

Figure 3: Overhead view of the fifteen organizational figures rendered with walled perimeter.

SIMPLE ORGANIZATION CONTINUED

On the right, two illustrations render the previous formal organizational figures as walled figures. In contrast to simple extrusions, the presence of a distinct envelope hints at rudimentary construction.

The upper image shows the figures in overhead perspective (3). The lower image shows the same group in parallel projection (4). Notice that, even in perspective, a figure-ground reading dominates the plan view as compared with the preponderant volumetric aspect conveyed by the angled projection.

The top row of figures shows the ideal shapes as solid projections that illustrate their figure-ground dynamic. All three of the forms project their centers outward. However, there are differences. The square's orthogonal axes are parallel to its bounding perimeters and its diagonal axes pass through its corners. For the circle there exist infinite axes and tangents – the orientation of its conditional boundary will likely take cues from its context. The visual dynamic of the triangle reflects one of its principal features – each of its three axes pass through a corner, the center and a face.

The second row of figures exhibit related figure-ground relationships. Thus the octagon projects an axis every 22.5° and is similar to the square in its axis-boundary relationships. The pentagon's axes, like those of the triangle, pass through corner, center and face. Three of the hexagon's face axes share their geometry with the triangle, however, each corner axis has a companion face axis at 90°. The resulting ambiguity is not dissimilar to that of the circle.

These forms allow us to understand the organization of the more complex figures in the next three rows. The relevant formal difference, as we see in later chapters, is the active negative space both along the perimeter and/or within a center courtyard.

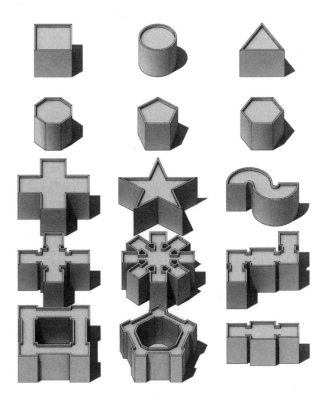

Figure 4: The same walled figures shown in parallel projection, mimicking a cabinet oblique drawing.

DEMONSTRATION 1·2
*The courtyard schema**

Diagram 1·1: Perimeter schema.

*SCHEMA

The schema is a representation of a plan or concept in the form of an outline or model. The plural form is schemata.

ENCLOSURE & AXIS

The courtyard SCHEMA follows an ARCHETYPE for organization. With origins in the campfire, ceremony and fortification, examples appear in the architecture of nearly all cultures throughout time and across locale. They may be either open or roofed, geometric or organic, but all share formal themes of center and edge.

Diagramming courtyards as Big Ideas begins with distinguishing the relationships between perimeter and path, enclosure and axis. The images to the left use the square form as their starting place.

· In the first diagram, the perimeter schema shows a continuous form surrounding a central space (1·1). Rectangles and other straight-sided figures, circles and ellipses all follow from this basic idea.

· The second row demonstrates single-axis schemata. Each diagrams a path or parallel paths through or across the central space (1·2–4). In the examples, the axes cross through the space at or near edges. Incomplete transit and central locations are also possible.

· The third row illustrates dual-axis schemata. Diagrams 1·5&6 both show incomplete transit, leading in and out of but not through the courtyard, the first located centrally, the second at the extreme corner. Example 1·7 contains both central and edge paths, complete and incomplete transits.

· In the fourth row, three cross-axis schemata demonstrate complete axial symmetry (1·8) and two varieties of partial or hybrid symmetry (1·10).

· Diagrams 1·11–13: show perimeter schemata augmented to include satellite forms.

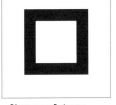

Diagram 1·2: Single-axis schema.

Diagram 1·3: Single-axis schema.

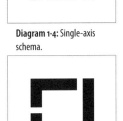

Diagram 1·4: Single-axis schema.

Diagram 1·5: Dual-axis schema.

Diagram 1·6: Dual-axis schema.

Diagram 1·7: Dual-axis schema.

Diagram 1·8 Cross-axis schema.

Diagram 1·9: Cross-axis schema.

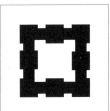

Diagram 1·10: Cross-axis schema.

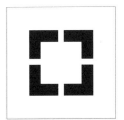

Diagram 1·11: Perimeter with corner satellites.

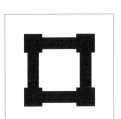

Diagram 1·12: Perimeter with center satellites.

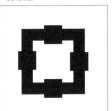

Diagram 1·13: Perimeter with corner and center satellites.

Figure 5: Thirteen courtyard schemes beginning with a simple perimeter and showing nine path variations and three symmetrical satellite configurations (*left*).

DEMONSTRATION I·3
Courtyards as objects

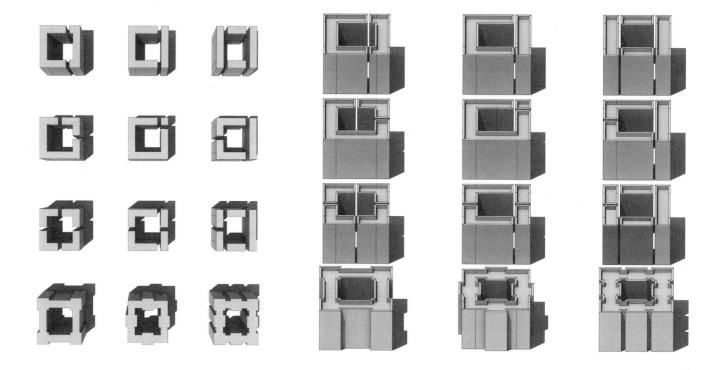

Figure 1: Overhead view of the twelve courtyard figures rendered as pure extrusions.

Figure 2: The twelve courtyard figures rendered with walls in parallel projection.

Figure 3: The character of satellite perimeters can change dramatically when ordered around a dominant cross-axis scheme.

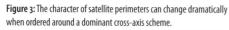

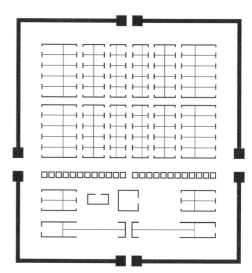

Diagram 3·1: Satellite perimeter with cross axis schema.

Diagram 3·2: Satellite perimeter interrupted by cross axis schema.

Diagram 3·3: Satellite perimeter modified by cross axis schema.

Figure 4: The organizational diagram of a Roman camp contains complex internal paths ordered around a dominant cross-axis scheme.

DEMONSTRATION I·4
Additional courtyard schemata

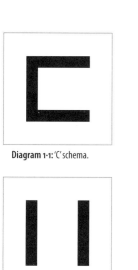

Diagram 1·1: 'C' schema.

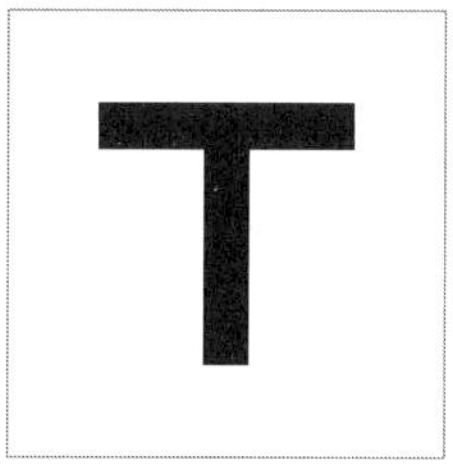

Diagram 1·2: 'T' schema.

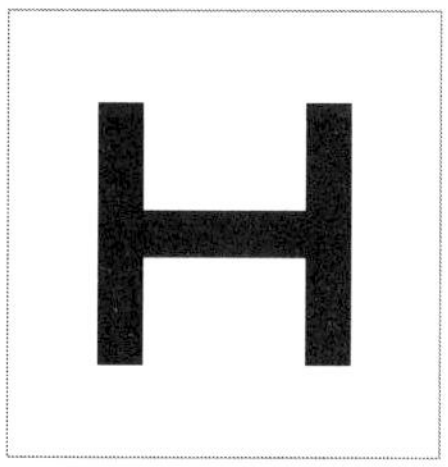

Diagram 1·3: 'H' schema.

Diagram 1·4: Parallel schema.

Diagram 1·5: 'L' schema.

Diagram 1·6: 'E' schema.

Diagram 1·7: Pinwheel schema.

Diagram 1·8: Cruciform schema.

Diagram 1·9: Hybrid 'U' schema.

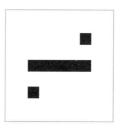

Diagram 1·10: Hybrid elements schema.

Diagram 1·11: Hybrid elements schema.

Diagram 1·12: Hybrid elements schema.

Figure 1: Twelve partial courtyard figures shown as figure-ground diagrams (*above*).

PARTIAL ENCLOSURE

Along with the fully enclosed courtyard, partially enclosed organizations also define interior space using perimeter forms. Their geometries vary broadly, but they result in defined and implied allied spaces.

· One category, the alphabetic schemata, derives its name from letter-form figures. They relate easily to ideal geometries by virtue of their regular form (1·1–3, 5&6, 8&9). In this context, there is little difference between the square and most rectangles – they both have four sides, parallel and perpendicular. Similarly, the circle and ellipse correspond closely to one another and the all triangles share a common identity.

· Parallel (1·1–4) and perpendicular (1·7–8) forms can also suggest archetypal configurations while partially enclosing space.

· Linear elements and smaller figures – dots – take the architectural structure of walls and columns and, by changing scale, define quite nuanced courtyard enclosures (1·10–12).

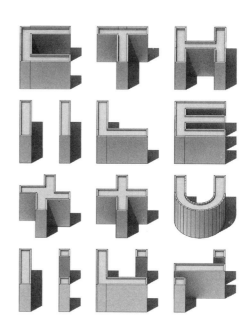

Figure 2: The twelve partial courtyard figures rendered with walls in parallel projection.

CHAPTER **2**
Sorting through ideas

Diagrams as method

We have defined the diagram as an agent of analysis. The diagram reveals or proposes an underlying conceptual organization of some aspect of the physical environment. Further, we have proposed that diagrams, in addition to representing architecture, actually constitute a kind of architecture, in and of themselves in the sense that they demonstrate or embody intellectual structure.

In architectural study, diagrams are ubiquitous. They are also frequently idiosyncratic. At first glance, there appear to be few generalized conventions with which to read and to generate diagrams. The reasons for this intertwine with the historical narrative wherein architecture became a formal discipline of both study and practice. It is a complex tale. However, our focus here is practical, not historical. The underlying visual principles and intellectual attitudes interest us. History aside, the lack of agreement upon a common practice results from the diagram's strengths – its inherent adaptability to purpose and context.

The definitions in two dictionaries point to a first issue: do diagrams represent?* We believe they do, but that they are selective representations. They demonstrate, through abstraction, a particular subset of the fullness of reality. In the same way that we recognize x-rays as a selective picture of the body, diagrams tell us more by showing us less. More precisely, this suggests the diagram as a form of modeling. A MODEL, after all, chooses particular characteristics and places them in relation for common study and comparison. It translates select properties of a system or object into an alternate framework. In mathematics and the sciences, models make the very large and very small manageable and graspable. Similarly, in mythology, models explain the unfamiliar with elements of the familiar.** In both cases, they act through representation.

Categorizing the diagram as a subset of the model clarifies its principal role: analysis, during or after the design process. A diagram attempts to understand something by selectively defining and isolating specific components. To analyze, after all, means to unbundle or pull apart, thereby enabling us to abstract the relevant from the whole. By utilizing only a fraction of the data available of its subject, the diagram operates with a high signal-to-noise ratio. It makes things obvious (1).

A good diagram engages simple elements to separate and convey complex interactions for study and verification. The elements depend on the recognition of fundamental representational tactics and strategies to function. Thus,

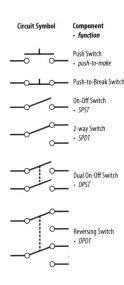

Circuit Symbol	Component · *function*
	Push Switch · *push-to-make*
	Push-to-Break Switch
	On-Off Switch · *SPST*
	2-way Switch · *SPDT*
	Dual On-Off Switch · *DPST*
	Reversing Switch · *DPDT*

Figure 1: Electrical diagrams for switches. Even for these most elemental functions, the diagrams show a highly developed symbol system at work.

* TWO DEFINITIONS

Webster's defines the diagram as a 'graphic design that explains rather than represents; especially a drawing that shows arrangement and relations (as of parts).' In contrast, the *Oxford English Dictionary* describes the diagram as 'a simplified drawing showing the appearance, structure, or workings of something; a schematic representation.'

** ON MYTH

'A myth is not a fairy story, it is the presentation of facts belonging to one category in the idioms appropriate to another.' Gilbert Ryle, *The Concept of Mind*, p. 8.

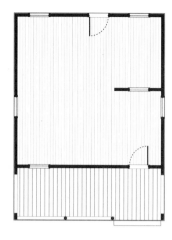

Figure 2: The image to the right shows a moderately complete floor plan adjacent to a perspective, far right.

Figure 3: Compare the conventional plan to the images of plan view diagrams below. The sequence of examples demonstrates all three types of diagramming:
- Reduced drawing (3·1)
- Abstraction (3·2–4)
- Drawing with overlay (3·5&6).

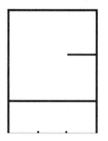

Diagram 3·1: Reduced drawing.

Diagram 3·2: Footprint; an abstraction.

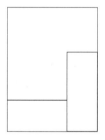

Diagram 3·3: Organizational *parti;* an abstraction.

Diagram 3·4: Openings; an abstraction.

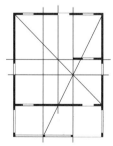

Diagram 3·5: Measure and proportion; an overlay.

Diagram 3·6: Path arrows; an overlay.

the better diagram tends to be self-evident. Among the least ambiguous elements found in diagrams is the arrow. It is safe to say that an arrow always represents direction by virtue of its formal structure: it points.

At the same time, the relative abstraction of the arrow reminds us of a challenge to the notion that the diagram both explains and represents. The dispute arises over a question of degree, of how complete a representation this entails. For us, this question seems perilously close to counting angels on the head of a pin. Abstraction always accompanies representation. A duplicate may be a representation, but not all representations are duplicates, just as a square is a rectangle, but not all rectangles are squares. In recognizing that diagrams may encompass varying traits of an original, we uncover one root of the diagram's diverse conditions: it represents only that which it aims to analyze.

Diagrams may visualize analysis, intent or both. Their purposes vary with context. The variety of purpose raises some questions. Are they not just private, circumstantial notations, useful perhaps in a utilitarian way, but without real function? Setting aside the use/function distinction, we propose a taxonomy of diagrams by way of example to sort out the issue of tool and purpose, and to make the larger case for the diagram's intrinsic role in the design process.

Diagram types

To begin, we limit ourselves to the two-dimensional, black and white diagram. We suggest that diagrams of this sort act as a special subset of drawing. In the simplest list, they comprise: reduced drawing, abstraction and drawing with overlay. These three categories fundamentally subtract from and add to comprehensive architectural drawings. We find them on both the creator's and the critic's desks.

A reduced drawing presumes a more complete referential image (3·1). It limits itself to details deemed relevant to the intent, and excludes the superfluous for clarity. The schematic 'you are here!' floor plan is an obvious example. In design, reduced drawings include common conventions of architectural representation – for example; plan and section; the schematic POCHÉ – and can vary in their inclusiveness.

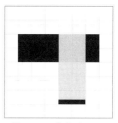

Diagram 4·1: Figure-ground.   **Diagram 4·2:** Defined space.

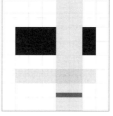

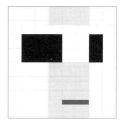

Diagram 4·3: Defined path and implied span.   **Diagram 4·4:** Implied grain.

Figure 4: The four diagrams to the right illustrate the example cited in the text. They form a sequence from simple figure-ground through more complex ideas of defined space, span, path and grain. The translucent fields adhere to the diagram type of **drawing with overlay** cited in the previous illustrations.

Abstraction is a subtler notion, for the reason given in the previous section: all drawings are intrinsically abstract to one degree or another. Abstraction follows seamlessly from the reduced drawing, and notably designates diagrams with more singular intent (3·2–4). Thus, a *parti* drawing diagrams the Big Idea, a structural diagram follows load bearing and a circulation diagram maps path. A figure-ground plan is a paradigm case in architectural abstraction. It substitutes simple building footprints for a more complex aerial rendering.

Drawing with overlay runs the gamut from adding a simple arrow – or other ensign – to full-blown collage, with the drawing serving as background (3·5–6). The overlay can be as simple as placing abstractions over drawings – PLANS, SECTIONS and ELEVATIONS among others – reduced or otherwise. As we move beyond black and white diagrams, translucent layers, tone and color are common devices for the overlay, re-purposing a drawing through addition.

Diagramming & design education

Design is a thoughtful enterprise. It is also a precursor to construction or manufacture. Because it is impossible to act responsibly without forethought, learning to design is also learning how to devise a plan of action. Planning is the quintessential human endeavor. Drawing is one measure of that activity – it both comprises and follows from the act of making diagrams.*

When learning to design well, it is imperative to consider before acting. Such forethought requires a conceptual vocabulary as well as an awareness of relevant practices. Pattern recognition comes first. It brings with it categories of form and shape – including an understanding of their essential properties, what we might call their ORDER. It also brings with it an intellectual structure that bears on later analysis of more complex endeavors. These early exercises lay the foundations for the analytical diagrams of future design work.

By way of example, consider the following design sequence. We begin with simple figure-ground compositions (4·1). To this, we add a visual element that manifests a defined space within the arrangement (4·2). From there, we proceed to place further elements showing defined and/or implied path, span and grain (4·3&4).** Throughout the sequence, these ideas aid coherent development and in the process become the *de facto* analytical tools of advancing design work. They become the diagrams.

These basic exercises simplify more intricate design methodologies, and render them as self-contained activities. Making things simpler is an abstraction, however, the abstraction should point in two directions. It should lead to iterations that are more complex and reveal underlying principles at work. Without this two-way reference, these exercises succeed only to the degree that they form the analytical backbone of future design learning. By doing double duty, they permit beginning designers to advance to ever more nuanced methods without risk of losing the clarity of their intent.

*DISEGNARE/DESIGNARE

And it is good to remember that the Latin root for design, *designare* – to designate – describes both the process and the intent.

** PROJECT SEQUENCE

The project sequence referred to is a subset of the examples that populate CHAPTERS 4 and 5.

* STRATEGIC LANGUAGE

Strategies and tactics comprise a rough hierarchy. In any game with rules, a strategy designates any plan of action with an overall goal. A tactic, in contrast, identifies an action to achieve a specific end. Therefore, tactics serve strategies, while a strategy may embody several tactics.

** GESTALT IN DESIGN

A term borrowed from psychology, gestalt refers to our perception of an overall form or composition rather than our separate assessments of its components. For design, it provides a coherent language of description.

Learning diagrammatic form

Mastering effective diagramming begins with learning the fundamentals of visual form. We identify tools and tactics as a preface to learning any skill. Knowledge of visual structure must therefore precede explorations in possible content.

Previously, we identified a general taxonomy of diagram types. To enhance our understanding of the architectural diagram, we identify three primary categories of diagrammatic form: ENSIGNS, FIGURE-GROUND elements and GESTALT strategies. These three identify the basic elements of any mix-and-match approach to teaching diagrams. The first two categories employ tactics, the third demonstrates combinational intent – hence the use of strategies.*

Ensigns comprise the most direct and readily identifiable elements within our taxonomy (5). The arrow is a universally recognized ensign. A light bulb or radiant sun might stand in for several things, but both act distinctly as emblems of meaning. This prompts some particular gestalt strategies discussed more fully in the next chapter. We borrow the term 'ensign' from heraldry and thus include emblems as well as icons, symbols and signs.

Figure-ground – a gestalt term – makes visual the solid-void relationship of architectural reality. At its largest scale, it identifies that 'here is a built form'. At smaller scales, it distinguishes form from space. The polarity may originate in visual phenomena, but the analysis that it fosters is broader. Figure-ground has the grace to clarify the intent of any composition under study. Thus, openings in a wall might best reveal a pattern when distinctions between a door and a window vanish. A more detailed discussion of figure-ground occurs in the next chapter.

Gestalt strategies, being combinatory, are inherently more speculative than are the two previous groups.** When different visual tactics play simultaneously, they reveal the interaction of their elements. The extension of purpose thus implied works as a gestalt of implication. The combination of tactics – each multiplying the other – acts by way of gestalt theory. This may be as simple as text supplementing an arrow, or as complex as shadows foregrounding surface. A gestalt strategy combines several visual or non-graphical tactics into an overall graphic schema (6).

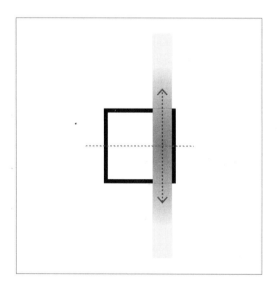

Figure 5: The plan image to the left shows elements of figure-ground to indicate walls and openings, as well as various ensigns, dotted lines, arrows and fades to describe spatial experience related to motion.

Figure 6: In comparison, the image to the right focuses on static elements of the spatial gestalt: center, edge and surround.

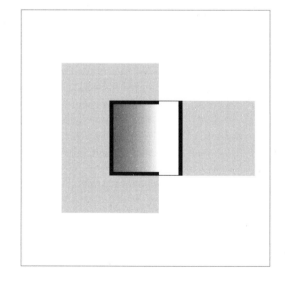

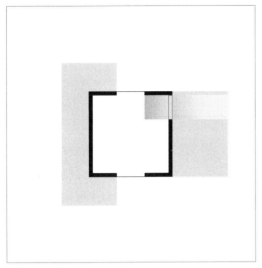

Figure 7: Examples of gestalt strategies depicting the three sub-categories:
1. Layers
2. Collage
3. Annotation.

Diagram 7·1: Layers.

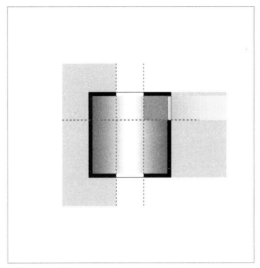

Diagram 7·2: Collage.

Gestalt sub-categories

Within either of the two first groups, which we define as tactical categories, one quickly notices that each tactic may play a role in the third, strategic, category. A figure-ground image combined with an ensign exhibits certain gestalt properties, but the overall effect is non-complex. By employing a gestalt strategy, we aim to generate the appropriate tension between two elements – tactical or otherwise – that produce what we might describe as a certain visual tremor. Without relying on ambiguity, gestalt strategies produce competitive readings of a diagram. It may be as simple as the friction between words and spaces, or as subtle as the play of colored geometric layers against a more sober, upright figure-ground plan.

The sub-categories of gestalt strategies are: layers, collage and annotation (7·1–3). All three are varieties of additions or combinations. The intent of layers is that we view each element of the drawing literally in a conceptual space with one atop the other. In the better examples, that positioning is also the source of multiple related readings, hence gestalt. Similarly, a true collage-as-diagram strategy ultimately derives its tension from the formal and pictorial qualities of each element. Technically, this means that these diagrams play from readings where the elements are visual only – collage – to those readings where each element brings with it some independent meaning – montage; but in this instance, the distinction is unnecessary. Annotation designates the addition of text to image, fact to picture.* In this instance, two communication modes, each capable of independence, work corroboratively as ideological force-multipliers.

The diagram & visual order

Our three diagrammatic forms are categories within a larger practice – visual order. Their proper use enables effective diagramming. A general vocabulary, used in speaking of design, should also have a visual counterpart. Some of these notions are general and familiar, such as PROPORTION, SYMMETRY, SHAPE, COLOR and SURFACE, ORGANIZATION and COMPOSITION. They inhabit most drawings as part of their structure.

With its arsenal of arrows, sightlines, environmental notations and geometric correspondences, the diagram helps to clarify intent as well as verify result.

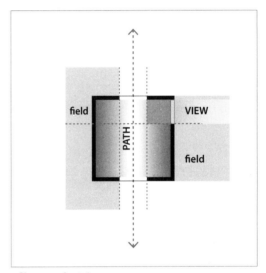

Diagram 7·3: Annotations.

* TEXT AS IMAGE

One of the more famous pronouncements on the independence of language and image comes from the philosopher Ludwig Wittgenstein in his *Tractatus Logico-Philosophicus*, 'Some things can only be spoken of, some things can only be shown' (¶4.121–4.1212).

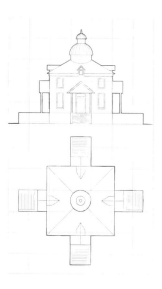

Figure 8: In this small sketch, the grid geometry already suggests an analysis of the organization of both plan and elevation. This is a common feature in the architecture of the Renaissance and Neoclassical periods.

***LEARNING RESPONSIBILITY**

The larger pedagogical ideal is to gradually place the responsibility of coherence on the apprentice beginning designer. There are no formulae to blindly follow to make judgments. As with good writing, the burden of clarity is the point of the practice.

It is an engine of efficiency in thought and practice. Because clarity is paramount, order is a requirement. The more comprehensive the skill set brought to bear by the designer, the greater the potential for both clarity of form and intent. Good diagrams are deceptive in only one respect: they are at their best when they conceal the ingenuity of their design. Their powerful clarity makes them appear obvious. A diagram's revelation seems self-evident, even when its creation has entailed tireless effort. An architect bears the responsibility of making a good drawing – one without excuses – in making her ideas clear to herself.*

Less obvious, perhaps, is the diagrammatic life of a building itself. When we draw a cube as a beginning gesture, we have begun to diagram space. Any measurements that we make within the drawing to locate openings or paths, depends upon the visual order of that diagram. To divide a cube into a three-dimensional nine-square – *à la* Palladio – is to engage with geometry diagrammatically as a set of possibilities and a working procedure (8).

Diagrams, as with all traditional drawing forms, hold performance distinct from analysis. Whatever utility the diagram offers, its more important function, as proof, shows that we know what we are doing and what we did (8). At the end of the design process, a final diagram becomes the ultimate argument for the project. It says 'this is what I did.' That diagram, as with any argument, is how we know whether our intentions are clear.

Our purpose

To those unfamiliar with design thinking, terms such as 'traditional' and 'vernacular' usually identify the familiar, whereas 'contemporary', 'modern' or 'post-modern' might characterize the unaccustomed. To a designer, these labels are less value laden and useful only in specific ways. Traditions abound and often conflict, and vernacular classifies practices relevant to the context at hand.

The present is contemporary by definition, while modernism and postmodernism serve best as reference to historical movements one hundred years and fifty years in the past, respectively – yet other forms of tradition. Rather than fuss over nomenclature, it is far better for designers to focus on ensuring fit,

Figure 9: Analysis of the organizational geometry of an elevation led to this diagram. Proposed changes attempt to unify the visual character of the entrance.

appropriateness and requirements. Design is not about style: it is either competent, or it is hapless.

Form and order interact in a way similar to language and syntax. Informed practice in both defines competence. It does not embrace either formalism or pedantry. The suggestion that canonic knowledge limits personal expression may be understandable, but it remains an error. Acquiring ability through thoughtful structure defines the possibilities of invention. Accidents may occasionally be happy, but only if seen in the context of intent.

Our collective experience teaching beginning designers affirms the possibility and need for shared practice and principles. In an era where architecture increasingly arrives via pixels and 3D printers, common practice becomes more difficult to discern. Along with the ultimate possibilities that the computer appears to open up, the prescriptive tools nested in software often reduce design choices to procedures bought blindly off the shelf. In response, we advocate restoring a frame of reference to the discipline of architecture as a means to foster, rather than hinder, personal expression.

As teachers, we believe it essential for students to question their work in new media relative to traditions that constitute the practice of architecture. Techno-pop is still music; it still bears relation to music's practical history. Moreover, just as music has keys and chords, architecture has proportion and order. For students to learn the craft of the diagram is to empower them to amend and augment the practice of architecture. Making buildings without making diagrams is certainly possible. Designing architecture within the tradition of the diagram is preferable.

GLOSSARY OF TERMS

ATTRIBUTES: Qualities or characteristics inherent in any composition.

BALANCE: A distribution of elements visually equal to each other. Balance may be symmetrical or asymmetrical.

·   SYMMETRICAL balance is equal in weight and tone on both sides of a composition.

·   ASYMMETRICAL balance is unequal in position or intensity using the tension between positive elements and negative space to achieve parity.

CENTER: A point equally distant from all sides, the middle point.

COLOR and SURFACE: Properties that characterize objects and shapes.

COMPOSITION: The elements that comprise any intentional arrangement, form or shape. The formal configuration of parts within a whole.

CONTEXT: In architecture, the circumstances of a form or design, may include environment, setting or formal composition.

CONTRAST: An abrupt shift in weight and/or intensity.

EDGE: The outside limit of an object, area, or surface farthest away from the center. Often synonymous with BORDER.*

ELEMENTS: The major components of a composition: color, value, line, shape, form, texture, and space.

GESTALT: In psychology, an ordered whole that we perceive as greater than the sum of its parts. The overall form that we perceive rather than the components that we assess.

LINE: A long narrow mark that divides, penetrates, encloses, or defines form or space.

MASS: The visual or physical weight of an element or the collective weight of a group of elements.

MODEL: A translation of an idea or object into another medium of particular characteristic for the purposes of study and analysis. For those purposes models place select properties into an appropriate framework.

ORGANIZATION: The structure or arrangement of objects in a group or system. Related to COMPOSITION.

PATTERN: The repetition of any element in sequence or arrangement in a design.

PLAN, SECTION and ELEVATION: Three drawing types commonly used in architecture, see main glossary for more specific definitions.

POSITION: The placement of elements in a specific area. Position demands an understanding of space as an organized total to which elements are applied according to the various principles of design.

PROPORTION: The relationship of one thing to another in terms of quantity, size, or number; the ratio. The comparative measurement of parts to a whole.

RELATIONSHIP: The connecting principle shared between or among elements.

REPRESENTATION: A description or portrayal of something in a particular way.

·   A depiction in a picture or model in a visual medium.

·   A likeness or reproduction of something.

SHAPE: The outline of an area or figure (compare to FORM).**

SOLID: Any unbroken area that has a definite shape.

SPACE: The area in which all elements act and occur.

SYMMETRY: Exactly similar parts facing each other or around an axis.

TEXTURE: Interwoven patterns of tones or surfaces.

TINT, TONE and SHADE: In printing, *tint* refers to the addition of white to a color. *Tone* is the addition of black and *shade* is the addition of gray. In conversation, all three may refer to degrees of light and dark.

---

* ABOUT EDGE

·   A BORDER is that part of a surface nearest to its boundary. It may also refer to the boundary line itself.

·   A MARGIN is a border of a definite width usually distinct in appearance from what it encloses. Distinct from border, it commonly refers to a void around a shape or form such as the margin on a page.

·   Both terms refer to something circumscribed, while edge refers to only a part of a perimeter, or the line where two planes converge.

** ABOUT SHAPE

·   SHAPE and FORM, commonly used interchangeably, usually refer to two- and three-dimensional objects respectively.

·   AREA refers to the defined interior of a shape, whereas VOLUME refers to the spatial content found in a three-dimensional form.

·   MASS, in contrast, refers to the solid content of a form.

DESCRIPTION 2
The essential hut

Indigenous diagrams

The origins of architecture have long fascinated designers and historians. Many have studied primitive dwellings in an attempt to yield evidence of principles fundamental to architecture. The mid-eighteenth-century theorist Marc-Antoine Laugier illustrated his notion of the natural origins of architecture by describing a primitive hut formed by the trunks and woven branches of a quartet of closely spaced oaks. Nearly a century later, architectural historian Gottfried Semper similarly used a 'primitive' dwelling as the principal archetype of his *Four Elements of Architecture* (1). For Semper, this vernacular Trinidadian hut came to represent a distillation of those four essential elements: the hearth, the mound, the roof and the partition.

For our purposes, we draw attention to minimal dwellings because they reveal fundamental principles of architectural order. In Semper's hut, for instance, we witness a simple yet nuanced hierarchy of spatial thresholds. Approaching it, we first encounter the edge of the low podium upon which the dwelling sits. The covered porch provides an intermediate threshold to the more fully enclosed portion of the hut. The open hearth, covered yet placed outside the interior in the balmy Caribbean climate, establishes an additional threshold, separating an open space equal in size to the sleeping cell, and an entrance 'hall' centered between the two larger, square spaces. A doorway centered on the adjoining wall provides an additional threshold, followed by another around the raised platform within. If we examine the plan for axial relationships, we immediately recognize two: the centered alignment of the hearth with the doorway between porch and interior and a perpendicular access centered on the porch 'hall', balancing the equal spaces on either side.

At first glance, Semper's hut appears to share little with the circular dwellings – c. 4500 BCE – excavated at the Yanshao settlement of Banpo, near the modern-day city of Xi'an (2). Upon closer analysis, we begin to recognize the pattern. Built upon a low earthen podium, the Banpo hut offers up yet another set of thresholds. The circumferential wall folds in on itself, providing a covered exterior vestibule. Beyond, the four-square arrangement of posts

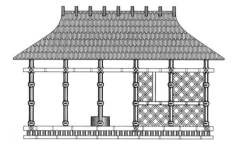

Figure 1: Semper's *Essential Hut,* a Caribbean dwelling he first saw housed within the Crystal Palace, London, at the Great Exhibition of 1851.

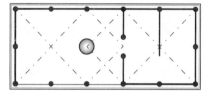

Diagram 1·1: Plan diagram of axes and paths.

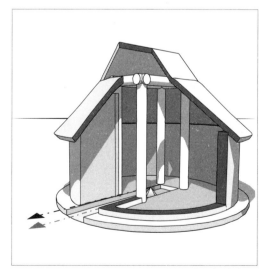

Figure 2: Cutaway view of *Banpo Hut* showing entrance, hearth and axis.

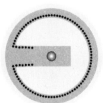

Diagram 1·1. Perimeter and flooring schema.

Diagram 2·1. Hearth and spatial scheme.

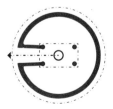

Diagram 2·1: Axis and spatial features.

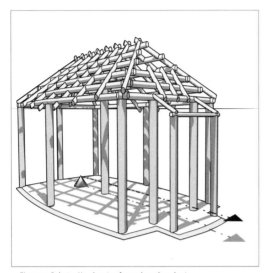

Figure 3: *Palatine Hut* showing frame, hearth and axis.

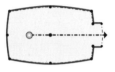

Diagram 3·1: *Palatine Hut* showing walls, hearth and axis.

Diagram 3·2: Axes, columns, perimeter and roof.

supporting the raised center of the roof provides a second space, nearly identical in shape, separating the entrance vestibule from the further recesses of the interior. An open hearth at the center of this interior vestibule further divides into fore and aft halves. The hearth lies, by extension, at the center of the larger cylindrical volume defined by the circuit of the enclosing wall.

Half a world away, the eighth-century BCE settlements excavated atop the Palatine Hill in Rome reveal distinct similarities with the Banpo dwellings (3). Here the ridge beam is held aloft by a single central post rather than the quartet we see at Banpo, but the axis of clerestory openings, hearth and doorway remains the same. As with both the Banpo and the Trinidadian huts, the entire enclosure sits upon a low podium of hardened earth protected by the overhang of the roof. An entrance vestibule frames a further threshold. The Roman penchant for establishing overt alignment with the cardinal axes in their settlements, through the ritual act of *inauguratio* discussed in the previous chapter, is mirrored by the cruciform arrangement of the center and perimeter posts of the Palatine hut. This practice establishes a clear visual correspondence between even the earliest Roman settlement and the cosmic order denoted by four-square division of *cardo* and *decumanus*.

For a more modern, if equally minimal and ostensibly 'primitive' dwelling, we might study Henry David Thoreau's design for the cabin he constructed near Walden Pond (4). Here we find a relatively modern shelter devoted to sustaining the basic requirements of shelter and sustenance. Yet, apart from the replacement of hand-hewn timber by milled dimensional lumber, Thoreau's cabin contains many of the same fundamental attributes of its ancient forebears. The parallel ridge of the roof overhead reinforces the axial alignment of doorway and hearth. The arrangement of windows centered within the flanking walls establishes a significant cross-axis. Built for a distinctly northern climate and therefore understandably devoid of any open-air appendages, the single-room cabin still manages to articulate a series of distinct thresholds and spatial divisions. The sill of the door rests two steps up from the ground. The single doorway provides the most significant threshold, while framing a view of the fireplace centered in the wall opposite. The positions of the two largest objects in the room – a bed and table – reinforce the centered openings of the windows to either side of the cabin.

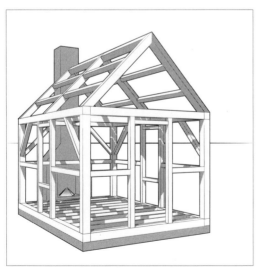

Figure 4: Thoreau's *Cabin at Walden Pond,* showing the framing scheme.

Diagram 4·1: *Walden Cabin* structural scheme.

Diagram 5·1: *Walden Cabin* occupation scheme.

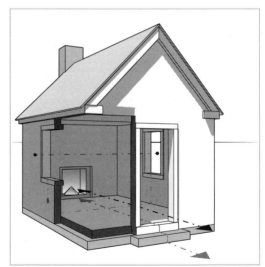

Figure 5: *Cabin at Walden Pond,* cutaway view with the axis for entrance and hearth.

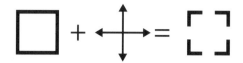

Figure 1: Gestalt combination diagram; path display #1.

DEMONSTRATION 2·1
Diagrams and context

Combining simple diagrams

Diagrams can take many forms depending on their intended use. In plan, the most common starting point is enclosure followed by the logic of path or circulation. In the first three illustrations to the right, we see evolution of the same basic idea: a simple perimeter and cross-axis openings (1–3). Each diagram offers the same combination but presented using different means.

The first diagram shows the simple removal of perimeter to display openings on axis (1). The next illustration adds a sense of movement, emphasizing circulation through the center (2). The third image adds representation of thresholds and reduces the visual emphasis on the motion along the path. In its place, the center appear as a static locale (3).

Symbols and ensigns can also exhibit variations that reflect context of purpose. An arrow can remain simple, become volumetric or transform into a sign (4). In this, the arrow mimics certain figure-ground diagrams (5) and care must be taken to avoid confusion as diagrams evolve toward complexity. The illustrations of a simple entrance way plan show several common additions to reduced plan diagrams (6). The arrow defines egress rather than entry. The gradient path shows the transition from light to dark without demonstrating preference. The cast shadow suggests both volume and general orientation without being precise about either.

The final diagram (7) includes information of preferred direction (the arrow), orientation, and shade and shadow, added to a display of organizational geometry.

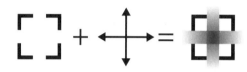

Figure 2: Gestalt combination diagram; path display #2.

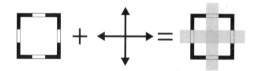

Figure 3: Gestalt combination diagram; path display #3.

Figure 4: Ensign based diagrams: arrows.

Figure 5: Figure-ground based diagrams, various.

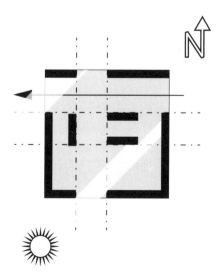

Figure 7: Diagram demonstration including abstractions for path, spatial hierarchy and solar orientation.

Figure 6: Gestalt based diagrams marking path, entrance and transparency.

Gestalt reading of form

Diagrams follow basic visual rules and yet remain capable of deliberate nuance even in their simplest form. The examples below all show variant characteristics of a simple square figure and its visual properties as seen in a field.

The first three diagrams display figure-ground, perimeter and axial path (8). The next four demonstrate appreciation of the same square figure with emphasis on a spatial reading of the figure's gestalt character as it relates to the field (9).

The two elongated diagrams show the effect of the field's proportions on our reading of the figure (10). The final image translates four axial paths into a three-dimensional diagram.

Figure 8: The square in a square field – as a solid, as in-line form (as walls) and with axial paths.

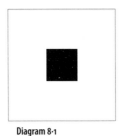

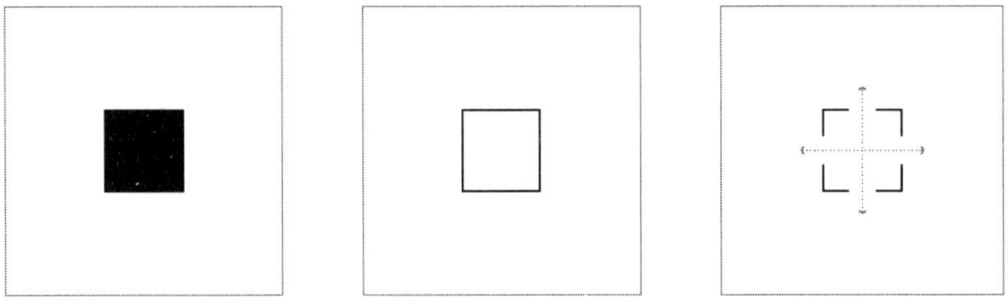

Diagram 8·1

Diagram 8·2

Diagram 8·3

Figure 9: Diagrams of space and paths – combination forms, linear drawing, spatial tone and radiant forms.

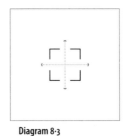
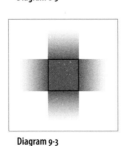
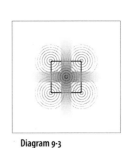

Diagram 9·1

Diagram 9·2

Diagram 9·3

Diagram 9·3

Figure 10: Diagrams of a square in a directional field shown as combination forms and linear drawing. The diagrams hint at the origin of the axial datum.

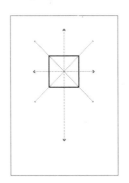
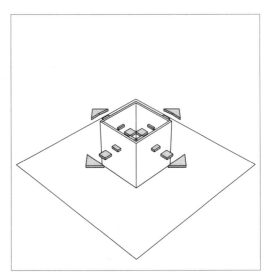

Figure 11: Diagram of a cube and its axes in a square field presented in perspective.

DEMONSTRATION 2·2
Plan as diagram

Imagining fields within

The ubiquity of wall *poché* often hides its intrinsic visual character. Beginning designers often make the misstep of viewing plan as informative but 'sketchy'. Viewed carefully, however, the diagrams can lead to valuable speculation wherein patterns suggest themselves not only a possible improvements but also as opportunities for exploration, question and learning.

The simple images represent examples of commonplace themes in design. From the first diagram, we move through a evolving sequence of theme and variation exploring openings and their effect on spatial form. As before, the intent is to illustrate design thinking in diagrams.

Starting with a single opening on a square perimeter (1), the diagrams reveal a sequence of theme and variation concerning entrances and their effect on spatial experience (2–7). The diagrams shown are without scale. At this point they merely array some options for formal pattern.

Alternate sequences might begin focus on variation in the size of the openings, more complex arrangements or proportions. The example implies no ideal as to form. These sorts of pattern exercises simply display schematic ideas as definite form. Remembering to observe plans as visual artifacts as well as design documents can encourage fresh views of the design conventions used in most projects.

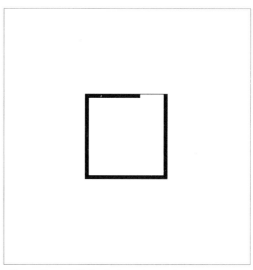

Figure 1: Diagrammatic plan of entrance along an edge.

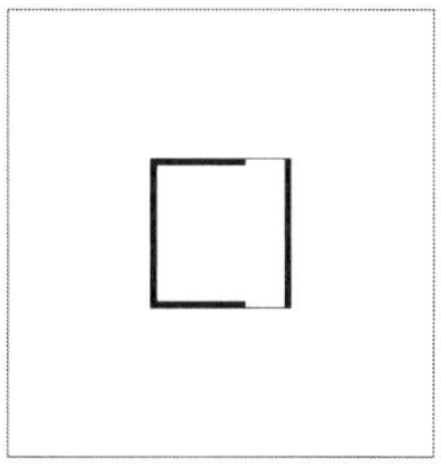

Figure 2: Two entrances face opposite along an edge.

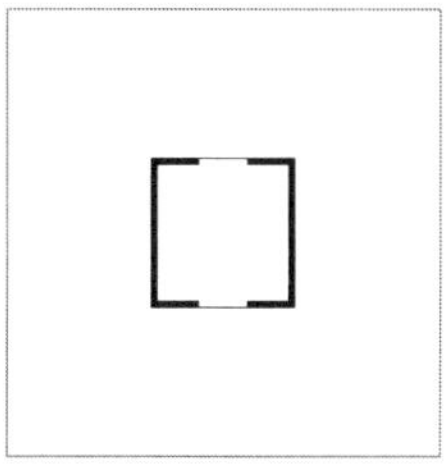

Figure 3: Two entrances opposite across the center.

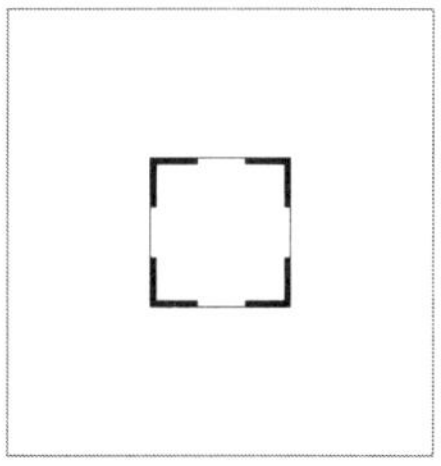

Figure 4: Four entrances create a crossing.

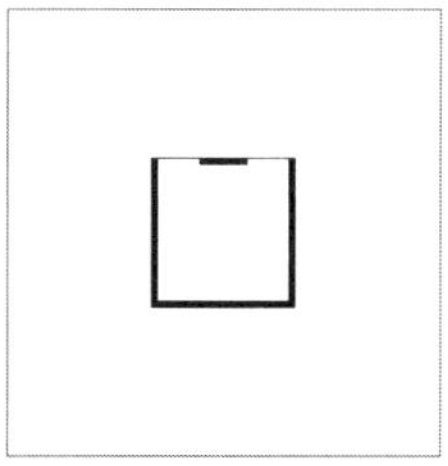

Figure 5: Two entrances face occupy the same edge.

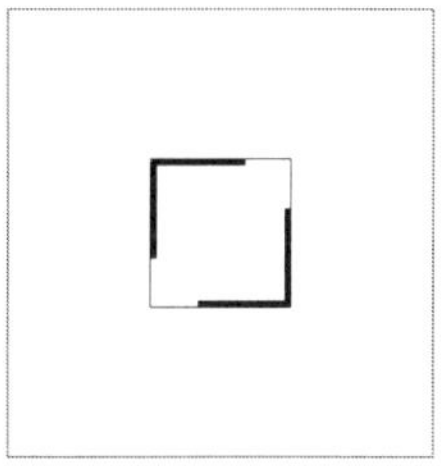

Figure 6: Two corner entrances create diagonal path.

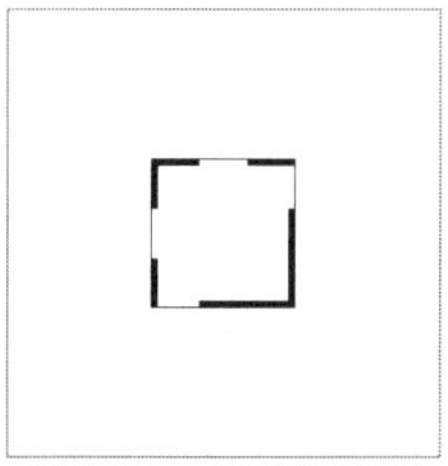

Figure 7: Multiple entrances articulate the volume.

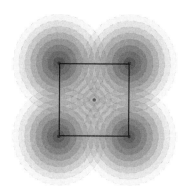

Figure 1: Our psychological response to the visual presence of a square leans in the direction of finding its center and axes.

Figure 8: Edges lead us to follow the axes outward extending the diagrammatic dynamic of the figure into the ground.

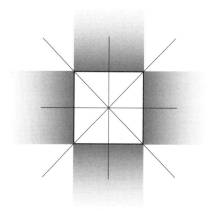

CHAPTER 3
Order first

On order

Order surrounds us as part of our everyday experience of the world. We see this in the games we play, the tables that we eat at and even the books that we read. On a football field, a line defines sides, a perimeter defines borders and a frame defines the goal. A place setting structures a meal and defines it as either casual or formal. Text presents itself as words, sentences, paragraphs, sections and chapters. As you read this page, you rely on its organization, its division of space. A large vertical portion holds the text while off to the side is a smaller portion holds illustrations and notes. This is the architecture of this book – its order.

Our book uses a common organizational strategy for its pages: big piece, small piece – primary and subordinate. As we add other typographic furniture – headers, footers, notes, etc. – this also conforms to that basic architecture to keep things clear. We experience such strategies as relationships of parts to whole. Ordering those relationships is what composition means as a practice.

One of the ongoing debates for architects and designers concerns whether compositional form is part of the content, or only a means. We find that debate irrelevant to learning composition. After all, good writing reflects its composition, whether that writing is a poem, an essay or a set of instructions. Similarly, composing music requires a sense of, if not a theory for, harmonic principles. It is fair to admit that we, the authors, find form intrinsic to architecture and not merely a means to an end.

It is improbable that we would make a building without placing a stake in the ground, literally or figuratively. We start from somewhere and proceed to define a figure. Even the architecture of the space station defines a particular place relative to the universe and its boundaries describe its perimeter. This focal reality, 'centeredness', derives from both our expectations and our visual perception.

Gestalt psychology informs us that when we see a square, we perceive its center at nearly the same moment (1). As we observe the figure of the square, we measure it and apportion it. We recognize its center, its corners and its middle (2). We do much the same with other shapes. Such perceptions lead us to organize the world in terms of the components of visual composition: edges, axes, centers, and subdivisions. The clarity of these perceptions depend on a perceptual capacity that we term FIGURE–GROUND.

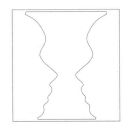

Figure 2: Line drawing of the classic figure-ground ambiguity towards reading either face or vase as the figure.

Figure 4: Tonal shapes of the same figure-ground example. The emphasis of this version lends some figure dominance to the faces.

Figure 3: A third, volumetric version demonstrates a surprisingly strong figure-ground ambiguity.

Figure 5: Another classic figure-ground ambiguity, the young and old woman.

Figure 6: A related modern variation of figure-ground ambiguity, the young woman and the saxophone player.

Roughly speaking, figure-ground identifies our perception of edge. It is how we establish order amidst visual ambiguity. It is the visual framework that helps us locate an object in space with our eyes. We mention this psychological term because it affects the practice of drawing. Ordering visual ambiguity is how a drawing becomes a coherent image. In order to comprehend a drawing, we must respond correctly to its formal qualities. Ultimately, comprehension also involves us in a cultural framework of convention and expectation, but all of that follows from perceived visual order (3–9).

The history of drawing embodies a long tradition of recording what we observe, and projecting what we imagine, a tradition shared with the history of architecture. Therefore, to understand architecture – whether to sustain it or challenge it – requires an understanding of how drawing, composition and architecture intertwine and conflate.

Drawings exist on a page, a surface real or virtual. They can either float in a near-infinity, or exist within a visible boundary. They show things in a two-dimensional format utilizing contrast to either illustrate two-dimensional

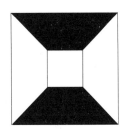

Figure 7: Perspective figure-ground ambiguity, in which the spatial/volumetric character of the form resists clear resolution.

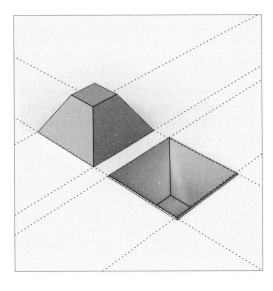

Figure 8: This perspective shows the two possible resolutions of the ambiguity – a truncated pyramid or frustum and its hollow inverse.

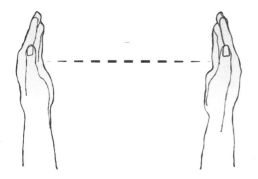

Figure 9: We use common references to speak of measurement. Here the two hands indicate a distance between them.

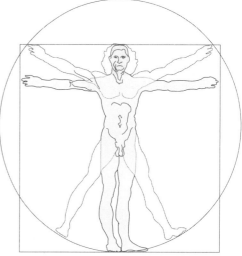

Figure 10: Leonardo DaVinci, the great Renaissance master, left us this classic interpretation of the *Vitruvian Man* – shown above redrawn after the original.

shape and area or suggest three-dimensional form and space. Comprehending an illustration requires interpretation, and provokes questions. Does a drawing reference something besides its own example? How big is the thing that it references? What is its size and scale? Such questions lead us readily to ideas of measurement.

On measure

Rulers and their units of measurement are so nearly ubiquitous that we can scarcely imagine them as not pre-existing. If someone asks 'How big was the fish?' you might find yourself illustrating the answer as a space between two hands (10). You might also add, 'It was twelve inches across,' never seeing the gesture and description as conflicting or distinct. This brings us to an important if subtle point. The gestural measurement is relational: it uses something that is actually there – the space between your hands – to refer to something absent – the fish. The verbal description makes use of yet another absentee, the unit of measurement.

The inch (from the Latin *uncia*) signifies one twelfth, a relation without a necessary parent or source. We make sense of the fish's size if we know that an inch in this instance is the twelfth part of a foot and by also knowing – from prior experience – how large a foot is, however approximately. Someone with a background in the metric system might not be able to sort it out at all.

The verbal description – twelve inches across – leads us back to ideas of drawing. How do you find a twelfth, one might ask. It turns out that the basic action, finding a center, helps us find halves and fourths and eighths, thirds, sixths, and twelfths as well. This sort of practice resides at the heart of our earliest understanding of geometry.

Geometry – the art of measuring ground – begins with the simple tools of the straightedge and the compass. It is an elementary practice that founds itself in the perception and measure of the world. To understand architecture requires that we also understand how we go about measuring things. Subdividing a square works from the outside inward. In contrast, the Cartesian grid starts from an origin – the zero point – and works outward. This is an important distinction. The world of the infinite grid and the ruler, by extension, is an unbounded world. Infinity is a scary proposition for human beings.

Figure 11: The architect, Le Corbusier, also had a great interest in the relationship of human proportion to design. His famous *Modular Man* set about measuring the golden section in relationship to the body.

The familiar, by contrast, anchors us to reality. Distinguishing relationships between the familiar and the alien occupies much of the history of humanity and architecture. One of the first tasks in architecture is making a safe place, a familiar place, a defined place. Geometry arises from this need, and shapes its practice.

Dividing the square

As we observe a rectilinear figure, a square perhaps, we note the points of contrast against a background – usually its corners. Thus, we establish the square as a figure differentiated from its ground. Once we connect the corners, we clarify its perimeter, but we also perceive its center, a particular form of middle. Further on, implied lines crossing the center from the midpoints of its boundaries divide the original figure into four quadrants.

We may also perceive each one of the quadrants as smaller figures within the larger one. This makes of the original square a ground for the smaller figures. Similarly, we may divide each of those smaller figures toward their centers, creating a grid of yet smaller squares. The result of all of this subdivisions leaves us with a hierarchy related to the original figure – quarters and halves measuring linearly, or sixteenths, eighths, etc. measured by area.

As we begin with the drawing of the subdivisions – the halves – a diagonal that bisects the half also serves to subdivide the square into linear thirds. This likewise can generate sixths, twelfths, etc. (13). We encounter this sort of subdivision folding paper to make origami, paper airplanes or cootie-catchers. A side-to-side or corner-to-corner fold will divide a page in equal halves. A top-to-side fold will measure a square from a rectangular page. Repeated folds will continue with subdivisions and reflect the underlying geometries.

Geometrical procedures enact how we might begin to measure and apportion the world. Visual mechanisms – figure-ground, perception of center, etc. – share this nascent geometry. Our front-back, left-right, top-bottom sense of our bodies – our cruciform selves – also play a part in this (14). Our perceptions help construct our understanding and organization of place (15&16). Both our perceptions and our systems analyze and propose order. They relate to the architecture of the world for us, whether they cause it, or merely share in it. They are native to our selves.

Figure 12: A simple method for deriving geometric quarters and linear thirds using straight line geometries. Further divisions show the extension into eighths and sixteenths as well as sixths and twelfths. The resulting compound grid is often referred to as a tartan grid due to its resemblance to traditional Scottish fabric weaving.

Note that dividing the form down the horizontal and vertical centers yields linear halves and quarter areas (13·1). Similarly, linear thirds yield ninths as areas (13·2).

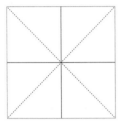

Diagram 13·1: Finding the center and quartering the square.

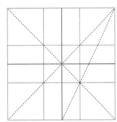

Diagram 13·2: Finding the thirds within the square.

Diagram 13·3: Further subdivisions into fourths.

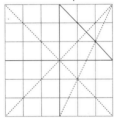

Diagram 13·4: Halving thirds to find sixths.

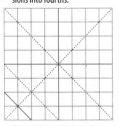

Diagram 13·5: Continued subdivisions into eighths.

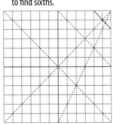

Diagram 13·6: Half again to determine twelfths.

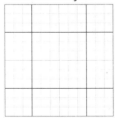

Diagram 13·7: The resulting tartan grid.

Diagram 13·8: The grid and its geometry.

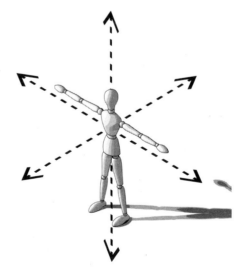

Figure 13: Standing upright with our hands outstretched, we easily apportion the world to reflect our orientation. We perceive things as ahead or behind, left or right of and above or below us.

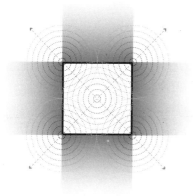

Figure 14: The diagram to the left shows the perceptual pattern of boundary and center in a square figure.

Figure 15: The variation to the right diagrams the proportioning of space from within the square figure.

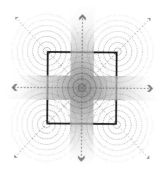

As we measure things in relationship to one another, we eventually encounter scale. The continuing subdivisions and relationships simply overwhelm our point of view. At some point, the web of lines outstrips our capacity to discern pattern, just as the size of the paper limits the number of folds. We might further ask what happens when one group of measurements overlaps another. Can we measure dissimilar things similarly?

One scenario is to impose the method first defined by Descartes, thereby ordering from without, using a neutral method or tool. The usefulness of the Cartesian grid resides in its abstraction and purity of method. The grid can provide a common expression for things with or without intrinsic form or shape. Algebraic formulae are just one example of how we gain form through the grid.

Aside from classes in geometry, algebra and physics, a contemporary experience of the grid occurs at the computer monitor. The screen composes the world as dots of light, or pixels. The lower left-hand pixel of the viewing surface serves as the arbitrary zero point. Two numbers assign subsequent pixels to rows or columns. This is the practical Cartesian grid. It can count to infinity, although in practice it ends at the screen's boundaries. An image can be larger or smaller, but it starts at zero and moves up in increments without real scale, albeit with practical size limitations.

The grid of the computer screen exists outside of meaning until we assign it a proper interpretation. As the digital environment evolves the character of its conventions becomes ever-more important. One reason to understand the evolution of earlier conventions – what we might call 'local relational geometry' – is that they provide a ground from which to critique the digital realm. In this text, we discuss the universal Cartesian grid after we explore the fundamentals of the relational grid. Half as many pixels is different from half of a form or shape. The difference is nuanced but vital to considering measure and order.

Rules of engagement

The history of architecture intertwines with the histories of mathematics and philosophy. Criteria for how to do things well compete in the marketplace of ideas.* Relational calculus and the grid both make use of scale and order to

* NOTE ON THE IDEAL
The architecture of both the narrative and the family demonstrate that order, whether perceived and imposed, or perceived and distilled, participates in how we make sense of the world. It is inevitable perhaps that some forms of order come to be seen as either clearer or more desirable. Philosophy, aesthetics in particular, describes competing views about preferred, better constructions. From that discussion there emerges, almost inevitably, notions of an ideal.

The histories of both architecture and philosophy encompass much debate about whether there is an ultimate 'best form', an ideal. We encounter some of these as we describe architectural procedure. And although we are not without opinion, our goal is to present the terms of the argument without pretending to any ultimate conclusion.

Figure 16: Stones strewn randomly, encountered by chance in a field.

Figure 17: Viewed as a set of four, they may describe an irregular quadrilateral figure.

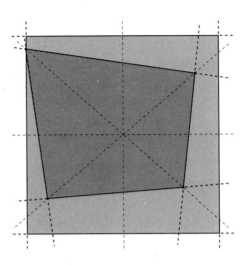

Figure 18: The drawing shows the boundaries and axes center point of the figure identified by the four stones.

Diagram 19·1: Viewed in plan, the stones define this irregular figure.

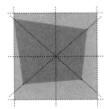

Diagram 19·2: The simple assumption of corner diagonals allows us to bound the form using a larger square with the same center point.

Diagram 19·3: This second variation shows the diagonal center point locating a smaller, enclosed square.

Diagram 19·4: This alternative sharing of the diagonal center point defines a square of equal scale to the original.

represent the world. Stories commonly have beginnings, middles and ends. Modern narratives may rearrange the parts, but their structures remain a matter of scale, moving from the episode to larger compositional entities: fables, epic poems and novels. Similarly, one might begin with an individual and move on to siblings, parents, etc., continuing to extend the family tree by branching forward, backward or laterally. Such an enlarged set of relationships might construct a clan, community or even a nation. These sorts of calculus emerge from both a starting point and perceived boundaries or rules of enclosure.

Imagine coming across several stone markers in an open field (17–18). If we identify the stones as a group, we might start to perceive figures and boundaries in the open space (19). In doing so, we begin to structure the hitherto unstructured terrain. We begin to make architecture within space.

In our example, the group may be seen as an irregular quadrilateral – four sides neither parallel nor at right angles. Such a figure might result from tossing four stones from a single place while attempting to construct a square. If this were our intention, it would also be possible to adjust the stones to achieve the more regular figure of a square. This is not simply a rhetorical gesture; regular figures follow sets of rules by definition. In the case of the square, the rules are exceedingly simple. All four sides are of equal measure, as are the two diagonals. Middle divisions follow accordingly. We make sense of an irregular quadrilateral by overlaying it with the simpler architecture of a square. In doing so, we construe both figures as diagrams.

With diagrams in mind, we can easily perceive three possible relationships. The square can surround the first figure, or vice versa; the two figures can share alignments at their diagonal center or share corner adjacencies. They might also be merely near one another. Diagrammatic geometry helps us to organize and analyze the forms as well as to visualize and act on the relationship. The diagrams to the left (19·1–4) illustrate the relationship of three squares that share an axial center with the irregular figure.

In practice, irregular figures commonly appear within a site, the tangible context for building design. Site boundaries may result from irregular landforms, prior orientations of roadways and rivers or from more abstract and circumstantial conditions arising from a site's particular history. Strategies for

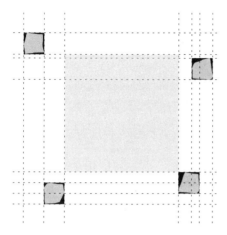

Figure 19: The drawing to the left shows an amalgam of multiple orthogonal relationships between the figures. These include edge and center relationships, groupings and shifted dynamics.

The diagrams to the right (20·1–8) identify each separately.

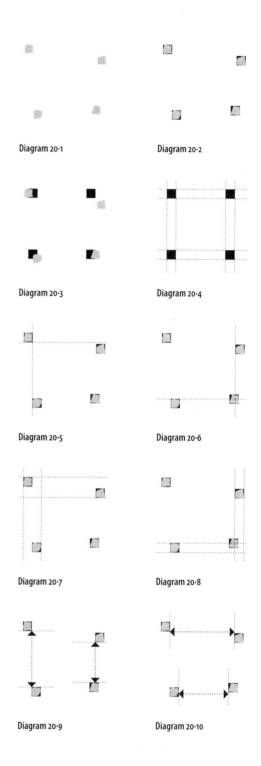

Diagram 20·1   Diagram 20·2

Diagram 20·3   Diagram 20·4

Diagram 20·5   Diagram 20·6

Diagram 20·7   Diagram 20·8

Diagram 20·9   Diagram 20·10

working through the nuances of irregularity derive from overlays drawn from the simpler architecture of regular figures.

Returning to the four stones, we can demonstrate how elemental spatial relationships clarify such strategies (20). Here, the relationships hinge upon three simple notions: center, edge and boundary. We can identify centers and edges of each individual stone and the entire composition. Boundaries derive from relationships between two or more stones. As we characterize those relationships, we discover four fundamental visual concepts: CONTRAST, REPETITION, ALIGNMENT and PROXIMITY. In our diagrams, we note that the four stones are approximately the same size, thereby exhibiting little contrast in dimension (20·1&2). The image of four similarly sized objects arrayed in a roughly orderly manner prompts an acknowledgement of repetition (20·3&4). Visualizing the relationships between centers and edges depends on ideas of alignment (20·5–8). Comparing the intervals between objects in their arrangement defines their proximity (20·9–10).

Contrast includes a larger number of differences, as we shall discover in CHAPTER 4. Here, as we measure the irregular forms of the stones, we see that they are approximately the same scale and likeness. The square boxes drawn around the shapes in 20·2 help us approximate and represent that similarity. Recognizing that the arrangement easily fits within a square wherein the stones roughly occupy the four corners, suggests an interpolation of basic repetition on both horizontal and vertical axes. Diagram 20·3 compares the ordered repetition to the actual placement of the stones, while 20·4 illustrates the ideal with all elements aligned and evenly spaced.

Measuring the ALIGNMENT of the forms, we discover that alignment relationships outside of that ideal nonetheless use the same boundaries of each stone to construct sight lines from edges and centers. Comparing 20·5 with 20·6, we note the former gathers two edge relationships at the fulcrum of the farthest outlying stone while the latter organizes a grouping in which the center of one stone relates to the inner edges of two others. As we continue our observations by completing the boundary lines of the upper-left and lower-right stones, we see that the edge relationships (20·7) govern a broad horizontal and vertical area, whereas the centered relationships (20·8) form a more tightly constrained visual area.

Our last observations measure horizontal and vertical distances between pairs of stones (20·9&10). These comprise the proximity of elements within the whole arrangement.

Positive & negative space

In the next chapter, we explore fundamental figure-ground relationships that utilize these observations as part of the purpose of ordered visual design. The groundwork for order is a fundamental visual concept that grows from figure-ground – the perception of POSITIVE and NEGATIVE SPACE.

When observing any black and white image, we identify figure and ground as separate entities. In the beginning of this chapter, we showed figure-ground images (3–9) that demonstrate visual ambiguity. In the diagrams, there is less ambiguity, but clear or otherwise, we identify two classes of shapes. The object in the field we call positive shape or space. The field itself we refer to as negative space. As part of the analytic process, we observe the form of negative space and ask ourselves whether that form is coherent or merely resultant. In the case of four squares placed in a corner arrangement, we read the squares as positive but we also observe the presence of the cruciform as a negative space of equal value and clarity (21).

In diagramming as well as in design itself, the observation of negative space is essential to the analytic process. This is more than a pretty coincidence; the resultant space should be part of the intent and part of what we observe as the order of architectural form. Just as with our cruciform, a courtyard scheme rendered as figure-ground can help explore the proportional relationship between the positive and negative space of an architectural composition (22).

In 1748, Giambattista Nolli published the results of his ten-year mapping project of the city of Rome. In addition to its unprecedented accuracy – Pope Benedict XIV granted him access to every building and apartment in the city – the map is significant for its use of negative space (23). Nolli made the fateful decision to distinguish between public and private spaces within the city. In his mapping, he displayed private spaces as block forms without interiors – FOOTPRINTS – while showing the interior forms of public buildings – churches and public offices – with plan elements of their interiors visible.

The comparison of context as mass with interior organization has since become a near-standard for architectural practice. This allows, among other things, the observation of relationships among interior plan elements, arrangements and proportions – *parti* – with the formal elements of the site. We explore those kinds of formal relationships in the next chapter.

Order & the orthogonal

Early in their first semester, our students generally ask why their exercises occur within gridded space. This is a reasonable question. The easy answer is that we start from simple and move to complex. A more nuanced explanation centers on orientation and our innate sense of place. In the introduction, we defined architecture as how we make sense of the world by establishing our place within it. Until relatively recently, humanity occupied a world of largely undifferentiated wilderness. Given our propensity to experience the world according to the geometry of our own bodies – front, back, up, down, center – when we first emerged from caves to modify our environment, we employed fundamental attributes of our corporeal sensibilities. Horizontals and verticals, axes and thresholds, pattern and proportion; these were the tools at

Figure 20: Four squares placed at the corners of a square – a positive shape – also create a cruciform negative space.

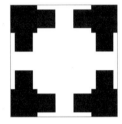

Figure 21: Four corner forms create the figure of a positive shape as well as defining the courtyard figure, a negative space.

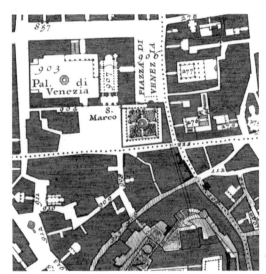

Figure 22: Fragment of the Nolli plan, 1748. Note the use of *poché* to indicate and differentiate public from private space.

our disposal to establish order in a large and scary place. Orienting ourselves may now seem so commonplace as to escape our conscious attention, but it remains essential. It may seem merely practical, but it is also philosophical. It is a sacred task that belongs to architecture.

As we observe an object, we draw a line of sight. Moving within the world, we draw thousands, perhaps millions, of these lines daily. Assimilating them, privileging some and ignoring others, is the fundamental mapping by which we construct and navigate a landscape from our own perspectives. Human beings share a propensity to organize toward the simply expressible. Recognizable figures, simple geometries and grids form part of that background precisely because of our innate desire for order. Deviation from order increases complexity and creates powerful exceptions. From an individual's perspective, exceptionalism is paramount. From a distance, exceptions disappear. Designers understand this – the fundamental context of everything particular is a harmony of all the particulars.

The emergence of pattern is a foregone conclusion. The question as to what pattern should emerge is the essential role of the designer. To excel, designers must grasp their discipline as well as they know their own efforts. Acknowledging history is not uncreative. We do not have to invent the pencil anew in order to draw. We do not have to program our own computers to work in a digital environment. Those contexts – pencils, computers, etc. – are the media of expression. They are the ground from which figures emerge. As we learn from gestalt theory, there is no object without a background. There is no *it* without a *where* and *when*. A single note requires silence to be heard and distinguished. Every work of architecture reduces to a single point at a great enough distance. It is a matter of scale.

The idea of scale suggests a hierarchy of composition. By both convention and in keeping with our perceptual mechanisms, we map the world to our pictures and sensations in an orderly fashion. It begins with acknowledgement of the limits of our perceptual field. The boundaries that we recognize form the scale of our actions. Both when we observe and when we design, we reference our actions to the constraints of that field. Placing things within and sizing those same things is the first order of business. This is how figures enter the ground and how, at a different scale, the figures propose dependent, additional elements. In this way, each field begets its figures, which in turn sponsor additional figural elements. This process of organized hierarchy manifests order and reflects scale and proportion.

The conventions of drawing within design embody the sequence of developing order. That is where we begin the next chapter.

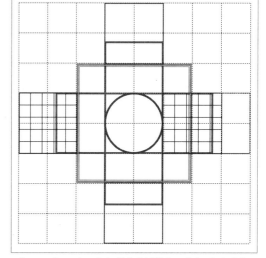

Figure 23: Geometric analysis of Palladio's *Villa Rotanda* showing underlying grid and spatial areas in overlay. Diagramming is the first step in the study of precedent.

THE LANGUAGE OF CONTRAST

In describing contrast of objects and their context, we encounter several terms that overlap in meaning.

- The term FIGURE-GROUND denotes the perception of an intelligible picture or pattern of organization by distinguishing objects from the background in an image. Architectural plans often borrow from mapping convention the particular use of figure-ground to depict buildings within a setting.

- Designers refer to NEGATIVE SPACE to identify compositional balance particularly when the space, not the object, presents itself as the more dominant shape. In that context, POSITIVE SPACE distinguishes the role of the object shape or form.

POCHÉ

A larger fragment of the Nolli plan, 1748. The *poché* creates a complex image of both positive and negative spaces.

GLOSSARY OF TERMS

ALIGNMENT: Arrangement along a straight line, or in visible relative positions.

CONTRAST: An abrupt shift in weight and/or intensity.

FIGURE-GROUND: The perception of images via distinguishing objects from background by contrast.

- Also refers to contexts wherein the distinction is ambiguous.

FOOTPRINT: In architectural convention, the reduction of buildings to the plan outline of the entire building without interior detail.

HIERARCHY: The order of dominance, or priority, of the various elements within the composition

PARTI: A diagram that delineates the dominant organizational or formal concept governing an architectural scheme. From French, literally, the big idea.

POCHÉ: The filled-in areas of a plan or section drawing. The convention reveals the parts of a building cut by an imaginary section plane.

- Giambattista Nolli's figure-ground drawing of Rome employed contrasting fields of black and white space to represent architectural objects and their context (*below*).

- Beaux-Arts drawings used black *poché* to distinguish walls and columns from (white) space.

POSITIVE and NEGATIVE SPACE: Terms used in discussing overall organization of an image or form. Related to FIGURE-GROUND.

PROXIMITY: Nearness in space to another element.

REPETITION: The recurring use of the same element or theme.

RHYTHM: The moving force, or flow, which connects elements within a composition.

SCHEMA: The representation of a plan or concept in the form of an outline or model. The plural form is SCHEMATA.

VALUE: An element of art that refers to the lightness or darkness of a color or tone. Value is an especially important element in works of art when color is absent, as with grayscale images.

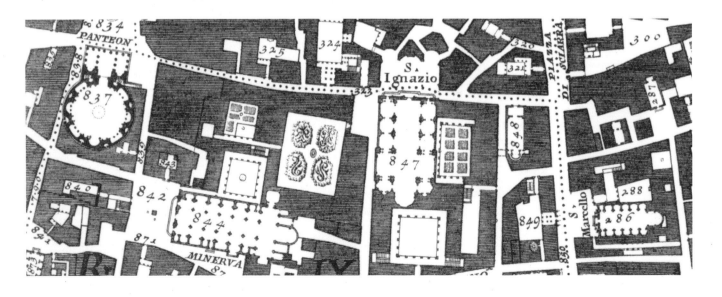

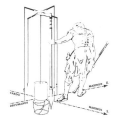

DESCRIPTION 3
Order, orientation & the orthogonal

Some may view the gridded city as a soulless by-product of the modern era. The truth, as we might expect, is altogether more compelling. Ancient cultures commonly employed orthogonal geometry. Apart from any pragmatic advantages they may have offered ancient builders, right angles frequently signified loftier connections. As we observed earlier, the intersection formed by the cardinal axes frequently served as a symbolic template for the sacred order of the cosmos. At the same time, the right angle reflects the intrinsically human capacity for orientation within the world, with our embodied symmetries of up/down, front/back, left/right and before/after.

As such, ancient cultures commonly employed orthogonal geometry in rites that ordained the construction of buildings both sacred and mundane. Temple structures like the great complexes at Karnak or Angkor Wat consistently demonstrate the widespread use of orthogonal geometries to arrange sacred precincts. Their designs embodied intricate theological schema of hierarchic spatial subdivision. Most often, these practices extended to the planning of urban settlements.

One of the clearest examples from the ancient world of a gridded settlement is that of the *castrum*, the Roman military encampment built to house and protect soldiers, equipment and supplies. Using a standardized, orthogonal template and the *groma*, a Roman legion could erect a *castrum* in a matter of hours (1). In conquered regions where military garrisons remained, the structure of the *castrum* served as an underlying grid for the establishment of more permanent towns and cities.

Timgad, located in present-day Algeria, is a vivid example of a Roman city laid out along the lines of a legionary *castrum*. Its distinctive central intersection of *cardo* and *decumanus* organize the orthogonal grid of blocks and open spaces. Because desert sands covered Timgad not long after its abandonment in the seventh century, its original Roman grid remains particularly well-preserved (2).

Other cities, despite centuries of continuous inhabitation after the fall of the Western Empire, still hold clear vestiges of their Roman origins. The map

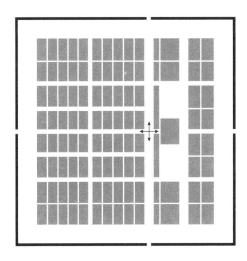

Figure 1: The template for a Roman legionary encampment, the *castrum*, provided for ordered spatial hierarchies and expedited construction.

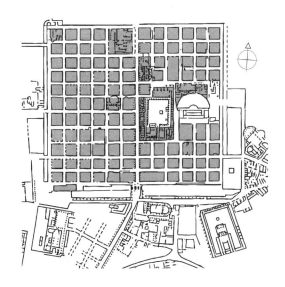

Figure 2: Plan of the Roman city of Timgad, in present-day Algeria. The structure of the original *castrum* determined the layout of the city center.

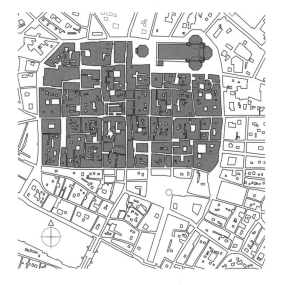

Figure 3: The center of Florence retains a pattern of street and blocks reflecting its origins as a gridded city of Roman origin.

of the city of Florence, for example, reveals a distinctly orthogonal pattern of gridded blocks at its center, evidence of the original settlement established by the Roman general Sulla in 80 BCE (3).

Orthogonal city planning in the ancient world was not restricted to the West. In China, the Zhou Dynasty city of Chengzhou – now Luoyang – was planned on a regular orthogonal grid as early as the eleventh century BCE (4). The layout of the city was similar to the plan of the 'well-field', a pattern derived from the Chinese character *jing*, meaning 'well'. The character was similar in appearance to an *octothorpe* (#), a form of nine-square grid that depicts the well-field plan, wherein eight identical square plots of privately cultivated land surround a communal central square. The Chengzhou nine-square diagram became the model for subsequent city plans throughout China. The *Rites of Zhou* – a third-century BCE compilation of Confucian texts – codified its principles. It included formal principles dictating planning practices across a broad range of scales, from individual residences to the layout of entire regions.

The nine-square well-field system served to establish equitable access to agricultural land during the Zhou Dynasty. The same impulse lay behind the Northwest Land Ordinance Act of 1785, which established what we now refer to as the Jeffersonian grid. Thomas Jefferson worried that the newly acquired federal lands west of the Appalachians might fall into the hands of a few large speculators or lead to the establishment of an American landed aristocracy. Jefferson believed that the best way to strengthen the democratic aspirations of the new nation was to ensure that the majority of its citizens owned the land on which they lived.

The initial surveys of the Northwest Land Ordinance divided federal territory into square townships, six miles by six miles and aligned with the cardinal axes. Each township subdivided into lots of one square mile, or 640 acres, quartered into sections of 160 acres, and further quartered into fields of 40 acres. The guiding principle behind this division was the belief that each section of 160 acres would provide enough land to sustain an individual farm. In areas that came to be towns or cities, the arrangement of streets and blocks followed a further pattern of subdivision. The image on the left is from a 1910 fire insurance map of Albia, county seat of Monroe County, Iowa (5). The town's square blocks are a vestige of the Jeffersonian grid, which organizes the entire state. Even the blocks themselves are quartered by the cruciform network of alleys. The heart of the town is the Public Square. As is customary for county seats in Iowa, the Monroe County Courthouse sits in the center of Albia's Public Square.

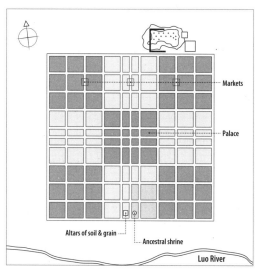

Figure 4: Plan – Chengzhou, China, Zhou Dynasty.

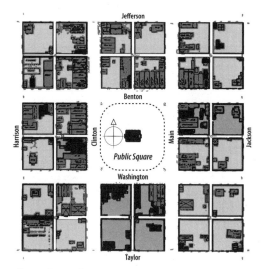

Figure 5: Nineteenth-century town square plan – Albia, Iowa.

DEMONSTRATION 3·1
Gestalt defined

Gestalt & pattern

Over the years, designers and artists have adopted language from several dis-ciplines to assist in their own discourse. The term 'gestalt' originates in the literature of psychology where it identifies a group of perceptual processes as well as a general theory and holistic approach to therapy. In visual studies, it provides a useful language for identifying common themes that confront the beginning designer sorting through observed patterns in studio practice.

Gestalt theory proceeds from a recognition that we tend to organize our experience toward regular, ordered, symmetrical and simple observations. This idea accepts as true that we observe objects in a context and that our per-ceptions result from our interpretation of both object and background taken together. The theory describes four interactive concepts.

When we observe a scene or image, patterns 'emerge' from the contrast of figure and ground (1). From those patterns, we 'reify' – accept as real – an interpretation of both object and context (3). We might find our perception stable or ambiguous – 'multistable' in the language of gestalt theory. Further-more, clearer shapes – often of simple form – tend to remain 'invariant' in their identity regardless of position, distortion or rendering (4).

In architectural plans, we typically observe dark areas against a lighter page. Drawing convention privileges this contrast as it helps us perceive both the building mass and surrounding space so that the presence of both *emerges*. In the example to the right, two simple forms in a field exhibit patterns that *reify* the total composition including proportion, placement and the result-ing courtyard between the forms (4). Our perception of the courtyard results from the *multistability* of the image, we infer its shape because of the contrast – a figure-ground convention – and the composition – the design. The simplic-ity of the two forms and the courtyard's spatial description allows us to recog-nize them even when we change the rendering from plan view to axonometric projection. They therefore also exhibit *invariance*.

Other characteristics

In designing and in learning to design well, we engage in ongoing analysis of visual evidence. Proceeding from the four operational insights described above and in support of the underlying assertion towards order in perception, gestalt theory also identifies a fundamental vocabulary referring to sensation that beginning designers should keep in mind. The language has the benefit of clarity, as do its underlying concepts.

As we move towards order, we also approach the succinct, meaning-ful, substantial and expressive. In gestalt studies, the German word *präg-nanz*, 'pithiness', identifies the order that occurs as rules within our percep-tual framework. Psychologists, in refining *prägnanz*, identify six precepts that hypothetically predict our interpretation of sensation – in this instance toward perceiving order. Often called 'gestalt laws', they attempt to define

Figure 1: The image depicts a Dalmatian amidst the shadows of trees and thus demonstrates emergence. We perceive the dog as a whole rather than inferring the dog from its parts.

Figure 2: Reification identifies perceptions that imply more spatial information than is explicit in an image. We perceive a white square in the figure on the left, although there is no drawn white square.

Figure 3: Multistability describes the tendency of certain ambiguous perceptions to oscillate between alternative visual interpretations. The infamous face/vase illusion is a multistable image.

Figure 4: Gestalt theory notes that we recognize simple geo-metrical objects regardless of rotation, translation, and scale. Invariance includes recognition through variations in illumina-tion, aspect and rendering. This insight helps account for us being able to regard both the plan view and the axonometric as representing similar object groups.

 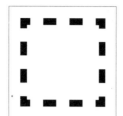

Figure 5: Two examples of closure.

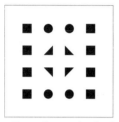 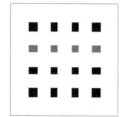

Figure 6: Two examples of similarity, one composed of three distinct shapes, the other showing overlapping groupings.

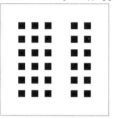 

Figure 7: Two examples of proximity. The first uses regular forms while the second pictures irregular shapes.

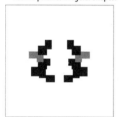 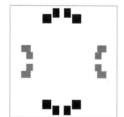

Figure 8: Examples of symmetry.

Figure 9: An example of continuity. The picture on the right shows the interpretation of the composition to its left as continuous.

 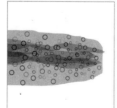

Figure 10: Examples of common fate.

patterns of observation that lead toward establishing visual expression and meaning. These laws demarcate perceptions of closure, similarity, proximity, symmetry, continuity and common fate.

In design, we find it useful to analyze form, both in precedents and in our own work. This is the heart of diagramming. It makes our analysis visible, verifiable and concrete. Architecture, the subject of our analysis, in both simple and complex expressions becomes clearer if we know what we are looking for. Thus, what begins as a set of psychological notions becomes for designers useful criteria for analyzing relationships among forms present in their work.

LAW OF CLOSURE

When we observe an incomplete regular figure, there is a tendency to increase its regularity by filling in the gaps toward completion of the form. This occurs in the instance of an inconsistent line, a staggered perimeter sequence or a grouping that only partially occupies a regular space (5). It is also why we may perceive the gap of an entrance and still recognize the overall form of an architectural figure

LAW OF SIMILARITY

Facing a number of objects, we tend to group similar elements into collective entities or totalities that reflect relationships of form, size or surface (6). Even as spatial intervals remain constant, a change in aspect has the potential to interrupt and subdivide our experience of pattern and order.

LAW OF PROXIMITY

The interval between objects can profoundly affect our perception of groups within a larger collective (7). This is easily evident when other contrasts are absent but even in irregular collectives, it holds as a powerful sense of affinity among differing elements.

LAW OF SYMMETRY

In figure-ground relationships, symmetry appears as the manifestation of an axis, the perception of a line or center around which objects disperse in regular fashion (8). When this occurs, we perceive the symmetrical components as a collective, regardless of distance to the axis.

LAW OF CONTINUITY

Once observed, patterns foster an urge toward extension. Having formed a pattern in our experience, we seek to continue the pattern into both space and time (9). Abrupt ends in music, movement or visible pattern arrest our attention in part because we expect them to continue. In this way, the conclusion of a figure or figured grouping creates a sharp reading of the ground implying continuity.

LAW OF COMMON FATE

We perceive elements moving in the same direction as a collective or unit (10). Armies march, because the soldiers move in unison. Observed on a field and against a ground, visual elements seem either static or kinetic. In images and diagrams, motion occurs by implication. In compositions, the implied provides a substantial signal toward both balance and asymmetry.

Gestalt in design

Gestalt images in their purer forms can seem a long way from practical application in design. An emerging dog or cow appears to have little in common with architecture. Similarly, reified images, while graphically tantalizing, do not immediately bring anything like buildings to mind. The same can be said of the other two characteristics, multistability and invariance. So why are they important?

As we said at the beginning of this demonstration, gestalt provides language particularly applicable to the visual aspect of drawings and diagrams. In particular, the gestalt laws expose the workings of images found in the process of design and design analysis. They explain what we look at and thereby help us work toward what we try to develop in architecture. As ideas about both vision and experience, they reveal the inner workings of design representation and built form.

Architecture is order reified, it makes something abstract – order – into something more real – architecture. The experience of buildings brings ideas about order to our attention through the senses. The underlying principle of closure comes to mind as we subconsciously respond to the way things are displaced and articulated in space. The illustrations below demonstrate simple ideas about enclosure and the sorts of patterns that express them (13).

Columns and walls forming a perimeter exhibit closure just as Stonehenge (PP. 11–12) appears as a circle because we fill in the gaps between the stones automatically. As designers, we can sort through ideas for built form better when we remain conscious of those sorts of possibilities. In this way, formal understanding leads to better practice.

The lower two images continue that basic exploration using columns and walls to articulate the perimeter and entrance more robustly. Although simple – and reduced to figure-ground – they represent a dialogue of formal concepts with gestalt principles (13.3&4). Moreover, the ideas designers discover through figure-ground drawings can set the standard for testing those ideas in three dimensions (14).

Aside from the simple recognition that we observe in an orderly manner, gestalt theories remind us that sorting through an abundance of visual material is what designers do for a living. It is the particular qualities of any given

Figure 11: The emerging cow.

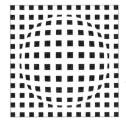

Figure 12: A single sphere emerging.

Figure 13: Right, four plan views of perimeter conditions and modeled extrusions of the same compositions that reflect several gestalt laws.

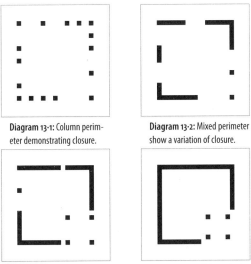

Diagram 13·1: Column perimeter demonstrating closure.

Diagram 13·2: Mixed perimeter show a variation of closure.

Diagrams 13·3–4: Two compositions of walls and columns exhibiting both closure and continuity.

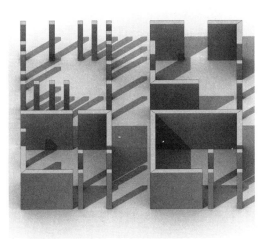

Figure 14. Extruded models of the four plans to the left.

space that interest us. It is not only what we worry over, it is the soul of what we practice. A vocabulary that describes what we do allows us to do it better. It helps us work through design and structure, analyze and evaluate alternatives.

15·1: A balance of walls and columns exhibits closure.

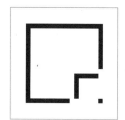

15·2&3: Two compositions dominated by walls illustrate close variations using both closure and continuity.

Figure 17: Emergence defines the process of forming complex pattern from simpler rules.

We perceive four spheres as emerging from within the pattern of the first image. In the next two diagrams we can readily identify both the cruciform and the rotated square as they appear from within the varied checkerboard patterns.

Figure 15: Three additional figure-ground examples of perimeter conditions continue the exploration of perimeter and entrance.

Figure 16: Extruded models of the three plans as shown on the left.

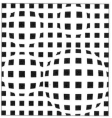

Diagram 17·1: Four spheres emerging.

Diagram 17·2: A cruciform emerging.

Diagram 17·3: A rotated square emerging.

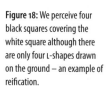

Figure 18: We perceive four black squares covering the white square although there are only four L-shapes drawn on the ground – an example of reification.

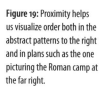

Figure 19: Proximity helps us visualize order both in the abstract patterns to the right and in plans such as the one picturing the Roman camp at the far right.

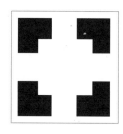

Diagram 19·1: Proximity reveals path.

Diagram 19·2: Proximity reveals hierarchy and path.

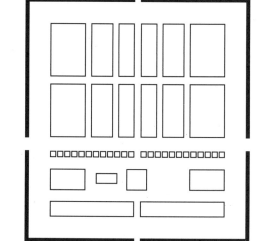

Diagram 19·3: Proximity allows us to confirm both hierarchy and path in this plan of a Roman camp.

Regular & irregular forms

Following the principles of gestalt studies we can make certain observations concerning the perception of forms in compositions. Basic perception follows certain patterns though the forms involved may be regular or irregular in contour.

Curves, angles and variegated edges affect the overall appearance but still fall into some general categories of figure-ground strategies. The first examples below show four form types as both regular or geometric figures and corresponding irregular or organic figures.

Note that despite obvious differences both versions share similar outline and position in their configuration.

DEMONSTRATION 3·2
Gestalt readings of basic form

Regular or geometric **Irregular or organic**

Intrude and erode

Basic geometries guide the perimeter, position and proportion of both regular and organic figures.

Diagram 1: Intrude and erode – the figure appears to intrude or the ground appears to erode.

FIGURE-GROUND STRATEGY ONE

When the figure connects with one edge, it either intrudes into the ground or appears as an erosion of the ground. Depending on the exact configuration, the effect is either definitive or ambiguous.

Center and wrap

The first example uses centering geometry to determine the position and proportion of the figure. The irregular example approximates the same visual effect.

Diagram 2: Center and wrap – as the figure defines a center of balance, the ground wraps around it.

FIGURE-GROUND STRATEGY TWO

As the figure moves from the edge, it begins to infer a center within the ground and the ground wraps the figure. The configuration and placement of the figure in relationship to the true center implies weight across both horizontal and vertical axes.

Traverse and divide

In both examples a figure traverses the ground positioned adjacent to the center and in proportion to the ground.

Diagram 3: Traverse and divide – the figure moves across the ground and divides the field.

FIGURE-GROUND STRATEGY THREE

When the figure moves from edge to edge it traverses the ground and the ground divides around the figure. This strategy is inherently axial. It suggests direction and, depending on the configuration of the ground, travels with or across the grain of the whole.

Displace and tear

Traversing figures shift over and back relative to the center of the composition.

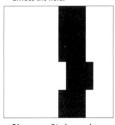 

Diagram 4: Displace and tear – the shift within the figure suggests lateral displacement while the ground appears torn.

FIGURE-GROUND STRATEGY FOUR

When traversing edges shift in relationship to its direction it can suggest an apparent motion, either displacing the figure's edge or tearing the ground. As a subset of the traverse and divide strategy, displacement is strongest when figure edges remain parallel.

Direct & derivative forms

As a composition evolves in its complexity to include more than one figure, it alters our perception. The tension of a compound figure expands the gestalt reading of figure-ground and creates multiple balances between objects and context. The examples here show the four form types as both *regular* or direct figures and corresponding modified or derivative compositions.

Below, both versions follow similar gestures and formal constraints in their configuration.

Regular or direct   **Modified or derivative**

FIGURE-GROUND STRATEGY FIVE

The facing edges of a regular figure composed of abbreviated traversing gestures crosses the same axis and creates a connecting negative space in the form of a sideways H.

Diagram 5: H-shapes – two figures traverse, dividing the ground on both axes.

H-shapes
Two figures intrude into the space and toward each other on the same axis, demarcating and connecting two spaces.

FIGURE-GROUND STRATEGY SIX

As a single figure traverses incompletely from the top edge, the ground appears to wrap the figure. The resulting negative space forms a surrounding U-shaped forecourt. Rotated 90°, the configuration changes axis and becomes C-shaped. Proportion and placement affect figure-ground balance.

Diagram 6: U-shapes – a figure intrudes and divides.

U-shapes
The space wraps around a single intrusion and defines a partial perimeter that moves around the form.

FIGURE-GROUND STRATEGY SEVEN

When similar figures occupy all four corners, their combined negative space defines a cross. Modifying the figures affects the regularity of the apparent field. Depending on the configuration, the effect may be either definitive or ambiguous.

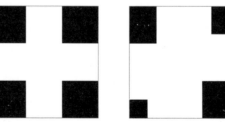

Diagram 7: Cruciforms – figures intrude at the corners.

Cruciform
Figures intrude at the corners, articulating the spatial cross-axes as negative space.

FIGURE-GROUND STRATEGY EIGHT

When diagonal edges converge, the resulting figure-ground is dynamic but multi-ambiguous. Changes in the symmetry or balance of elements may improve the figuration, however, many X-shaped compositions often prove difficult to evolve beyond their first bold gesture.

Diagram 8: X-shapes and diagonals – intruding figures suggest direction and apparent formal motion.

X-shapes or diagonals
The figure centers and intrudes resulting in a dynamic spatial gesture.

Varied rendering effects – set one

LINEAR REPRESENTATION

Changing to linear drawing from filled shapes of black and white generally renders figure-ground composition in a more subtle fashion. The character and weight of the outline play a key role in the intelligibility of the forms. In addition, the reduction of formal contrast allows greater scrutiny of the edge condition of both figure and field.

USING TONE

Color affects contrast. When we alter value – the light-dark aspect of color – away from the extremes of black and white we can profoundly effect figure-ground perception even though the composition remains unchanged.

INVERTING FIGURE-GROUND

Interchanging white and black values in a composition inverts both figure and ground as it reverses their roles in the image. We notice the inversion most where ambiguity – multistability – is least. In general, clear distinction between shape and field in a composition amplifies the visual effect of inversion.

Varied rendering effects – set two

LINEAR REPRESENTATION

As the elements of the composition grow in number and variety, the role of line weight in maintaining the intelligibility of the figure-ground relationship increases. In these examples, line weight remains constant – excepting the darker frame for the composition. Notice that the upper row's x-shaped composition, in particular, lacks clues to spatial intelligibility.

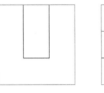 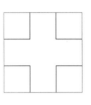

USING TONE

As compositions acquire more elements than a single figure, tonal possibilities expand – figures may contrast with each other as well as with the ground. With tonal shifts, visual similarity can alter relationships that seemed firm in black and white. In the case of the upper x-shaped composition, gestalt emergence produces an apparent three-dimensional image of a pyramid and resolves much of the previous ambiguity.

INVERTING TONAL VALUE

Value reversal of the figure and ground makes concepts of positive and negative space visible. What was previously figural may now appear as ground and *vice versa*. In general, the clearer the distinctions found in the original *compositional structure*, the clearer the reversal. Thus, the regular examples of the U-shaped, H-shaped and cruciform compositions exhibit their ground most clearly, while the dynamics of the x-shape remain highly ambiguous.

OVERVIEW
The first project

*THE SCALE OF THE EXERCISES

Throughout this text, we often deliberately omit exact dimensions for the exercises. In practice, we use a relatively modest 4"×6" index card for the project in order to fit the large number of responses from our students within available display space. The actual image size is 3.5", placed in the upper portion of the card, as shown below.

This chapter begins the four-project sequence that evolves throughout the text. In our first semester course, we use the first weeks of design studio to familiarize students with studio practice and rigor, in particular the use of theme and variation as a means for exploration and development. Comprised of three interwoven themes, we designed PROJECT 1 to introduce fundamental figure-ground composition, focusing on the relationship between figure and field in defining spatial organization within a ground.*

Spatial organization dominates much of our thinking about architecture. This seems normal. After all, planning implies determining our interaction with the environment. We want to know and predict where we are and what is near and far from any point in an organizational configuration. These sorts of maps depict order in a 'you are here' diagram of a building or a route path downloaded from the internet. Purposeful order illuminates our place in a designed environment. On a practical level, it helps us navigate the world. With greater ambition and application, it can also amplify meaning and wonder in our experience of the world.

The project set begins with proportional placement of two figures and thereafter evolves into a consideration of defined and implied fields. The exercises described here introduce beginning designers to basic tools used in formal analysis and generation. At the same time, presentations and critiques provide specific language for describing form in composition regardless of the character of the forms. These first descriptions form the foundation for all subsequent projects and discourse.

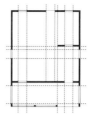

Figure 1: The schema for a small dwelling with no and a sheltered portico seen in CHAPTER 2.

CHAPTER 4
Design & drawing fundamentals

On drawing

Thus far, we have introduced some basic principles of visual order. In this chapter, we elaborate on our introduction to figure-ground, and articulate the pivotal role it plays in design thinking and drawing. The contrast between a figure and its ground or FIELD provides design with a setting for building. It governs how we visualize potential organization and construction. It becomes a kind of drawing where design anticipates action. The most common architectural drawing is the plan. Its name reflects its purpose – designers plan before committing to action.

Architecture and drawing form a close partnership. While it may be possible to build without drawing first, one or more diagrams still inhabit the architecture. When we survey a building, we can easily record our observations in a drawing. More importantly, we can tease out the inherent diagram that illuminates the intent of the designer. Drawings demonstrate the rules that inhabit the architecture.

We can represent most if not all objects, real or imagined, through drawing. Drawings may be clear or obscure, detailed or general, accurate or approximate, good or bad, but they always embody a specific view of an object. In this way, drawing serves as a record of both the object and our perception of it.

Imagining a building often begins with a drawing. It may be a plan, a perspective or another sort of visual convention. It might be entirely untutored, as in the case of a child's scrawl, or schematic in a more formal manner. The case for the diagram begins with the scheme. In turn, schemes begin with an assessment of their place in the world – the GROUND.

Drawings utilize a central feature of our vision – figure-ground distinction. Figure-ground, you will recall, refers to our capacity to distinguish and interpret dark and light shapes. In the classic examples of optical illusions, we encounter it as a sort of problem. If (2) is a picture of a vase, then the insistent appearance of the two faces creates an uncomfortable ambiguity wherein the silhouettes vie for our attention, their roles in the image oscillating between figure and ground.

Perspective drawings also exploit figure-ground, creating the illusion of depth (3). The same effect produces a three-dimensional image from tonal variations presented in two dimensions, allowing us to perceive patterns of tone as order in space (4&6). Architectural drawings exploit this capacity as they go about the business of representing form and space.

Figure 2: The classic figure-ground ambiguity. Compare to the perspectival space illusion below.

Figure 3: A perspective framework rendered as high contrast figure-ground.

Figure 4: The same sort of visual phenomenon structures the complex tonal image of this grayscale photograph.

Figure 5: Four values of gray emphasize the figure-ground structure while remaining within the image's color range.

Figure 6: This black and white reduction further amplifies the image's figure-ground as extremes of dynamic contrast.

Relevance to design

Orthographic drawings create views that project themselves perpendicularly from the spatial whole, without perspective. This is the fundamental convention for both visualizing and designing buildings. The chief value of these drawings – plans, sections, elevations – is that they are scalable, in that they maintain precise proportional relations to the original, or proposed object. As a result, they stress formal relationships over visual effects, and are diagrammatic by virtue of their scaled reduction. In order to understand them, a designer must fully grasp the basic conventions of orthographic projection as a foundation for subsequent forms of representation (7).

Understanding a drawing involves more than merely seeing it. It requires the ability to perceive and analyze the components of the drawing as a unified system construed with intent. When we define architecture as order toward a purpose, we proceed from the expectation that the order is perceptible and comprehensible. Architecture is never an accident. It results from ideas embodied in the strategies and tactics of its shared practice.

By analogy, being able to see the marks on this page is a long way from being able to read the book. The marks first need to represent a functioning language. Moreover, the language must be one that we understand. The deeper our knowledge of a language, the greater is our ability to comprehend and respond to the meaning within the text. When we watch a sporting event, familiarity with the rules of the game determines our appreciation of the events. A die-hard fan will better discern the nuances of executing a play than will someone new to the game, while a seasoned coach will be able to conceive an overall strategy and diagram the tactics at work in the match or game.

To the untutored observer, a building appears as a collection of features and impressions. Doors and windows, continuous and broken surfaces might capture their attention and perhaps their approval. It may be pleasant or not, of a familiar sort or a novelty. However, from such casual observation nothing important arises.

In contrast, for the architect such features must add up to a coherent composition ordered by a clear overall design strategy and executed using appropriate tactical elements. Without that, the design is without merit. Success may be a matter of judgment, but neither design nor judgment can or should be arbitrary. They embody a path of rules and exceptions, and design thinking proceeds from diagrammatic analysis. Order matters. This is where we begin to investigate the practice of design. Order also informs the procedures and demonstrations in this chapter and throughout the rest of this book.

Deriving order in drawing

There are two primary strategies for order in architecture: order derived from circumstance, and order derived from ideals. The ancient Greeks positioned their temples in response to the terrain. At the same time, they organized the measurements using various geometrical systems, derived from both their mathematics and their philosophical beliefs. In contrast, Roman town planning often embodied the same urgent sense of geometry that distinguished their military camps. Mediaeval towns proceeded almost entirely circumstantially, using local practices and contingencies.

Architects today utilize both circumstantial and preconceived systems of order. Contemporary practice allows for both a focus on abstract ordering systems and a concern with particular forms contingent on circumstance. Within

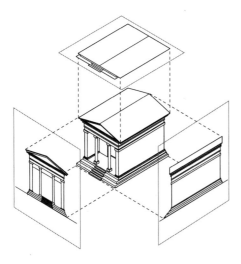

Figure 7: Architectural drawing conventions rely on orthographic projection. The drawings represent shapes parallel to the surface of the view. The example shows the derivation of two side elevations and the roof plan.

this duality, designers inherit both the Neoclassical concern with order and the Romantic penchant for effect.

Within the traditions of geometric order, there are two dominant tactics. The first is the relational subdivision of space and the subsequent location of forms and axes using the compass and the straightedge. The second traditions follows from the universal grid.

Relational tactics commonly identify diagonals that regulate subdivision and orthogonal lines that define boundaries. The subdivisions and the boundaries help identify AXIS, figure, FIELD, center and edge. These components provide a focus for the designer's intentions and help to organize design at several scales. We might best refer to this as relational geometries, that is, it begins with circumstance and interprets by formula. Physical and visual fields of differing proportions yield distinct divisional geometries, although the process of subdivision follows the same set of rules.

The universal grid, in contrast, arrives at shapes by counting off pre-set and – usually – equal units. The pixels on a computer screen follow this method, as does Cartesian mapping. As we will see in later chapters, the differences in procedure are conceptual. For the moment, we will begin with the first relational system: proportion.

The method of dividing the square shown in the previous chapter is a primary tactic of relational geometry using a straightedge and scribing tool – a pencil – to subdivide a rectangular field. We begin with a square divided by eighths and sixths (8). This generates the combination of two related but distinct grids. Often referred to as the 'tartan grid', multiple measurements form part of an overall strategy commonly used by architects since the Renaissance. The examples that follow use this divided square ground as the site or locale for simple rectilinear figures.

Exercises in relational geometry

There are four distinct phases to the sequence. The first is a planning mode that uses line to define figures. The second converts those lines to full figures on a field, displayed as high-contrast figure-ground. The third and fourth phases manifest perceived relationships between the elements and geometries of the total ground as fields. We begin with the first two phases.

Figure 8: Diagram showing the major construction lines used for the division of a square area into halves and thirds and their further subdivisions – quarters, eighths, sixths and twelfths – in a tartan grid.

We illustrate the individual steps to the right. A more embellished explanation may be found in DEMONSTRATION 5·1 that follows CHAPTER 5.

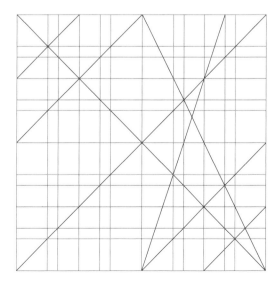

Step 1a: Define center.

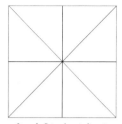

Step 1b: Extend centerlines in both axes.

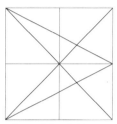

Step 2a: Define thirds by intersection.

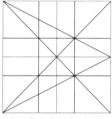

Step 2b: Mark thirds in both axes.

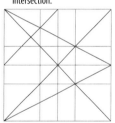

Step 3a: Subdivide halves into quarter measures.

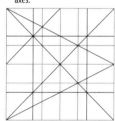

Step 3b: Extend lines from intersections in both axes.

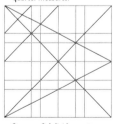

Step 4a: Subdivide quarter measures into eighths.

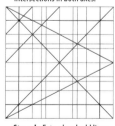

Step 4b: Extend and add lines from intersections in both axes.

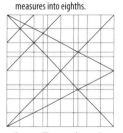

Step 5a: The same diagonal defines the sixth measure.

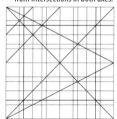

Step 5b: Extend lines from intersections in both axes.

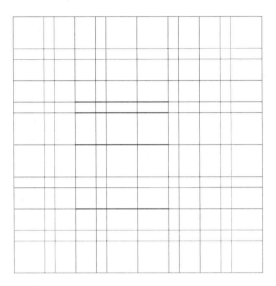

Figure 9: The image to the right shows the previously constructed grid with four abbreviated horizontal lines drawn across the field. The lines align on both edges and are of equal length.

Figure 10: The two resulting figures – shown as black – create the spatial gestalt as described in the text and shown below. The darker area between the two black figures marks the specifically defined area or field. The gradients identify the axial domains for spatial gestures implied within the composition. The relational grid subdivides both the defined and implied areas.

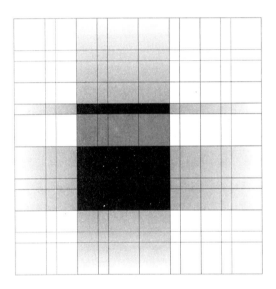

* CLOSURE

Closure, encountered earlier as part of gestalt theory, identifies the perceptual tendency to view a collective of lines or figures as a comprehensive shape – to connect the dots. The distinction between defined and implied figures or figural spaces refers to the relative completeness of the provided 'dots'. Thus four corners define a square, while two corners merely imply it.

In the case of substantial forms – a matter of scale – the shape of the spatial figure may respond to either the inside or outside boundary of the defining 'dots'. In the diagrams following on the next page, the dotted lines outline a completed form as defined or implied by four, three or two squares.

The first image above shows two figures defined by four horizontal lines drawn on the grid (9). Every two lines form a pair. All lines fall on one of two constructed grids of eighths or sixths. The lines do not touch the edge of the field, but instead stop at two elected intersections within the overall grid. The construction follows the pattern illustrated on the previous page and the eleaborated on in CHAPTER 5, DEMONSTRATION 5·1.

While multiple compositions might possibly follow the procedure, all will share certain traits based on the instruction set. The resulting composition uses contrasts of size and position, alignment of common edges, and the proximity of the elements to one another and the perimeter to generate a particular spatial character. With that in mind, we can describe the example composition as showing smaller and larger elements or figures. The larger lower figure lies closer to the smaller figure than to any other edge or BOUND-ARY. The upper form's distance from the top approximates its width. Seen in the context of the bounding lines, the figures' placement and construction reveal a nexus of relationships within our perceptions. Those observations might result in a diagram representing the spatial gestalt of the composition as seen in the next illustration (10). Within the composition, the field most clearly DEFINED by the two figures lies between them. The other areas identified in the gestalt diagram are IMPLIED FIELDS that result from the extension of the figures into and across the ground. Both terms refer to gestalt closure*, although implied space is open to more subtle description and understanding.

Defined & implied space

Defined and implied space holds the possibility of envisioning other elements to enrich a composition. Why is this important? The practical version might suggest that because building happens in a context, designers should be good at this. This is, of course, true. However, the larger point is that design proceeds from a central IDEA toward greater complexity in response to changing scales of design. Harnessing complexity through drawing is one way that designers create order in their projects, leading to buildings of merit and beauty.

The distinction between defined and implied spaces rests on a simple definition, although in practice it often bedevils beginning design students. The

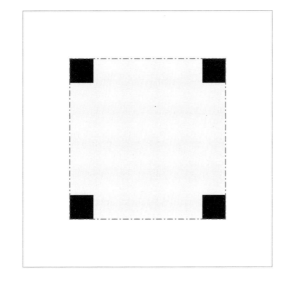

Figure 11: Diagram identifying the space defined by exterior boundaries of the composition. In this example the four squares occupy the space they define.

Figure 13: The diagrams below illustrate some of the other possibilities for defined and implied space in several related compositions. Dashed lines mark defined boundary lines while heavier dotted lines denote implied edges. The gray infill areas occupy some of the more apparent fields.

Diagrams 13·1–4 show examples based on four square figures. Diagrams 13·5–6 and 13·7–9 show variations with three and two figures respectively.

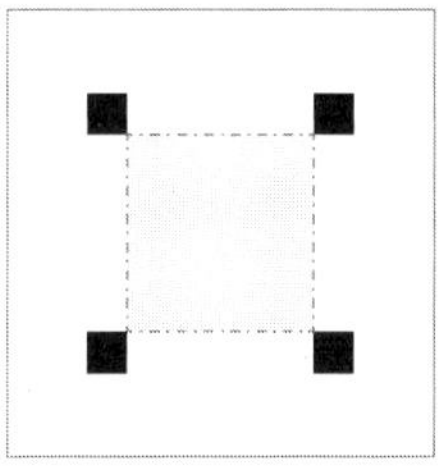

Diagram 13·1: Space defined by interior boundaries.

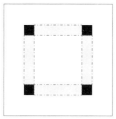

Diagram 13·2: Space defined by figure boundaries.

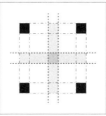

Diagram 13·3: Spaces implied by repetition.

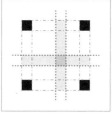

Diagram 13·4: Spaces implied by proportion.

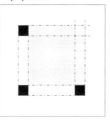

Diagram 13·5: Spaces defined by figure boundaries.

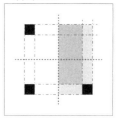

Diagram 13·6: Spaces implied by proportion.

terms characterize underlying gestalt features of form and space. Our perceptions emerge from the collective set of elements that exist in a composition. Defined spaces result from extending of boundaries present in an array. In the case of rectilinear forms such as our examples, boundaries coincide with the edges (11). Any rectangular form will project four boundary lines.

Implied forms, in contrast, generally refer to the underlying organizational structure. In the example below, the proportional geometries of both figure and field account for measurement of two centerlines (12). The gray field is thus defined on three edges and implied on the fourth.

In summary, figures generate boundaries that *define* edges while the geometries of the composition (including field geometry), repetition and gestalt closure *imply* other edges. Both kinds of edges can describe additional fields – or figures – as the composition evolves. The relationship that results from our four figures arranged as a square composition can develop in several directions depending on design intent. The original intention can be reinforced directly or subtly by the manifestation of suitable additions as it moves

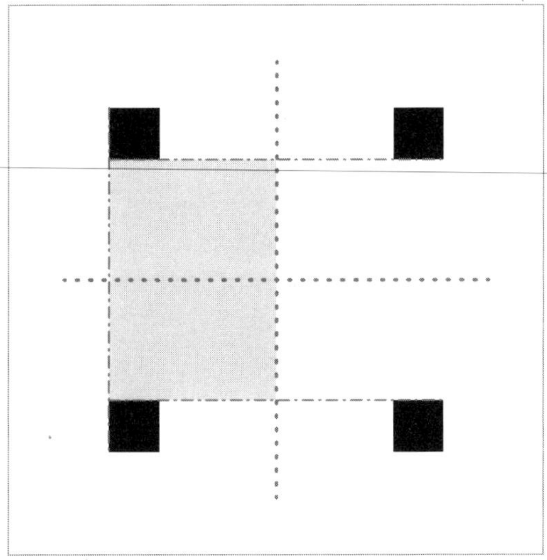

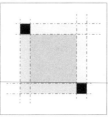

Diagram 13·7: Spaces defined by figure boundaries.

N.B. A comparison between Diagrams 13·7 and 13·8 reveals that similar spaces can result from both defined and implied boundaries.

Figure 12: Diagram showing a space defined on three edges by the composition with a fourth edge implied by the proportional center line.

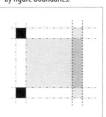

Diagram 13·8: Spaces implied by closure.

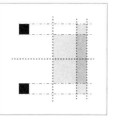

Diagram 13·9: Spaces implied by closure and proportion.

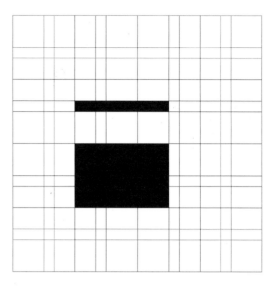

Figure 14: The two figure composition (10) placed within the tartan grid. The analysis seen at the far right corresponds to that underlying structure (16).

toward greater complexity and emphasis. This sort of formal design logic demonstrates the presence of a coherent, evolving central idea.

That a central idea underwrites good design may seem so obvious that its significance remains hidden. The word 'idea' comes to us from the Greek term denoting form or pattern. In Middle English, the root term *idein* meant 'to see'. To have an idea is literally to perceive something as distinct. As complexity arises throughout the design process, the designer responds with ideas – hopefully good ones – so that the result may be literally full of good ideas. However, they are not all of equal importance. At the heart of good design lies the Big Idea, the summoning picture against which we judge the design as a whole.

In a similar way, the first gesture in a design figures not only itself but also sets about creating visual cues for orderly evolution from the simple to the complex. In that sense, we can see in the simplest composition certain patterns that emerge within the drawing to define and imply space and form.

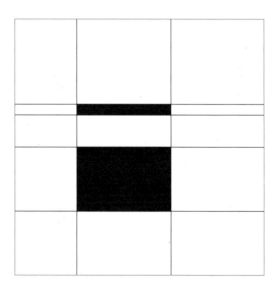

Figure 15: The drawing results in two black figures which in turn we mark with extended bounding lines.

Identifying those patterns gives purpose to our analysis: making visible the underlying possibilities of a simple thematic composition.

Analyzing the composition

Analyzing our two figures in a field reveals a formal inventory of related forms found within (15). The visible relationships within the composition expose the underlying proportional matrix and manifest both defined and implied extensions of the figure-ground structure. Thus, observing both the positive and negative spaces of the figure-ground in the context of the grid, we discover potential augmentations to the central compositional idea.

Such discoveries have a visual component that render readily as diagrams. In (16), we illustrate the following list of perceived primary proportional relationships:

1 Two horizontal figures – one shallow and one deep – share the same width (16·1). We show this relationship as a series of parallel gray fields.
2 The two figures align vertically at both edges, viewed here as boundary lines (16·2).
3 The top edge of the deep figure also aligns with the horizontal centerline of the ground. The deep figure thus resides in the lower half of the field (16·3).
4 The area of the deep figure added to the space separating the two figures – imaged as a gray field – constitutes a square (16·4).
5 The shallow figure added to the space above it forms a similar square (16·5).
6 The shallow figure is one square distant from the right edge of the ground (16·6).
7 The space between the figures is 1:3, that is, it holds three smaller squares of space illustrated as three gray fields (16·7).
8 The lower left corner of the deep figure intersects with a center diagonal drawn crossing the ground (16·8).
9 The deep figure is one square distant from the left edge. The lower left corner of the deep figure is also one square distant from the corner of the ground (16·9).
10 The distance to the right edge equals the width of the figure (16·10). This shows as an adjacent gray field.

The accompanying overlays to the composition demonstrate the first stage of diagramming – visualizing formal relationships (16). Although not an end in itself, this helps the designer see embedded possibilities for further compositional development. The particulars reflect a confluence of the component forms, the underlying grid, the rules of procedure, and decisions regarding the size and placement of figures relative to the field. How these resolve is clearer after altering one aspect of the composition and analyzing the resulting formal structures.

Three variant compositions

Using our initial composition of two forms, we move to a series of dependent compositions that vary the horizontal measure of one or both figures. The resulting series highlights the impact of alignment. Each variant represents a potential tactic for formal differentiation. The categories we illustrate build on each previous description. From our first composition – the figures aligned – we move to the figures staggered across one boundary. From there, we advance to figures aligned along one boundary, followed by figures fit between two boundaries. The correlation of the tactics used to the criterion of alignment should be apparent.

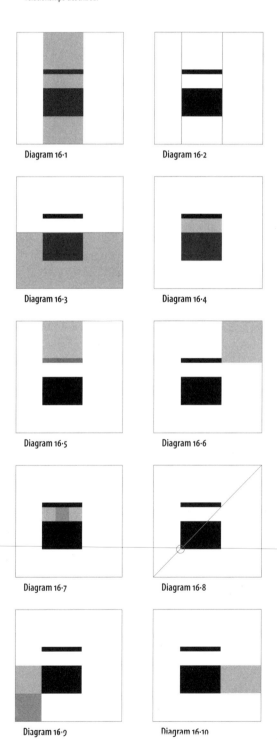

Figure 16: The ten illustrations below display the primary proportional relationships found within the composition seen in (14) and enumerated in the text. As diagrammatic overlays, they demonstrate those visual, formal relationships described.

Diagram 16·1   Diagram 16·2

Diagram 16·3   Diagram 16·4

Diagram 16·5   Diagram 16·6

Diagram 16·7   Diagram 16·8

Diagram 16·9   Diagram 16·10

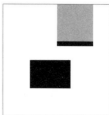

Diagram 18·1

Figure 18: Three analytic studies corresponding to the numbered list in the text.

Note that many of the formal relationships found in the initial parallel boundaries composition apply here. In particular, Diagrams 16·3, 16·8–10 remain pertinent as the lower figure remains unchanged from the original.

Diagram 18·2

Figure 17: The staggered figures composition and grid on the right relate to the three analytic studies show on the left (18).

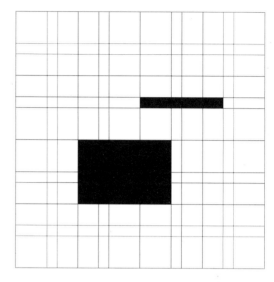

Diagram 18·3

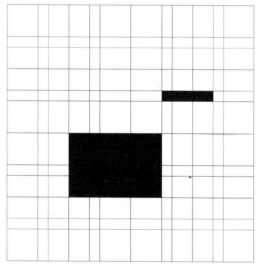

Figure 19: In this edge-aligned figures composition only one measurement and boundary change.

Figure 20: The related analytic studies to the right demonstrate the principle distinction of this condition as compared to the former. The nexus of *edge-aligned* composition often falls along the shared edge and is most likely linear or center-pointed. In contrast the focal condition for staggered figures is most often and volumetric area.

Starting from our aligned figures generated by widely and narrowly spaced pairings of lines in close proximity, our first variation shifts one of the figures laterally within the tartan grid. The shift results in an offset alignment of staggered figures that share a defined area of overlap (17). For our third composition, we shear the overlapping portion of the shallow figure to produce edge-aligned figures. These share a common edge (19). For our final tactical variation, we replace a portion from the far side of the larger figure with a new, third figure aligned horizontally with the pre-existing shallow figure. We label that composition fitted figures (21).

Analyzing the three variations, and in comparison to the first, we generate three abbreviated lists of primary differentiations that we observe. We might describe them as follows:

STAGGERED FIGURES

1 The space above the shallow figure is now a square; the lower figure is now narrower (18·1).
2 The field between the two figures at the overlap is now a single square (18·2).
3 The left edge of the shallow figure aligns vertically with the vertical center-line of the ground (18·3).

EDGE-ALIGNED FIGURES

1 The area defined by the lower edge of the figures, and bounded by the edges of the ground forms a square (20·1).
2 The area occupied by the two figures, measured from the lower left corner, thus establishes the presence of a larger foursquare centered on the lower left corner of shallow figure (20·2).

Diagram 20·1

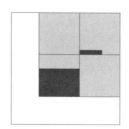

Diagram 20·2

Diagram 20·3

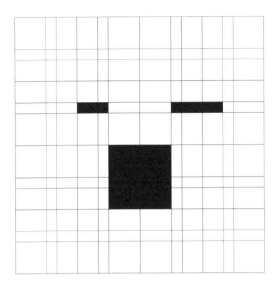

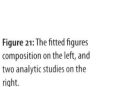

Figure 21: The fitted figures composition on the left, and two analytic studies on the right.

Diagram 21·1.

Diagram 21·2.

3 The figures, therefore, occupy square quadrants diagonally opposite each other (20·2).

FITTED FIGURE

1 The deep figure is now a square, centered vertically in the ground (21·1).

2 The second shallow figure sits atop a defined square area (21·2).

Observing contrast, repetition, alignment & proximity

These tactical variations and the description of the set-up introduce a more nuanced gestalt reading of figure-ground. With two or more figures in each composition, we also observe the relations categorized in CHAPTER 3: contrast, repetition, alignment and proximity. Contrast in this instance identifies differences in size, shape and orientation (22). Repetition addresses any feature that repeats or varies along a continuum (23). Alignment recognizes relationships of center and boundary of any forms (24). Proximity determines near and far adjacencies (25).

Thus, the two figures in our base composition (14) exhibit contrast in their shape and demonstrate proximity, both to one another and to the boundaries. Alignment, constrained in the example, assures visual connection along parallel edges. With two figures, repetition identifies those features that do not contrast, in this instance the measure of positive and negative spaces as shown in the earlier diagrams (16). The variations – staggered, edge-aligned and fitted – employ the four relational categories as part of their description and rule structure.

The variations considered

The staggered composition scheme shifts one of the figures from its original alignment and in the example affects the contrast – size and proportion – in the process (17). Both changes still accord to the underlying grid and underscore an important character of geometric order in spatial compositions. Orthographic order – occurring at right angles – derives a sort of hierarchy from the cross-axial structure of the underlying grid. As in our earlier encounter with boundary gestalt, this reminds us that there exists a deep kinship between balance and axial order.

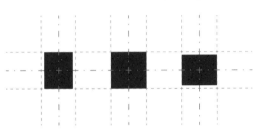

Figure 22: Contrasts include size, shape, orientation and negative space or interval.

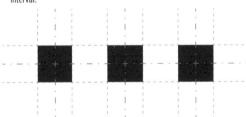

Figure 23: Repetition occurs in the figure shape, the interval between, the centerline and boundaries.

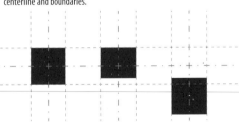

Figure 24: All vertical edges remain parallel but the horizontal edges exhibit variation in alignment.

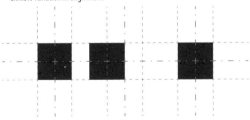

Figure 25: Proximity in the example results from differences in interval

Figure 26: Two images show each composition in two expressions: on the left, the figures and boundary lines and on the right, the figures as white and the negative space as gray. The darker gray identifies the internal defined space and the lighter gray the boundary condition.

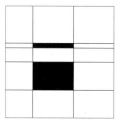 

Diagrams 26·1 a&b: The initial composition of two parallel and equal width aligned figures.

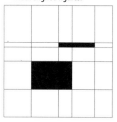 

Diagrams 26·2 a&b: The staggered figures composition.

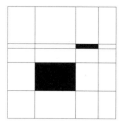 

Diagrams 26·3 a&b: The edged-aligned figures composition.

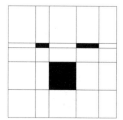 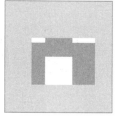

Diagrams 26·4 a&b: The fitted figures composition.

In a composition ordered in a regular orthographic area, balance suggests itself not only at the center – as shown earlier in Figure 10, but also at points defined by both symmetric cross-axes whose dimensions reflect proportionate measure. In a square field the strongest correspondence occurs at equal measures from the cross axis (11&12). This intersection diagrams a relationship of rectangles similar to the boundary geometry of the ground – in this instance, squares.

With two figures defined by parallel horizontal lines, multiple cross-axial relationships suggest themselves at the vertical boundaries (26·1). By examining the comprehensive visual gestalt of the existing figures, we can see possible variations of figural balance. In our second example, the upper edge of the larger form abuts the horizontal centerline of the ground (26·2). The smaller form abuts the vertical center and the overlap between the figures demarcates a square. This produces a sense of stability within an active compositional space. The result is both an image and a diagram of spatial relationships.

For the third – edge-aligned – variation, we reduce the smaller figure (26·3) to align with the edge of the larger. This action removes the negative square of the previous composition and alters the center of balance. The negative space now divides along an edge rather than around a figure. This simplifies the defined spatial character of the whole by increasing the prominence of the bounding perimeter of the two figures.

The fourth and final variation adds a third figure parallel to the existing upper figure and changes the lower figure to fit in between with two sets of aligned edges (26·4). The result is a highly defined composition showing an articulated formal grouping. A gestalt reading – closure – yields a U-shaped figure from the three separate figures while also recognizing the inverted U-shape of the internal negative space.

General observations

The example compositions are only possible responses to the compositional sequence. They do reveal, however, a coherent architecture of figure-ground. This narrative explains the underlying approach to the development of a design idea through a simply articulated formal grouping.

Further examination also reveals important ideas about linear figure-ground images. The first is that the quality of the drawing should allow us to identify component elements of the composition – in this instance: line, grid and ground. We should be able to distinguish among the faint lines of the underlying grid, the slightly darker lines of the boundary or ground, and the character of the lines designating the figure.

As we sort out the composition, the figure and ground will demonstrate particular attributes of form. Attributes include the following:

· Alignment – in this instance all alignments are either parallel or perpendicular,

· DOMINANT and SUBORDINATE relationship either by relative size, position or both,

· PRINCIPLES of organization.

Taken as a whole the three examples embody the fundamental design concepts discussed thus far. They exhibit and rely on figure-ground for clarity of expression. We see the shapes because of the structure of contrast. In addition, the definition of apparent shapes between the figures prompt a reading of them as defined form, in this instance a negative space. The compositions make visible axial relationships resulting in balance – a product of visual symmetry and asymmetry. In the second and third examples, the perception of implied edges at the cuts creates an implicit edge condition. This is an example of visual gestalt, the formal resolution implied within any composition of multiple interrelated parts.

Motif, pattern & theme

There is something else to mine from our simple gestalt reading. We have spoken before about order and it is appropriate to add to those comments. Pattern, by nature, repeats and varies. In composition, those elements go by the name of MOTIF. In decorative settings, motifs can be as simple as repeated geometric forms or as complex as varied thematic elements, such as scenes from a story. In all cases, the elements act as the core variables, the irreducible relationship that helps us make sense of the whole.

The framework for discussing motifs in composition finds its most robust use in music. There it refers to simple melodic and harmonic relationships between a set of notes as MOTIVIC themes. The four notes that begin Beethoven's Fifth Symphony (three repeated short notes followed by a lower, longer note – dah·dah·dah *duhmm*) announce the thematic core of the entire work. In a similar fashion, a gestalt framework for design can identify simple pattern generators as motivic in function. These basic formal relationships help identify the inner workings of repeated and varied elemental sets. Not surprisingly, they also identify potential relationships of contrast, alignment, proximity and repetition. It is in this context that our four compositional variants make the most sense.

Figure 27 shows an archetypal arrangement of a nine-square figure on a five-by-five gridded ground. In the eight diagrams to the right, the resulting motifs demonstrate minimally inflected expressions of the compositional sequence. The defined field areas complete the square figure, filling the center of the composition (28). Comparison of this sequence with the diagrams on the facing page (26) shows that the internal negative spaces share a similar motivic structure. The principal difference between the two compositional sets results from the proportional variation of the figures. The thematic gestures remain constant: a rectangle, a pinwheel, a two-part adjacency and a modified U-shape.

Figure 28: Images of prototype motifs for the four variations use highly regular geometries to demonstrate a base case for compositional gesture. A grid marking the ground in fifths governs size and placement. The resulting figures, therefore, act within an enclosed archetypal *nine-square* schema.

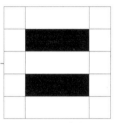 

Diagrams 28·1 a&b: The base composition of parallel figures defines an equal internal space.

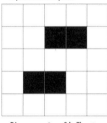 

Diagrams 28·2 a&b: The staggered figures arrange around a square internal space and define equal spaces in a pinwheel formation.

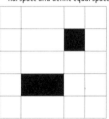 

Diagrams 28·3 a&b: The edge-aligned figures define proportional spaces in adjacent positions.

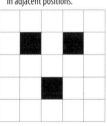 

Diagrams 28·4 a&b: The fitted figures' near-V-shape defines multiple adjacent spaces that approximate a reciprocal configuration.

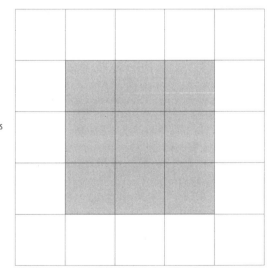

Figure 27: An underlying grid of fifths shown with the nine-square field at its center.

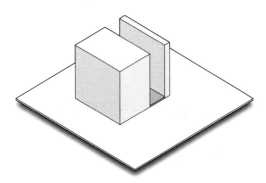

Figure 30: The field rendered as a ground plane lying between the original motivic figures.

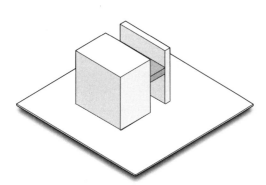

Figure 31: The field rendered as a horizontal figure between the original figures in proportion to the original composition.

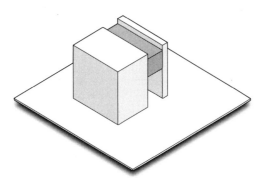

Figure 32: The field rendered as a figure placed so that the elevation mirrors the 1:3:6 geometry of the original motif.

Figure 29: The single defined field of this composition fits between the overlap of the figures' boundaries (29·1). Compare the same figures illustrated as a line drawing and absent the field (29·2).

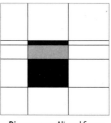

Diagram 29·1: Aligned figures and defined field.

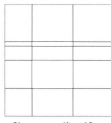

Diagram 29·2: Aligned figures drawn as line absent the field.

In music, there are almost as many motifs as there are melodies, which is quite a large number. Similarly in architecture, there are as many motifs as there are arrangements of form – also a large number. However, the four relationship categories help identify simple motivic structures. Between two or more figures, naming contrasts of size, shape and orientation, including the interval between them, identifies their elemental structure. Alignment specifies their spatial gesture, repetition marks the scope and principle of arrangement, while proximity designates any groupings. Thus the geometric motif for our first aligned composition might read:

·   Two horizontal figures separated, proportioned as 1:9 and 2:3, the smaller figure above and separated by an interval proportioned as 1:3.

·   The figures are parallel and aligned vertically such that the larger figure and the interval describe a square.

Notice that this description does not include any reference to the motif relative to the ground. Once we expand our point of view to include the larger field that is the ground, the dynamics of the composition become more involved.

Recalling the earliest analytic diagrams of the four compositions, we recognize that the fields drawn within those analyses make visible the formal relationships within the composition. When we mark those as fields of tone, we begin to turn from the procedures of analysis to the possibility of extending the composition based on the original formal structure of the base compositional structure. If we assert that our initial simple composition acts as the Big Idea – the diagram of controlling order, then the analysis should lead us to visualizing a structure for coherent additions and modifications that fit within that order. The changes may alter the image of the project but the result remains connected to its intent.

Defined fields

Picking up from our earlier discussion, we start with a simple defined field – one that results directly from the boundaries of existing figures. In the case of the two parallel horizontal figures, there is only one, the 1:3 proportional negative space between them (29). The illustrations on the left show three variations for interpreting the defined field. In all three variations, the figures have a height equal to the width of the original compositional element resulting in near-cubic volume. As a result, the section along one axis mirrors the plan.

In the first illustration, the field remains as a ground plane, creating a courtyard connecting the two figures (30). In the second, the field sponsors a slender connecting volume proportional to the elements in the two-dimensional plan but rearranged (31). The final example shows another spanning volume that transfers the initial plan geometry on to the elevation of the compositional solids.

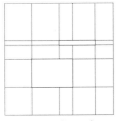

Diagram 33·1: Staggered figures drawn as line.

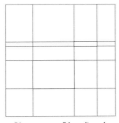

Diagram 33·2: Edge-aligned figures drawn as line.

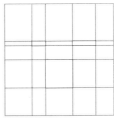

Diagram 33·3: Fitted figures drawn as line.

Figure 33: Three other compositions – staggered, edge-aligned and fitted – shown as line drawings.

As we examine all four of the original compositions – aligned, staggered, edge-aligned and fitted – as simple line drawings, we can perceive a degree of visual correspondence between the depiction of the figures, the boundaries and the underlying rules (29·2&33·1–3). Such linear diagrams reveal alignments and proportions among the elements. However, as we have seen in locating the defined field for the first composition, when we depict them as black figures on a white ground, we enhance the contrast between figure and field and objectify their spatial correspondence. This makes the gestalt dynamics more visible, helping to visualize additional elements in the ground that sustain or counter the basic motif.

The aligned forms define a single bounded, in-between field (34·1). In contrast, the other three compositions define other possible fields of two kinds - ADJACENT and HYBRID (34·2&3). Adjacent fields border a figure's side and extend to the parallel boundary of the other figure. Hybrids also border one form but derive their other measure from both the parallel and perpendicular boundaries of a second figure. Analyzing the complete set exposes subtle similarities and helps to illustrate the sequence of development of the compositions. Examining the figure-ground diagrams, we find the following:

· The staggered figures define one in-between field, two adjacent and two hybrid fields – five areas in all (35·1a). There are two adjacency-hybrid pairs and adding the hybrid areas to the in-between raises the total to ten rectilinear fields (35·1b).

· The edge-aligned figures share no in-between space, only two adjacencies and two hybrids totaling four fields (35·2a). There are three available pairings, bringing the total to seven defined rectilinear fields (35·2b).

· With three elements, the fitted-figures composition defines twelve fields. In-betweens, adjacents and hybrids accrue to six fields. Adjacent pairs and a set of three betweens define six more rectilinear fields.

Variations in the figural elements will affect the character of each composition type. This reminds us that the project is an exercise in proportion as well as an introduction to figures and fields on a ground. Our next observations will isolate individual fields and continue our analysis.

Figure 35: The three derived compositions – staggered, edge-aligned and fitted – offer the possibility of multiple fields defined by various combinations of edges. The diagrams illustrate individual and grouped patterns to help visualize a complete inventory.

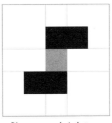

Diagram 34·1: An in-between field.

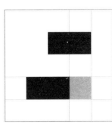

Diagram 34·2: An adjacent field.

Figure 34: Three general field types – in-between, adjacent and hybrid – arrayed in a prototype staggered motif.

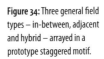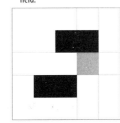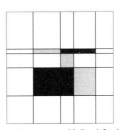

Diagram 34·3: A hybrid field.

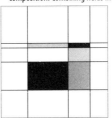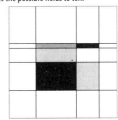

Diagrams 35·1 a&b: Five defined areas result from a staggered figures composition. Combining fields increases the possible fields to ten.

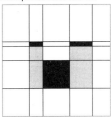

Diagrams 35·2 a&b: Four defined areas result from an edged-aligned figures composition. Combinations increase the possible fields to seven.

Diagrams 35·3 a&b: Six defined areas result from a fitted figures composition. Combinations increase the possible fields to twelve.

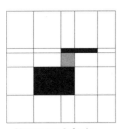

Diagram 36·1: Defined in-between field.

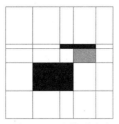

Diagram 36·2: Defined hybrid field.

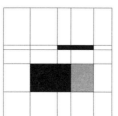

Diagram 36·3: Defined adjacent field.

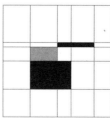

Diagrams 36·4: Defined hybrid field.

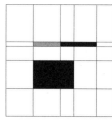

Diagram 36·5: Defined adjacent field.

STAGGERED FIGURES

Figure 36: Five defined fields in the staggered composition – in-between, adjacent and hybrid – shown above in sequnce, starting at the center.

Figure 37: Two diagrams on the right show paired adjacent/hybrid combinations.

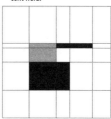

Diagram 37·1: Defined adjacent/hybrid combined field.

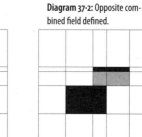

Diagram 37·2: Opposite combined field defined.

Figure 38: Combinations of the two hybrid areas with the in-between field yield multiple occupations of the visual middle as shown on the right.

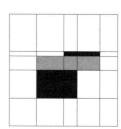

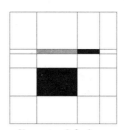

Diagram 38·1: Defined combined field to the left.

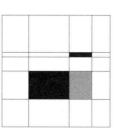

Diagram 38·2: Opposite defined combined field.

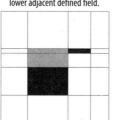

Diagram 38·3: Central, shared defined combined field.

EDGE-ALIGNED FIGURES

Figure 39: The four defined fields found in the edge-aligned composition consist of two adjacencies and two hybrids, shown on the right.

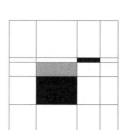

Diagram 39·1: Defined upper adjacent field.

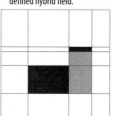

Diagram 39·2: Companion lower adjacent defined field.

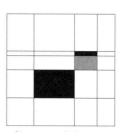

Diagram 39·3: Leftward defined hybrid field.

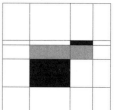

Diagram 39·4: Rightward defined hybrid field.

Figure 40: The three combined defined fields found in the edge-aligned composition occupy distinct precincts as shown on the right. Note their effect on the overall balance of the composition.

Diagram 40·1: Defined combined field to the left.

Diagram 40·2: Opposite combined field to the right.

Diagram 40·3: Central combined defined field.

Sorting through results

Scanning the defined fields, we can sort them using a few basic observations.

· Single adjacent fields extend visual gesture within boundaries and along one axis (36·3, 36·5, 39·1, 39·2, 41·1–3), as do some hybrid fields (39·3, 39·4, 42·1–3). This is also the case with some combined fields (38·1, 38·3, 43·1–3).

· Some extending combined fields touch two figures and create more complex L-shape figure-field outlines (40·1, 40·2, 43·1, 43·3).

· Certain hybrid fields also result in L-shape figure-field outlines (36·2, 36·4).

· In some instances, the field connects two figures, resulting in a negative space that suggests a courtyard figure (37·1, 37·2, 44·1–3). We can see a similar suggested effect resulting from some hybrid fields (36·2, 36·4).

At this point, we should recognize that the interplay between figure and field follows from the precept of gestalt in which shapes and forms combine within a field to create a unified visual effect. The challenge of this exercise is noting where those effects are clearest and where further adjustments or additions to the fields can lead to a more coherent overall composition.

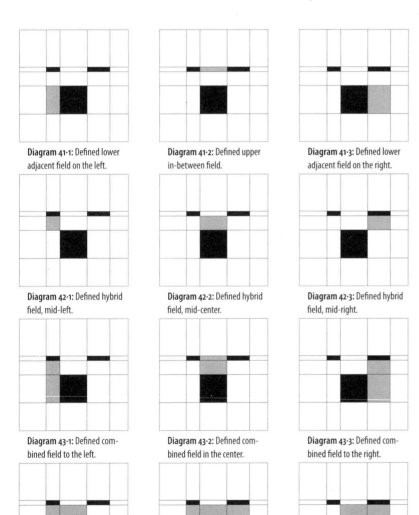

Diagram 41·1: Defined lower adjacent field on the left.

Diagram 41·2: Defined upper in-between field.

Diagram 41·3: Defined lower adjacent field on the right.

Diagram 42·1: Defined hybrid field, mid-left.

Diagram 42·2: Defined hybrid field, mid-center.

Diagram 42·3: Defined hybrid field, mid-right.

Diagram 43·1: Defined combined field to the left.

Diagram 43·2: Defined combined field in the center.

Diagram 43·3: Defined combined field to the right.

Diagram 44·1: Defined combined field, left center.

Diagram 44·2: Combined field, spanning the center.

Diagram 44·3: Defined combined field, right center.

FITTED FIGURES

Figure 41: The in-between defined field found in the fitted figures composition occupies a key position, reflecting the structure of the underlying nine-square diagram. In contrast, the two adjacent fields accent our appreciation of the negative space.

Figure 42: The hybrid defined fields found in the fitted figures composition middle positions – shown on the left – reflecting the strategic structure of the basic nine-square diagram.

Figure 43: Three combined defined fields found in the fitted figures composition shift the balance. Those to the side of the composition tend to isolate the opposite figures, while the center field connects and unifies the overall configuration.

Figure 44: The other three combined defined fields found toward the center of the fitted figures composition also connect the upper and lower elements. Those on the left or right suggest apparent mass or weight, while the center field unifies the whole.

Comparing similar compositions holding different figures can improve both visual judgment and bolster the language for describing visual events. The image pairs to the left afford just such a comparison (45·1–4). The left-hand column repeats examples from our four compositional strategies using figures we can describe as large and small, and in close proximity. The right-hand column presents similar compositions that use more equally sized figures at greater distance from one another.

In the first pair, we observe the effect of scale and proximity in an aligned composition (45·1). The defined field in the first composition relates easily to the figures, effectively bridging and completing the proportional figures. In the second example, a larger field between two similar, mid-size figures forms a composition of opposing and independent elements.

The second set of examples, representing staggered figures, connects normal faces to suggest partial courtyards within the negative space (45·2). The illustration on the left is the more intimate, the enclosure seemingly limited to enclosing the smaller central square bounded by the lower figure (compare to 36·1). In the second diagram (45·2b), the negative space stretches to the bounding edge of the upper figure. Both of these observations respond to the relative scale of the field as a visual influence.

In the third set, the scale of the field compared to the edge-aligned figures also leads to divergent gestalt readings (45·3). The primary visual sense of the first composition notes the field's dependence from – and proximity to – the upper smaller figure, adding weight to the corner of an apparent rectangle and corresponding to the outer boundaries of the entire group (compare to 40·1). In the example (45·3b), the dominant scale of the dependent field combined with the upper figure favors the negative space to its left from which the lower figure depends.

The final example set, being more complex, yields more subtle gestalt observations (45·4). The combined fields in both connect two figures in an L-shaped amalgam. In the first instance, the contrast of the larger square figure emphasizes the negative space above, while the smaller figure on the upper right anchors within the negative space below and to its left. Together, they suggest two L-shaped areas interlocked around the center. In the second composition (45·4b), the similar scale of the three figures and the combined field fuse into a more balanced assembly. The defined interior negative space merges, field-like, and the arrangement conveys a nuanced rectangle caught between the bounding perimeters.

Reviewing the diagrams prompts two observations. First, changes in proportion and proximity radically affect our apprehension of figure-ground, particularly our awareness of resulting negative space (further examples can be found in DEMONSTRATION 4·2.). Second, marking discreet defined fields modifies the overall composition profoundly and can shift our perception of the whole. Refining and adding to these observations brings us to implied fields, which further alter and add to our understanding of figures in composition.

Implied fields

The next stage of the project builds on the diagrams thus far, developing additional figurative fields within the composition. An implied field is not arbitrary. Instead, it may call upon the latent geometry of the underlying grid, the proportions of the figural elements already present or visual qualities of the negative space. These fields also often conform to some of the boundary con-

Figure 45: A comparison of two related composition sets with differing figures illustrates the effect of proportion on our sense of composition. Each pair of diagrams illustrate similar defined fields for steps in the sequence.

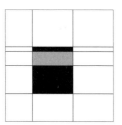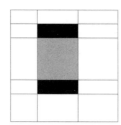

Diagram 45·1 a&b: Aligned figures and defined central fields serving as connecting elements.

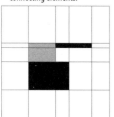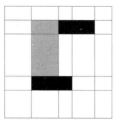

Diagram 45·2 a&b: Staggered figures and defined combined fields result in negative space courtyard schemes.

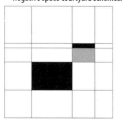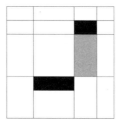

Diagram 45·3 a&b: Edge-aligned figures and defined hybrid field. Note the contrasting negative spaces in each scheme.

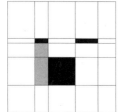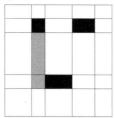

Diagram 45·4 a&b: Fitted figures and defined combined field. Note the overall spatial difference between the two L-shape groupings.

ditions found in defined field. Furthermore, this sense of 'implied' illustrates the point of the exercise – control of formal composition in figure-ground.

Adjusting one edge of the defined field to correspond to a visual intent allows the designer to alter the composition profoundly with a small change. In the aligned figures composition, one edge of the previously observed defined fields shifts to create a three-sided, enclosed negative space (46·1). These simple alterations also anchor the composition more firmly to the centerline of the ground and allow the direction of the field to counter the grain of the figures.

In contrast, the variations shown for the staggered figures reemphasize the sense of movement along the horizontal axis (46·2). In each composition, there is a general sense of progression across the ground, balanced by the defined residual negative space. This negative space is clearer in (46·2b), in part because of the overall homogeneous scale of the figures and the residual space within the boundaries.

The fields in the third diagram pair also represent tactics meant to balance the figures' dynamic position (46·3). In the first instance, we observe a field set as a sort of broad beam that infers three negative spaces adding weight to the left of the composition (46·3a). The second diagram, in contrast, places a larger, detached square field whose proximity and contrast act to anchor the two figures (46·3b). This gambit is more visually ambiguous, the apparent 'looseness' brought on by the fields separateness begins to suggest a third dimension to the visual resolution.

In the series' fourth example, adjustments expand to overlap one figure while remaining tangent and aligned to the other (46·4). The result in each instance adds to the visual weight of the left and bottom of the composition, increases the complexity of the negative space and draws the third figure inward by virtue of proximity and proportion. The right edge of the field in both examples also aligns to the vertical centerline of the ground to significantly improve overall balance. A glance at the illustration below, reveals the underlying structure of this composition and serves as a reminder that implied fields draw on what exists within the structure of the composition as firmly as the original figures (47).

Figure 46: For comparison, these diagrams show the two related composition sets – seen opposite – with implied fields in place. Each particular diagram illustrates a field related to previous examples of defined fields. The examples omit boundary lines to emphasize the spatial tenor of the figures and field combined.

Diagram 46·1 a&b: Aligned figures shown with implied central fields that connect elements and shape negative space.

Diagram 46·2 a&b: Staggered figures seen with implied fields that charge negative space to shape the perimeter.

Diagram 46·3 a&b: Edge-aligned figures and implied field. Note the contrasting negative spaces in each scheme.

Diagram 46·4 a&b: Fitted figures and implied field. Note the change in viewing each L-shape grouping for each iteration.

Figure 47: The diagram to the right includes both the underlying grid and the bounding lines for the figures. The composition is the same as that of **46·4b**.

The grid sponsors measurement of the implied field, aligning it to the ground and subdivisions of the lower figure.

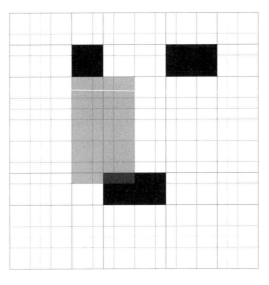

Figure 48: Additional examples of implied fields using the first aligned figures composition. The first image repeats the defined field. Thereafter, each diagram illustrates a tactic described in the earlier discussion of implied fields.

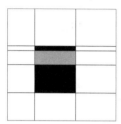

Diagram 48·1: Boundaries define a single enclosed field.

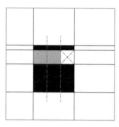

Diagram 48·2: Proportional subdivision – thirds – divides the defined area into three squares, two of which combine to comprise an implied field.

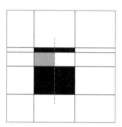

Diagram 48·3: The figural center axis divides the defined area to determine one edge of the implied field.

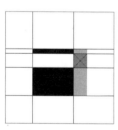

Diagram 48·4: Two implied fields resulting from both boundary and internal geometry. Both fields use the square of the defined area as a measure.

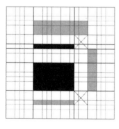

Diagram 48·5: These three implied fields make use of the underlying grid geometry and existing proportions to determine their size and location.

None of these compositions is absolute or closed to other interpretations and that is part of their charm and utility to the designer. By presenting compositions as open to interpretation, they admit and foster further speculation, as we will see.

Adding fields

Our examination of implied fields thus far has focused on identifying simple effects on overall composition. Given the complexity of the original grid, and even within the partial limits of existing boundaries, there exist many possible variations of implied fields within the four compositions.

Observing the diagrams to the left, we see examples of a previously seen defined field (48·1) and four tactics previously identified constructing implied fields (48·2–5). The first tactic is a hybrid (48·2). The composition follows the underlying grid but also, by subdividing its horizontal measure into thirds, identifies the unused square area of the in-between space as a courtyard.

The second tactic uses the compositional centerline, a measure that is absent from the underlying grid (48·3). The resulting negative space is similar to that of the previous example, however, its proportion energizes the composition differently.

The fourth tactic generates two related fields (48·4). The first, a square identified by the diagonal x-shape, extends the in-between space outward and within the ground. The second, a larger vertical field, occupies an area that places the composition symmetrically on the vertical axis. Note that the overlap between the two fields becomes a distinct characteristic of the visual totality.

The three fields in the last diagram each take part of their measure from the existing fields but their placement and proportion rely most heavily on the underlying grid – shown for clarity (48·5). All three lie outside the aligned figures and thus extend the composition further into the ground. The resulting visual centrifugal force – literally, moving away from the center – animates the overall figure-ground by creating multiple negative spaces.

These examples remind us that diagrams not only analyze existing form and shape but also serve to propose new elements in a composition. If we combine all the fields just seen, we create the image seen below, a dense, multi-articu-

Figure 49: Image of the combination of all fields shown in (**48**). Although not a part of the project, the visual density opens the way to observation of greater figure-field complexity.

lated composition open to several interpretations (49). This is the final object of this project sequence – the combination of defined and implied figures used with purpose to activate figure-ground.

Combining fields

To demonstrate the possible effects of combining fields we begin with the composition sequence seen earlier in the chapter. The diagrams to the right show two copies of each of four compositions in the series – aligned figures, staggered figures, edge-aligned figures and fitted figures (50).

To each copy of these compositions, we add a second, transparent implied field, observing two variations of each. The added field in each relates to the existing figures, field, underlying grid or a combination thereof. Other characteristics of the addition are as follows:

· The implied field may remain discrete, touching neither figure nor field.
· The field may overlap the existing figures, field or both.
· The added field may cross the existing figures, field or both.

Adding the implied field affects the existing visual grain increasing the overall complexity of the composition. Note particularly the conditions of transparency and opacity that are a product of the second field. The fields are not arbitrary. Instead, their role should be to increase the clarity of intent in the overall gestalt of the composition.

The first pair of diagrams demonstrates two tactics for using the implied field to extend the aligned figure composition laterally (50·1). In the first diagram (50·1a), the implied field overlaps the defined field and shifts the balance and grain of the figures while suggesting a lateral center for the entire grouping. In the next diagram (50·1b), the vertical field, although discrete, relates to the other elements through the resulting negative space. Together, they amend the horizontality of the figural grain and focus the composition inward.

In contrast to the aligned figure composition, the second pair of diagrams acts to counter the lateral motion of the staggered figures (50·2). The vertical implied field in the first does so by adding visual weight at the overlap. The resulting negative spaces – one vertical and one horizontal – also help balance the overall conglomerate. The second diagram (50·2b), by comparison, uses the added square element as a foil for the figures, providing a subversive static anchor that results in two negative spaces. The result is a play of back and front patterning that undermines the lateral thrust of the original.

The edge-aligned figures and defined field present a different formal challenge (50·3). Cast with the first field as a suggestive L-shaped cantilever, they combine to create a duality which is neither moving nor completely static. In the first instance, a large implied field overlaps and crosses the left side (50·3a). By size and position, this effectively divides the entire composition in half and causes the largest visual element to counter any residual action. The implied field in the second iteration uses an opposite tactic to achieve a similar end (50·3b). Resting under the projecting figure, completely detached, it nevertheless completes a static rectangle by position.

The fitted figure composition present a variation on the off-balance of the previous examples (50·4). The defined field on the left anchors the visual whole by suggesting an unequal stability of large and small halves around the horizontally centered square figure. In the first of the diagrams, we note that the implied field adds weight to the left, while at the same time, the tonal variation suggests a gridded complexity that activates the negative space to the right, thus joining and supporting the previously isolated figure on the right

Figure 50: Paired examples of four composition for the sequence demonstrate a range of results from adding implied fields. Each diagram on the left demonstrates *overlapping* fields, while those on the right use discrete implied field to compliment the existing defined field.

Diagram 50·1 a&b: Aligned figures composition with defined and implied fields – either overlapping or discrete.

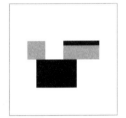

Diagram 50·2 a&b: Staggered figures composition with defined and implied fields – either overlapping or discrete.

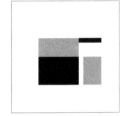

Diagram 50·3 a&b: Edge-aligned figures composition with defined and implied fields – either overlapping or discrete.

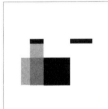
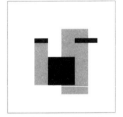

Diagram 50·4 a&b: Fitted figure composition with defined and implied fields – either overlapping or discrete.

Figure 51: Another hybrid image combining multiple defined and implied fields for a composition used in the previous diagrams. Again although it is not a part of the project, it prompts consideration of figure-field density.

(50·4a). In the second diagram, a large implied field crosses the rightmost and the center figures, suitably stabilizing the whole (50·4b).

Summary

Formal design premised on figure-ground gestalt – interpreting figures and fields on a ground – exhibits more nuance than the simple multistable 'face or vase' illusion. Throughout the presentation of this project, we have offered complex visual examples as products of simple means. The multiple interpretations of highly ordered diagrams serve an important purpose for the designer. It allows her to continually ask 'what if?', and then to proceed with additions to or alteration of the scheme in front of her. It enables her to imagine something that is not yet present. It provides a tool for analysis and improvement.

We began this chapter with an argument for including drawing and diagramming as part of the arsenal for design thinking. When we work with our students through this first project, they do not learn anything absolutely or finally. Rather, they pack up their experience, write and compare notes and sketches, and begin looking at composition differently – not as an endeavor to identify right and wrong, but as an open-ended inquiry into the possible.

GLOSSARY OF TERMS

ADJACENT: Describes anything – particularly a figure or field – next to or adjoining something else.

AXIS: An imaginary straight line that divides any space or figure into two portions. (Further remarks on 'axis' appear in later glossaries.)

BOUNDARY: Any line that marks the limits of an area, a boundary divides a figure from its ground.

· In diagrams, BOUNDING LINES (or BOUNDARY LINES) extend a figure's boundary past the figure and across the ground to provide visual evidence of formal influence – most often alignment.

DEFINED and IMPLIED FIELDS: Terms used to distinguish kinds of related boundaries and corners found within compositions.

· Defined fields directly correspond to an existing edges.

· Implied fields correspond to locations inferred by existing pattern and measure either through interpolation or extrapolation.

DOMINANT and SUBORDINATE: Terms used to describe elements as if within a perceived visual hierarchy.

· A dominant figure appears as the most influential field in a composition.

· A subordinate figure acts seems as less influential or dependant on another figure or field in the configuration.

FIELD: In visual composition, any area observed as an independent region. In gestalt, both figures and ground are potential fields for other elements.

GRID: A network of lines crossing each other to form a series of similar units, usually squares or rectangles.

· A RELATIONAL GRID results from the geometric subdivision of space relative to an initial field.

· A UNIVERSAL GRID represents infinite lines that cross one another at right angles at regular – sometimes numbered – intervals to precisely locate and measure objects and space.

GROUND: In composition, the largest field in which figures may interact.

HYBRID: A thing made by combining two distinct or different elements.

IDEA: A mental event about a possible course of action, often synonymous with the aim or purpose of that action. In its broadest sense, an idea can reflect concepts, opinions or feelings about something as probable, desirable or possible.*

MOTIF: A distinct group of simple elements that creates a single impression. Motifs most often accrue in larger, more complex compositions. Thus, two walls abut to create a corner and four corner motifs aggregate to form a square composition. The term also describes thematic variations perceived among formal sequences, for example a closed corner, a folded corner and an open corner.

· MOTIVIC: Of or relating to a motif.

PATH: A course or direction in which a person or thing can move.

PRINCIPLE: A proposition that serves as the foundation for a chain of reasoning. Also refers to a theory with multiple applications in a practice. Thus a PRINCIPLE OF ORGANIZATION identifies the basis for a fundamental attribute that determines the arrangement of objects in a collective.

*ABOUT IDEAS

The term IDEA generally refers to something either perceived through the senses, visualized or imagined. It is a comprehensive word that includes most aspects of mental activity.

· In contrast, a THOUGHT results from meditation, reasoning or other intellectual activity.

· The term NOTION denotes any vague or capricious or unreasoned idea.

· We define any widely held idea that identifies something particular as a CONCEPT.

· External phenomena often trigger an IMPRESSION, something less mentally rigorous.

DESCRIPTION 4
The courtyard

Figure-ground & solid-void

When asked to think of a work of architecture, many tend to picture an object-building – a building that appears as a singular, freestanding object. This is understandable, given the unambiguous image that an object-building presents to the mind's eye. This tendency is also understandable within the context of suburban North America, with its preponderance of single-family houses, box stores and fast-food outlets.

Yet much of the built environment, particularly in cities, provides a substantially richer context for architecture, one wherein figure-ground relationships are both more tangible and more nuanced. Traditional urban patterns of settlement tie individual works of architecture to multiple fields and grounds simultaneously, with boundaries defined by uniform setbacks, block plans and party walls, among others. Here, buildings not only comprise figures, they can also act as fields, containing their own, internal figures. Because buildings are inherently inhabitable three-dimensional entities, diagrams of positive and negative space provide us an additional set of analytic tools to further our understanding of compositional strategies in architecture.

Il Tempietto di San Pietro in Montorio

DONATO BRAMANTE

The *Tempietto* is an object-building *par excellence*. Formed from austere volumes and radial symmetry, Bramante's concise essay in Renaissance central-plan architecture demands to be perceived as a singular, freestanding entity (1). Nevertheless, its visual impact depends greatly on its immediate physical context: it resides within a courtyard (2). Despite its modest dimensions, the *Tempietto* exerts a powerful presence within the ordered confines of its rectangular *cortile*. Set within a larger, less uniform environment, Bramante's jewel would arguably lose its luster, overwhelmed by the spatial and scalar variability of its new surroundings. Simply put, our perception of a figure is dependent upon its field. To extend this analogy into three dimensions, we say that our impression of the *Tempietto*-as-object is wedded to the enveloping negative space of the courtyard.

There are further, more subtle reciprocities at work here. At first glance, when considered against its field, we might imagine a figure as a solid. However, such is rarely true of buildings. The interior of the *Tempietto* comprises two rooms, one void atop the other along the central vertical axis (3). Between its enclosing wall and the encircling colonnade, we see the space of a narrow ambulatory. Even within the *poché* of that wall, we identify the undulating rhythm of apses and alcoves. The reciprocities found among figure and ground, solid and void, and positive and negative space would be further enhanced

Figure 1: *Il Tempietto di San Pietro in Montorio,* Donato Bramante, 1503, after Letarouilly, *Edifices de Rome Moderne,* 1840.

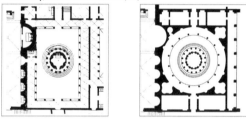

Figure 2: Extant state and proposed design for *Tempietto* courtyard.

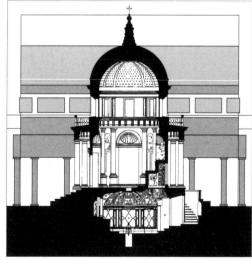

Figure 3. Section through *Tempietto* with proposed courtyard scheme.

Figure 4: *Palazzo Farnese,* after an etching by Giambattista Piranesi.

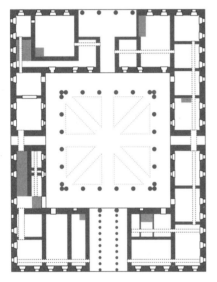

Figure 5: *Palazzo Farnese,* ground floor plan.

Figure 6: *Palazzo Farnese,* view of the courtyard.

had Bramante's circular courtyard been completed. Its design recalls the richly layered annular geometries of the *Maritime Theater at Hadrian's Villa,* a structure Bramante is said to have measured extensively just prior to designing the *Tempietto.*

Palazzo Farnese

ANTONIO DA SANGALLO, MICHELANGELO, *et al.*

Another example from Rome of an object-building is that of the *Palazzo Farnese,* a freestanding block facing a large, orthogonal piazza (4). Designed initially by Antonio da Sangallo, the project subsequently engaged many of the leading Italian architects of the sixteenth century, including Michelangelo, Vignola and Giacomo della Porta. Commissioned in 1517 by Cardinal Alessandro Farnese, the building served as home and headquarters for one of the most powerful families of Renaissance Rome. When the Cardinal ascended to the Papacy in 1534 as Paul III, plans for the palazzo grew considerably to reflect his newly acquired status.

The design of *Palazzo Farnese* marks the apex of the Italian Renaissance palace, a building type whose impetus came from enterprising patricians eager to forego their fortress-like ancestral compounds, enlarged willy-nilly throughout the Middle Ages, for the tempered clarity of an architecture in tune with the spirited poise of fifteenth and sixteenth century Italy. Despite the typically cramped confines of their urban sites, these grand dwellings strove for a formal autonomy, characteristic of the modern object-building. Nevertheless, while these buildings acted as distinct figures within the larger field of the city, they held within themselves a field essential to the type: the courtyard (5).

The central courtyard solved a fundamental practical problem: the provision of daylight throughout buildings with a large footprint. Yet, for architect and patron alike, the central void was also a matter of order and orientation. As the essential 'heart' of the design, the courtyard organizes one's experience of the building, providing the primary point of reference for navigating its interior spaces (6). The robust, ordered exteriors fulfill a significant objective of the design: to project a sense of strength and permanence to passersby, an impression heightened by the large plaza opposite the main facade. However the courtyard governs the experience, ennobling its patrons – the Farnese clan – and impressing their privileged guests.

Phillips Exeter Academy Library

LOUIS KAHN

Schooled in the traditions of the École des Beaux-Arts, Lou Kahn was profoundly influenced by history, particularly that of Rome. Yet, he also stood among the front ranks of heroic Modernists determined to re-invent the world from square one. A rich amalgam of historical precedent and modernity permeates Kahn's architecture, nowhere more so than his library at Phillips Exeter Academy, in New Hampshire (7). Completed in 1971, the brick-clad cubic volume provides an initial impression of muscular solidity, not unlike *Palazzo Farnese.* At the same time, the reductive geometric order of its severe exterior, stripped of all apparent ornament, defines the Modernist object-building *par excellence.*

It is in the arrangement of the interior, however, that Kahn's striking synthesis of tradition and innovation finds full expression. The prevailing plan-type of the library featured a large, centrally-placed reading room, surrounded by book stacks placed toward the building's periphery. Kahn's approach at

Exeter literally turned this convention inside out. He began with a consideration of the individual reading carrel, ensconcing them within the foursquare perimeter of the plan for optimal proximity to natural light. Abreast of this outer band lies a second, inner ring, that of the stacks: adjacent to the carrels, yet placing the books beyond the reach of direct sunlight.

At the core of the library, Kahn replaced the traditional reading room with a communal void. The enclosed, sky-lit courtyard allows for comprehensive views of the library's collection throughout the building, and affords a particularly vivid impression upon arrival at the top of the entrance stair. Identical to the role it plays in the *Palazzo Farnese*, the central courtyard here provides the essential point of reference for inhabiting the interior. The apparent simplicity of the figure-ground relationship in the plan reveals, upon closer inspection, a complex, interwoven web of proportional relationships; we examin this at length in CHAPTER 9 of this book.

Figure 7: *Exeter Library,* Louis Kahn, 1971.

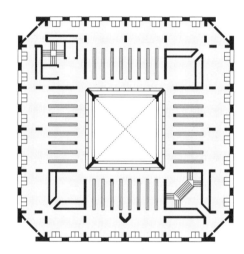

Figure 8: *Exeter Library,* Louis Kahn, 1971; plan view.

Figure 9: *Exeter Library,* Louis Kahn, 1971; interior courtyard.

DEMONSTRATION 4·1·1
Figures & field in variation

Sequence explained

The two example sequences in these demonstration pages attempt to show the similarities and differences of two divergent approaches to the composition illustrated in CHAPTER 4. The first set begins with differently massed forms in close proximity. The second starts with similar masses set more distantly from one another. Obviously other combinations are possible, but these allow for ready comparison.

As the sequences proceed, each set evolves into three variant compositions. To create a composition of staggered figures, one of the original figures shifts laterally to produce an offset alignment. To make the next configuration, we shear the overlapping portion of one figure, resulting in figures edge-aligned along a common side. In a similar fashion, we displace a portion from the other side of the dormant figure with a new, third figure aligned horizontally with the pre-existing shifted figure. We label that final arrangement as fitted figures.

Below and to the right are a rehearsal of the first set of compositions and their development. The demonstrations that follow illustrate the spatial implications of each of the variations.

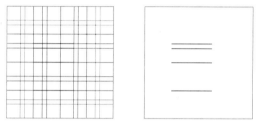

Figure 1: The first step showing large and small partitions in close proximity with and without the underlying measuring grid.

Figure 2: The large and small partitions in close proximity sponsor four variations.

The images on the right present each variant as both a set of boundary lines (above) and as filled fields of black (below). Dotted lines represent the previous composition and placement of elements.

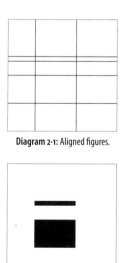

Diagram 2·1: Aligned figures.

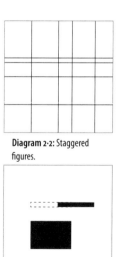

Diagram 2·2: Staggered figures.

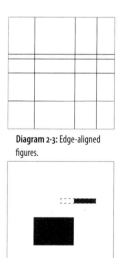

Diagram 2·3: Edge-aligned figures.

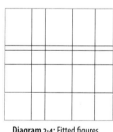

Diagram 2·4: Fitted figures.

DEMONSTRATION 4·1·2
Variation & elaborations

LARGE & SMALL MASSES IN CLOSE PROXIMITY

There are multiple ways of diagramming and representing the idea of space as it reflects an articulated figure-ground composition. The examples on the following pages display various possible diagrams taken from the four compositional types seen in CHAPTER 4.

Each figure-ground type generates its own unique spatial gestalt patterns within and beyond the boundaries of the ground. They imply force fields perpendicularly from all edges of the figures. We represent this phenomenon using gradient tone.

As we might expect, the alignment of the two figures in our first composition defines the middle shared space and implies both horizontal and vertical extensions of the spatial gestalt (3). A staggered composition necessarily produces an augmented, shared zone at the overlapping portion of the force fields (4). Edge-aligned compositions – as in the example – produce a more highly charged area defined by the common boundary of the figures (5).

The fitted figures in composition, by virtue of their proximity, suggest a negative space as a near-visible white figure (6).

To describe specific, bounded areas brought about by these examples of spatial gestalt, we might now add a third element to the dualism of figure-ground composition, the element we will call field

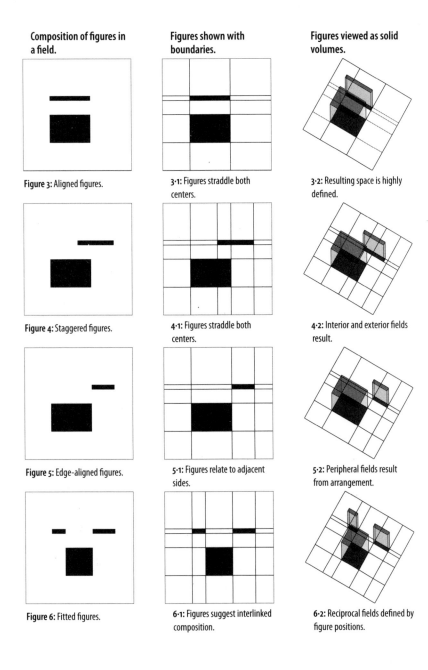

Composition of figures in a field.

Figure 3: Aligned figures.

Figure 4: Staggered figures.

Figure 5: Edge-aligned figures.

Figure 6: Fitted figures.

Figures shown with boundaries.

3·1: Figures straddle both centers.

4·1: Figures straddle both centers.

5·1: Figures relate to adjacent sides.

6·1: Figures suggest interlinked composition.

Figures viewed as solid volumes.

3·2: Resulting space is highly defined.

4·2: Interior and exterior fields result.

5·2: Peripheral fields result from arrangement.

6·2: Reciprocal fields defined by figure positions.

Spatial gestalt diagram using tone.

3·3: Diagram reveals the effective tartan grid.

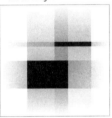

4·3: Spatial gestalt shows comparable density.

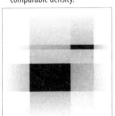

5·3: Gestalt implies a variable cruciform.

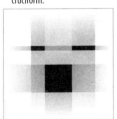

6·3: Gestalt diagram suggests field density.

Defined field shown as tone.

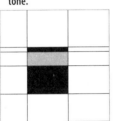

3·4: The courtyard field reveals the internal geometry.

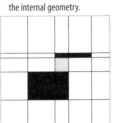

4·4: Small courtyard shared between forms.

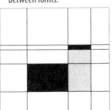

5·4: Side courtyard defined.

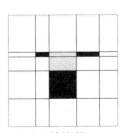

6·4: Central field addresses three figures together.

Alternative defined fields shown as tone.

4·5: Defined fields partially surround courtyard.

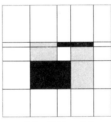

5·5: Alternate side courtyard defined.

6·5: Side courts connect the figures adjacently.

Additional defined fields shown as tone.

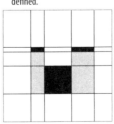

4·6: Defined fields extend from figures.

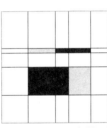

5·6: Twin, separate side courts defined.

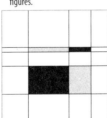

6·6: Side courts separate the figures into two parts.

DEMONSTRATION 4·1·3
Variation & elaborations

SIMILAR MASSES IN DISTANT PROXIMITY

In this set of examples, the alignment of the two figures the composition defines a larger middle shared space implying both horizontal and vertical space but enlarges the vertical dimension of that space – effectively placing greater distance between the two elements (7). The two figures begin as equals in size.

The staggered composition has more spatial tension and the slight difference in width is, as a consequence, noticeable (8). Despite the increased distance between figures, the edge-aligned composition sustain a charged sense on connection along the common boundary of the figures (9).

The increased distance has the greatest effect on the fitted figures composition (10). As there is greater scale affinity among the figures, the apparent figure found in the negative space is similarly clearer, despite the larger vertical separation.

Composition of figures in a field.

Figure 7: Aligned figures.

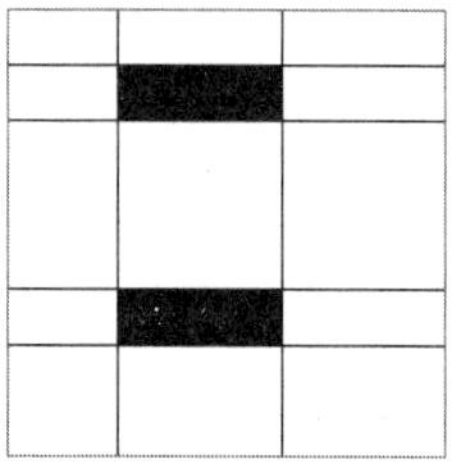

Figure 8: Staggered figures.

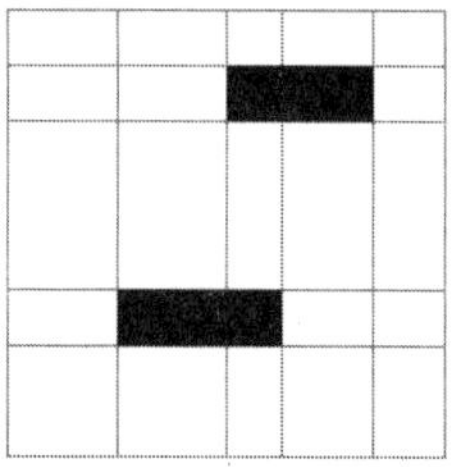

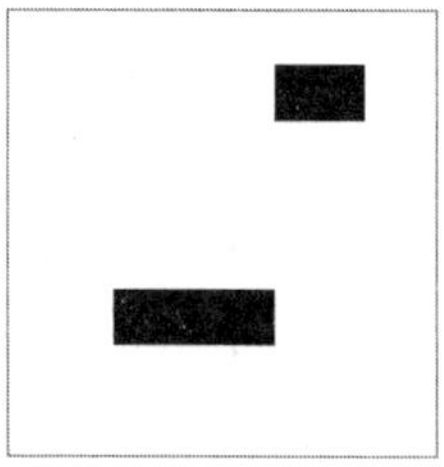

Figure 9: Edge-aligned figures.

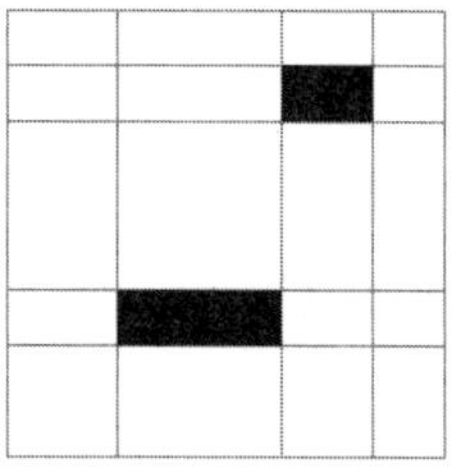

Figure 10: Fitted figures.

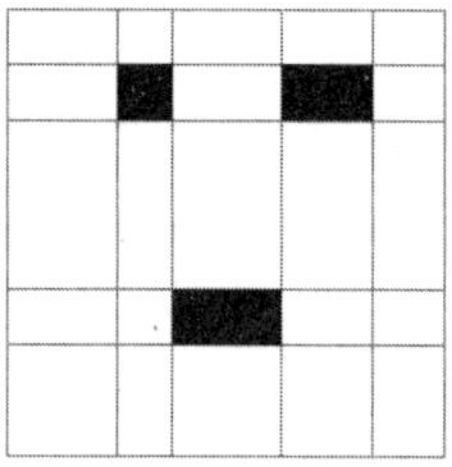

Figures shown with boundaries.

7·1: Figures shift from both centers.

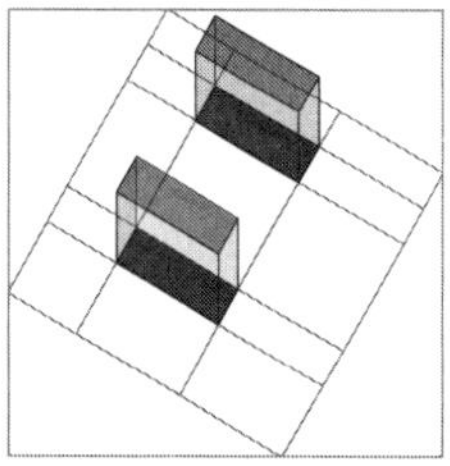

8·1: Figures approximate balance.

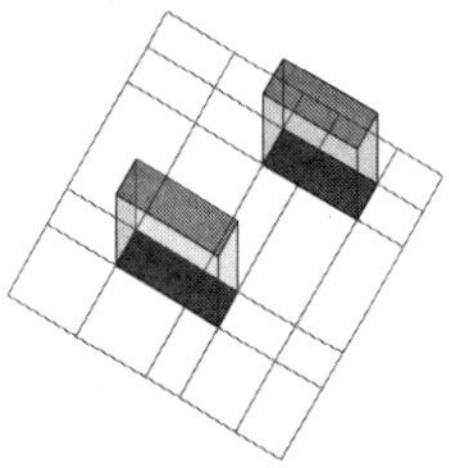

9·1: Figures oppose across the diagonal.

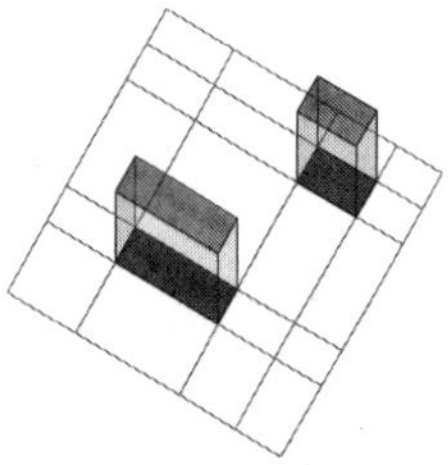

10·1: Figures shift balance to the upper right.

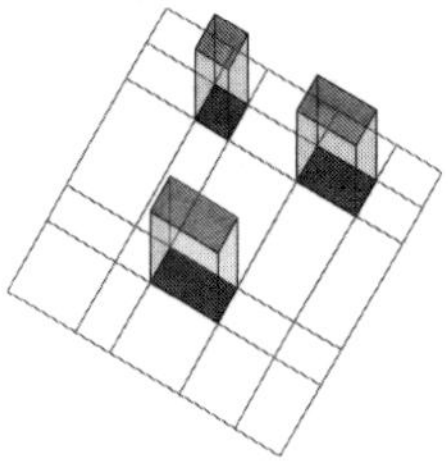

Figures viewed as solid volumes.

7·2: Resulting space remains clearly defined.

8·2: Exterior fields dominate the result.

9·2: Peripheral fields suggest larger figure.

10·2: Reciprocal fields aggregate toward the center.

Spatial gestalt diagram using tone.

Defined field shown as tone.

Alternative defined fields shown as tone.

Alternative defined fields shown as tone.

7·3: Diagram reveals vertical bias.

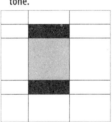

7·4: The courtyard field favors the internal geometry.

8·3: Spatial gestalt reflects balance.

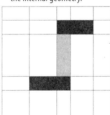

8·4: Small courtyard transits between forms.

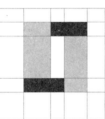

8·5: Defined fields appear to surround a connecting link.

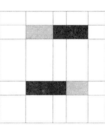

8·6: Defined fields expand from figures.

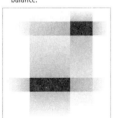

9·3: Center again dominates field gestalt.

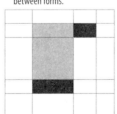

9·4: Forecourt dominates smaller figure.

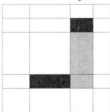

9·5: Alternate side court suggests sequence.

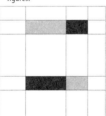

9·6: Side courts define sequential balanced composition.

10·3: Gestalt diagram reinforces dynamic reciprocity.

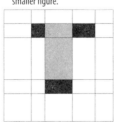

10·4: Central field suggest a balanced hierarchy.

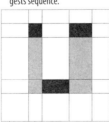

10·5: Side courts create a large connected figure.

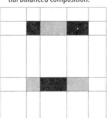

10·6: The two groups manifest the gestalt reciprocity.

DEMONSTRATION 4·2
Further variations

Figure 1: Four compositions of aligned figures illustrate changes in proximity and proportion.

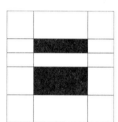

Diagram 1·1: Figures occupy a centered square.

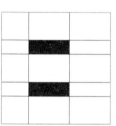

Diagram 1·2: Lower figure and negative space define a square.

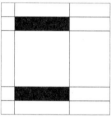

Diagram 1·3: Each figure and negative space define a square.

Diagram 1·4: Equal aligned figures spaced far apart.

Figure 2: As the figures stagger, overall proportions change as does the dynamic and balance within each composition.

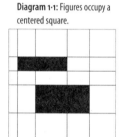

Diagram 2·1: Figures define negative space as a pinwheel.

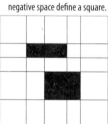

Diagram 2·2: Figures define a centered square.

Diagram 2·3: Defined negative space dominates.

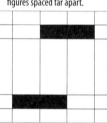

Diagram 2·4: Figures stagger across large central square.

Figure 3: The edge-aligned figures, occupying corners of the bounded space, stabilize each overall composition change, as does the dynamic and balance within each composition.

Diagram 3·1: Figures define serpentine negative space.

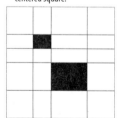

Diagram 3·2: Serpentine negative space occupy the square.

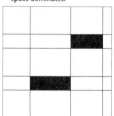

Diagram 3·3: Negative space balances the composition.

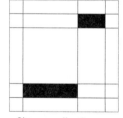

Diagram 3·4: Negative space dominates the composition.

Figure 4: The fitted figures, occupying the bounded space in a reciprocated rhythm and create a syncopated dynamic of horizontal and vertical counterpoint.

Diagram 4·1: Figures define syncopated negative space.

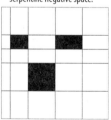

Diagram 4·2: Negative space completes the square.

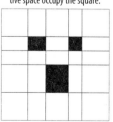

Diagram 4·3: Negative space adheres the figures.

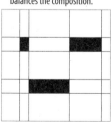

Diagram 4·4: Negative space emphasizes separations.

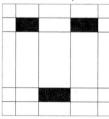

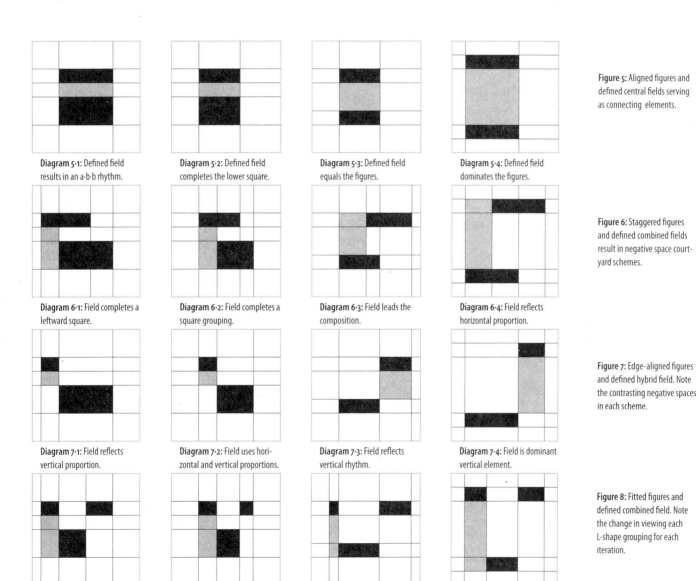

Diagram 5·1: Defined field results in an a·b·b rhythm.

Diagram 5·2: Defined field completes the lower square.

Diagram 5·3: Defined field equals the figures.

Diagram 5·4: Defined field dominates the figures.

Figure 5: Aligned figures and defined central fields serving as connecting elements.

Diagram 6·1: Field completes a leftward square.

Diagram 6·2: Field completes a square grouping.

Diagram 6·3: Field leads the composition.

Diagram 6·4: Field reflects horizontal proportion.

Figure 6: Staggered figures and defined combined fields result in negative space court-yard schemes.

Diagram 7·1: Field reflects vertical proportion.

Diagram 7·2: Field uses horizontal and vertical proportions.

Diagram 7·3: Field reflects vertical rhythm.

Diagram 7·4: Field is dominant vertical element.

Figure 7: Edge-aligned figures and defined hybrid field. Note the contrasting negative spaces in each scheme.

Diagram 8·1: Field borders virtual square.

Diagram 8·2: Field completes virtual square.

Diagram 8·3: Field stabilizes visual grouping.

Diagram 8·4: Field accentuates horizontal rhythm.

Figure 8: Fitted figures and defined combined field. Note the change in viewing each L-shape grouping for each iteration.

DEMONSTRATION 4·3
Contrast, repetition, alignment & proximity

Overview

This demonstration presents an overview of basic visual differences between multiple figures in a field. The four distinctions are contrast, repetition, alignment and proximity. The examples represent neither an exclusive nor complete catalogue. Instead, they serve to introduce language that describes the relationship among figures and fields. Consider the terms as useful tools for discussion and critique.

Contrast examples

Contrast generally refers to apparent formal differences and similarities between figures. These identify form and surface differences regardless of placement within a composition. Some common contrasts follow:

· Tone and color: identify the comparative qualities of the surface of forms.
· Shape: describes the outline of the perimeter of forms.
· Dimension: identifies the relative size or scale of the formal elements.
· Character: compares the means used to separate the figure from the ground.
· Orientation: refers to any apparent direction – or lack thereof – implied within the composition.

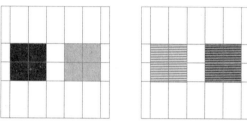

Diagrams 1·1&2: Two pairs of figures showing two forms of surface contrast.

Figure 1: Eleven images illustrating variations in graphical contrast.

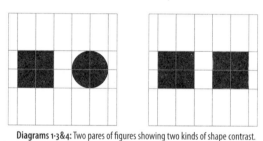

Diagrams 1·3&4: Two pares of figures showing two kinds of shape contrast.

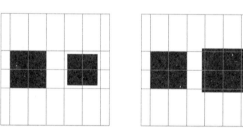

Diagrams 1·5&6: Two pairs of figures showing two varieties of dimensional contrast.

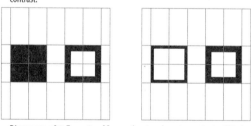

Diagrams 1·7&8: Two pairs of figures showing character contrasts of kind and degree.

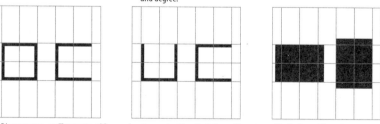

Diagrams 1·9–11: Three pairs of figures showing contrast in orientation with center and/or horizontal boundary alignment.

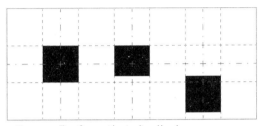

Diagram 2·1: Three figures with pairs aligned by edge.

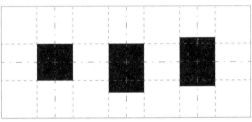

Diagram 2·2: Three figures with two aligned by edge and two aligned by center.

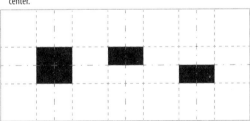

Diagram 2·3: Three varied figures aligned by center and edge.

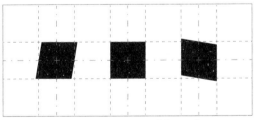

Diagram 2·4: Three figures showing horizontal alignment by center.

Figure 2: These four images show comparative examples of alignment for three objects arrayed horizontally.

Alignment examples

Alignment relates to axial and boundary differences and similarities among figures. Depending on the complexity of the forms within a composition, alignments can be simple or compound and can describe figure-field relationships as well as relationships between figures. Common terms for alignments are:

· Horizontal and vertical: identify the orthogonal directions for alignment in a field.

· Axial: identifies linear alignments regardless of direction.

· Edge: identifies the relative comparison of formal extremes of the perimeter of forms.

· Center: refers to the apparent center of forms as a measure of their alignment among formal elements.

This relatively simple vocabulary underwrites the often nuanced character of formal relationship.

Proximity examples

Proximity identifies the near and far relationships within a composition. As with alignment it also affects our visual sense of balance.

In addition, proximity includes not only the relationships among figures, but also the relative distances to the edges of a field. Some of the common proximity conditions on groups of figures are:

· Constant proximity: the spaces between figures are the same measure.

· Varying proximity: the spaces between figures change measure either randomly or sequentially.

When the boundary of the field is part of the composition, consideration and terms remain the same.

In addition, the scale of objects within a composition may affect the perception of proximity. Spaces that equal an object's footprint dimensions can lend a sense of repetition to a composition. Those that are lesser or greater can amplify the sense of proximity as well.

Figure 3: Five images showing examples of relative proximity using objects arrayed for the most part on the horizontal.

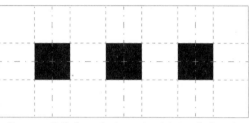

Diagram 3·1: Similar figures showing equal proximity to each other and the field.

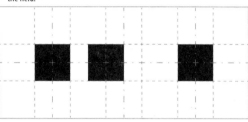

Diagram 3·2: Similar figures showing near and far proximity to each other and equal proximity to the field.

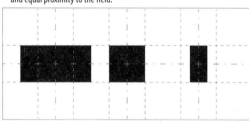

Diagram 3·3: Dissimilar figures showing near and far proximity to each other and the field.

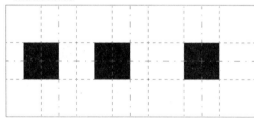

Diagram 3·4: Similar figures showing near and far proximity to each other and the field.

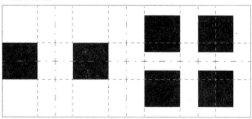

Diagram 3·5: Similar figures showing near and far proximity to each other and the field in two axes.

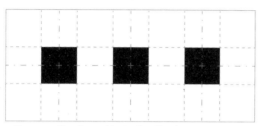

Diagram 4·1: Three figures with pairs aligned by edge.

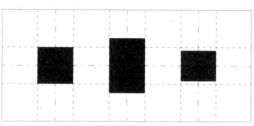

Diagram 4·2: Three varied figures with two **aligned by edge** and two **aligned by center.**

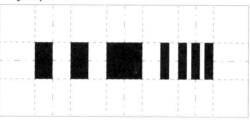

Diagram 4·3: Multiple figures aligned by center and edge.

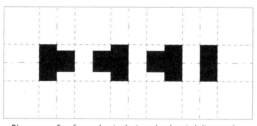

Diagram 4·4: Four figures showing horizontal and vertical alignment by edge.

Figure 4: Four images showing examples of relative proximity using objects arrayed for the most part on the horizontal.

Repetition examples

At its simplest we observe repetition when something reoccurs. As we consider the previous three formal categories, we recognize that in order to note differences, more than one thing has to be there for our consideration. In this way, repetition underlies many other principles of design. It is the form of similarity necessary for difference to occur.

Repetition can seem random like a field of rocks on the ground or, by exhibiting some measure of order, it suggests purpose or intent. In complex forms, repetition provides a base for identifying differences. Some common examples of this are:

· Series or sequential: repetitions suggest a beginning point of development.
· Rotation: such as the numbers on a clock or the columns on a round building.
· Linear: allowing the observation of rows, columns and grids.

The grid is the most common expression for repetition that allows for other observations. Separate illustrations of this follow.

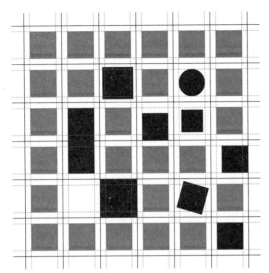

Figure 5: Example of a six-by-six gridded pattern showing ten combined formal variations including color contrast.

Repetition as context

Columns and rows beget the grid. In the particular case of figure-ground observations we use the underlying sense of pattern to observe special or extraordinary movements that interrupt the sameness of the grid.

COMMON GRID VARIATIONS

This relatively simple vocabulary underwrites the often nuanced character of formal relationships.

· Displacement: a shape moves out of the normal alignment for a pattern.
· Combination: the perimeters of two or more shapes merge.
· Scale: the shape changes in size relative to the norm.
· Proportion: the shape changes size along one or two axes resulting in an alteration of shape character.
· Orientation: the shape rotates about an axis.
· Shape: the shape exhibits a different figure.

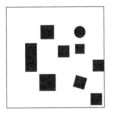 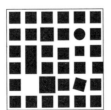

Figure 7: The combined formal variations from above without the regular figures (left), and without tonal variation (right).

Figure 6: Diagrams showing a sequence of formal variations in a nine-square grid.

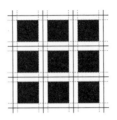

Diagram 5·1: Nine squares in a grid.

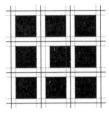

Diagram 5·2: Center square displaces on the horizontal.

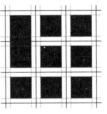

Diagram 5·3: Upper left squares combine.

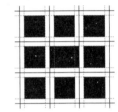

Diagram 5·4: Center square proportion expands laterally.

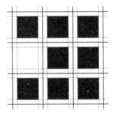

Diagram 5·5: Center left square disappears.

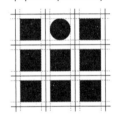

Diagram 5·6: A circle occupies center top – shape.

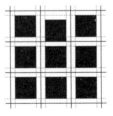

Diagram 5·7: Center top square displaces on the vertical.

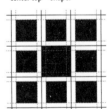

Diagram 5·8: Center square expands proportionally.

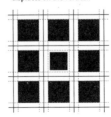

Diagram 5·9: Center square shrinks proportionally.

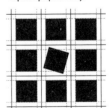

Diagram 5·10: Center square rotates within grid.

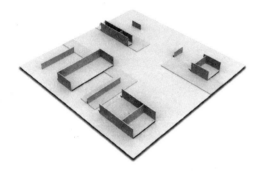

OVERVIEW
The second project

In this chapter, we present the first half of PROJECT 2. The exercises within build on the figure-ground language explored previously, so as to broaden the base for appreciating both composition and formal logic. In addition, the rhythm of the project's structure promotes a first understanding of the possible relationships between two-dimensional design and three-dimensional realities.

A consistent theme of our projects and our text is that the plan view in design allows for broader application than convenient, conventional representation. Building on the idea of the diagram as both record and analysis, this second project uses two-dimensional means to visualize relationships, as well as to construct figures and fields. In the process, the project evolves through multiple iterations of simple figure-ground to more complex groupings. The illustrations use drawings, cut paper figures, transparent fields and overlays to tease out an evolving dynamic.

We end this chapter with a three-dimensional artifact that will serve in CHAPTER 6 as a springboard to exploring the rigors of section through diagrams.

CHAPTER 5
Building on proportion

Object on a field

We noted before that every figure is potentially a field waiting to hold other figures. That observation follows from gestalt principles as a general trait of human perception: our senses move us toward resolution and completion. A charged form awaits an occupant, just as nature abhors a vacuum and silence beckons sound. Expectation should not be arbitrary, however, so here we take a critical view of what might happen during the design process and why.

In this chapter, we move on from generalized gestalt-informed analysis to explore basic pattern in an architectural construct. We take the reader on a journey from the abstraction of a figure on a field toward closer analogies of architecture on a site. In the process, we show how fields can multiply and subdivide. In a sequence similar to Russian nested dolls, as figures become fields, smaller figures enter the scene.

Placing an object in a landscape, or a figure on a field, results in a picture – a manifestation that suggests an idea. Ideas in architecture generally point to two things: the organization of a design, and its orientation to the site. Both of these are large concerns, full of possibility and interpretation. In developing those ideas, we describe the relationship of the design to its site and to its component parts.

As we perceive the world, objects either stand alone or associate to form collectives. From that fundamental observation, two ideas emerge as architectural possibilities. Buildings – in their simplest descriptions – either develop their complexity inwardly, as if initially a simple volume or they combine elements and express their complexity externally as multipartite. Following one approach or the other should result from the designer having a particular idea about results. The desired intent leads to adopting a basic strategic approach as an expression of the Big Idea.*

A figure in the relational field

In CHAPTER 4, we demonstrated the relationship of two simple forms in a field. In its initial iteration, the variations show two undeveloped volumes as solids and propose an analysis of their relationship. As the sequence evolves, relationships change, as each of the figures acts as a possible site for further development. In this way, a combination of two figures offers a relationship that can evolve towards greater complexity. This fundamental observation parallels the dichotomy between external and inward expression, an organizing principle that inhabits the middle portion of our narrative sequence.

*CREDIT WHERE DUE

In 1972, the architects Robert Venturi and Denise Scott-Brown published *Learning from Las Vegas*. Among their observations was the proposition that architecture offered up two strategic categories: the DUCK and the DECORATED SHED. The categories prompted lengthy discourse and multiple opinions. For us here, they inform our ideas about design strategies. Buildings that express complexity externally pay homage to the duck. Those that hold their complexity in a simple volume bow to the decorated shed. We do not suggest that Venturi and Scott-Brown would agree with us, but we admit that their observation lives in our premise.

We begin our investigation of the evolving figure the same way as the previous figure-ground episodes – by dividing a square ground into eighths and twelfths. We then place a single figure into the resulting relational grid and analyze the formal conditions. Generating multiple examples allows us to better illustrate the role that geometry may play in developing compositional integrity. The sequence that follows is a simple repetitive procedure followed by analysis, in the form of diagrammatic overlay.*

For each iteration, we place a black figure on the ground. Each figure obeys a few simple guidelines. These rules set the stage for later evolution, by eliminating extreme variants that might hamper or obstruct the sequence.

There are three guidelines:

1　No figure touches the perimeter of the square.
2　The figures' areas should fall between approximately one ninth and one fifth of the entire field in size.
3　The figures snap to the grid.

Four example variations appear below (1–4).

There are three distinct, related ideas to consider in creating the figures: PLACEMENT, ORIENTATION and PROPORTION. Placement, in its relation to order, should start with a general intent. Within the relational grid, the figure will reflect the underlying sense of either quarters and centerline or thirds and center space. Wherever placed, orientation of the figure on the grid can be horizontal, vertical or static – without overt direction. Ideas of proportion follow directly from orientation. The object can be tall or squat, wide or stubby, square or squarish – language is remarkably imprecise regarding proportion. Despite that potential imprecision, the resulting visual gestalt should yield to very simple verbal description – for example 'A relatively tall figure sits in the upper-left quadrant of a square field, its bottom touches the field's centerline' – if for no other reason than to practice verbalizing formal analysis (1). If you detect at this point that alternate verbal descriptions exist for the example, then you understand the underlying premise of starting here.

To appreciate the nuances of this seemingly simple scenario, we suggest repeating it through a minimum of eight variations. To understand the spirit of the idea, the eight should display diversity yet remain coherent as a group. They should achieve differences worthy of consideration yet remain related.

*DIMENSIONS FOR THE EXERCISES
Once again, we omit exact dimensions for the compositions. In the classroom, we continue to use index cards for the majority of drawn exercises – in this instance cutting them down to 4" squares. In some years, we used the entire 4"×6" to introduce students to the Gothic era's favored proportion. The project works equally well in either case.

Figures on a relational grid.
In the four examples below, regulating lines in a square ground define a single rectangular figure shown as a gray form. All figures are orthogonal and follow the general guidelines.

The general intent governing the set limit the figures in three ways:
• They avoid symmetrical placement.
• They vary the direction and visual demeanor of the figures
• Each example relates to the one before and/or after.

In addition, the set sequence demonstrates four interrelated variables:
• **Placements** cover all four quadrants, with three examples spanning the centerline.
• **Orientations** include horizontal, vertical and static.
• **Measurements** begin at both corners and edges.
• Therefore **proportions** interact with both centerpoint and center space geometries.

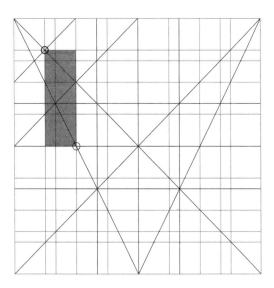

Figure 1: The figure originates in the upper left quadrant at a corner point defined by the regulating lines for the sixteenth interval. The intersection of the horizontal centerline and diagonal thirds regulating line defines the opposite corner.

Figure 2: The second figure uses the mirror regulating line in the upper right quadrant to define an edge point at the eighth interval. Following the line upward to the twelfth point and across to its semi-mirror in the opposite quadrant completes the figure.

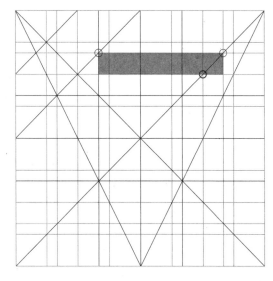

When our sixty first-year students compare their results, they quickly notice that what to them seemed obvious responses to the instructions prove to be remarkably individual. If they follow the rules of engagement, the final group of eight figures will share significant if subtle biases that provide a basis for engaging the ongoing design process.

A single figure on a ground exhibits basic compositional gestures. A horizontal figure might sit on top or settle to the bottom (2&3). It may relate to a side or the center, or occupy a particular quadrant. The figure may also either hold its place, or seem to move towards empty space to the left or right. A vertical figure – as seen in Figure 1 – acts similarly with differences reflecting the change in axial direction. Squares or other near-static figures seldom exhibit motion, instead appearing to possess a sense of gravity or stability (4).

These observations illustrate that while SYMMETRY may have a specific definition, the concept of BALANCE plays over a large range of possible equations. This seems an obvious point as a concept. In practice, however, refining one's sense of visual balance constitutes a subtle and ongoing challenge. Describing those observations accurately requires deliberate effort.

Being able to articulate the design act in the context of possible options broadens the capacity for design thinking. Speaking carefully becomes a verbal counterpart to analytic diagrams. Careful discussion of formal results reminds us that seeking one direction in resolving a design results from INTENTION, not from coincidence.

Language expands a designer's sense of intention. Taken on robustly, it helps clarify the context for judging one's own work, and thereby improves both the design and the designer. Addressing a design in language that suggests it as the only logical solution to a problem reduces the design act to formula. It also obscures the presence of intent, in pursuit of one tactic over another. We urge our students to separate personal taste from project possibilities, not because we eschew instinct, but because critical judgment lays a stronger foundation than instinct alone.* The four examples on the next page (5–8) further analyze the compositions shown below. Thereafter, a sequence of eighteen variations serves as a visual essay on compositional gesture, as described above.

*ON STYLE

Design discussions generally avoid using the word 'style' as it brings along a negative sense of the superficial. This pejorative connotation is leftover from nineteenth-century 'style books' that conflated apparent features with particular styles – e.g., pointed arches indicated Gothic style. 'Style without substance' more accurately describes such limited interpretation. In reality, genuine style results from well-applied technique and method – tactics and strategies. Correctly understood, style construes long practice wherein multiple decisions accrue as part of articulating ideas.

Working in simple forms toward internal complexity or from aggregate forms toward external expression are complementary styles of design practice. They are working methods that reflect different intentions.

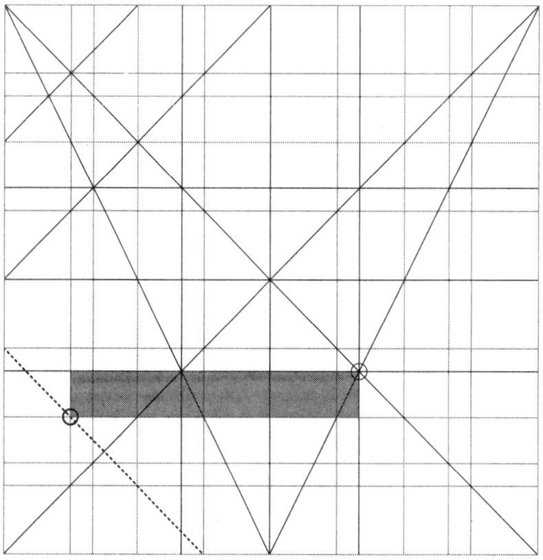

Figure 3: The third figure originates in the lower left quadrant at a corner point defined by the regulating lines for the eighth interval. The intersection of the diagonal thirds regulating line defines the opposite corner.

Figure 4: The fourth figure uses a subdividing regulating line of the upper right quadrant to define an edge point at the eighth interval. Following the line downward to the center diagonal and locating a point along the diagonal third in the same quadrant completes the figure.

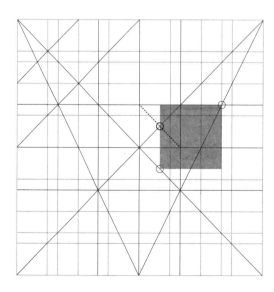

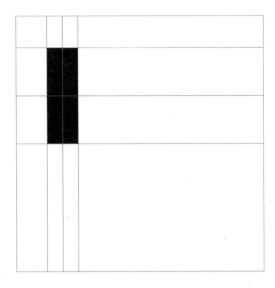

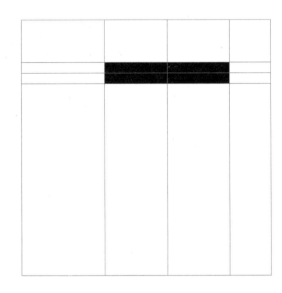

Figure 5: The figure's placement rests on the horizontal centerline. Its upper left corner marks a square, anchoring its position in the quadrant.

Figure 6: The second figure's placement mirrors the regulating line in the upper right quadrant to define an edge point at the eighth interval. Following the line upward to the twelfth point and across to its semi-mirror in the opposite quadrant completes the figure.

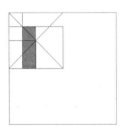

Diagram 5·1: The figure reflects repeated regular subdivision of the quadrant's square geometry.

Diagram 6·1: The figure uses regular geometric measure for proportion and placement.

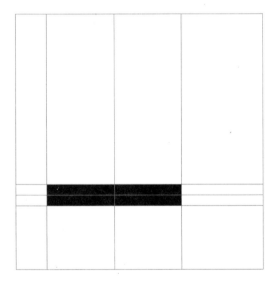

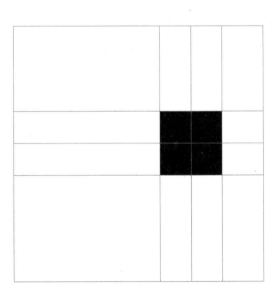

Figure 7: The third figure originates in the lower left quadrant at a corner point defined by the regulating lines for the eighth interval. The intersection of the diagonal thirds regulating line defines the opposite corner.

Figure 8: The fourth figure uses a subdividing regulating line of the upper right quadrant to define an edge point at the eighth interval. Following the line downward to the center diagonal and locating a point along the diagonal third in the same quadrant completes the figure.

Diagram 7·1: Underlying figure geometries show both regular intervals — the square — and the generation of the irregular measure.

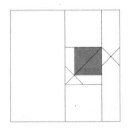

Diagram 8·1: Figure geometries reveal similar regular intervals of squares and the construction of the offset.

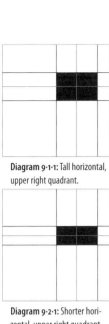

Diagram 9·1·1: Tall horizontal, upper right quadrant.

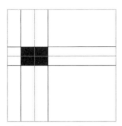

Diagram 9·1·2: Smaller variation, upper left quadrant.

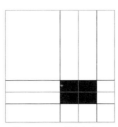

Diagram 9·1·3: Mid-sized variation, lower right quadrant.

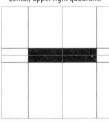

Diagram 9·2·1: Shorter horizontal, upper right quadrant.

Diagram 9·2·2: Smaller variation, upper left quadrant.

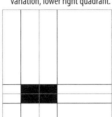

Diagram 9·2·3: Mid-sized variation, lower left quadrant.

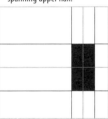

Diagram 9·3·1: Wide horizontal, spanning upper half.

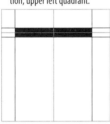

Diagram 9·3·2: Broader variation, higher up.

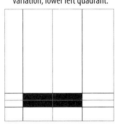

Diagram 9·3·3: Mid-sized variation, lower half.

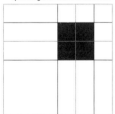

Diagram 9·4·1: Narrow vertical, spanning horizontal centerline.

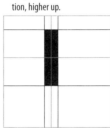

Diagram 9·4·2: Taller, narrower, adjacent to vertical centerline.

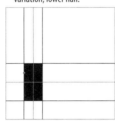

Diagram 9·4·3: Mid-size vertical, lower left quadrant.

Diagram 9·5·1: Square form touching centerpoint.

Diagram 9·5·2: Near-square occupying upper left quadrant.

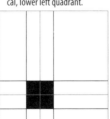

Diagram 9·5·3: Mid-size square, adjacent to centerline.

Diagram 9·6·1: Horizontal form touching centerpoint.

Diagram 9·6·2: Similar form occupies upper left quadrant.

Diagram 9·6·3: Mid-size rect angle, adjacent to centerline.

Orderly development of figures and variations

Figure 9: To the left, six related figures with three variations each demonstrate a sequential development. As with previous examples (1–4), all figures are orthogonal and follow the same general guidelines.

The general intent governing the set limits the figures in three ways:
- They avoid bilateral symmetrical placement.
- They vary the direction and visual demeanor of the figures.
- Each example relates to the one before and/or after.

The general organization for each row of three also follows a sequence of large to small to medium size – a papa, baby and mamma bear family of shapes.

The set sequence again illustrates four interrelated variables:
- **Placements** cover all four quadrants, with three examples spanning the centerline.
- **Orientations** include horizontal, vertical and static.
- **Measurements** begin at both corners and edges.
- **Proportions** therefore interact with both centerpoint and center space geometries.

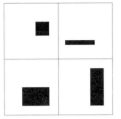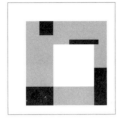

Figure 10: A deliberately uneven sequence group shown with a possible organizing figure resulting from select bounding lines.

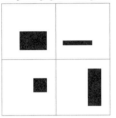

Figure 11: Exchanging the two left figures shifts the balance of the group and lessens the bounded center.

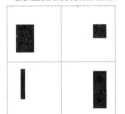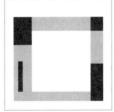

Figure 12: Rotating the two horizontal figures and displacing the square expands the bounded center, creating distinct left and right sides.

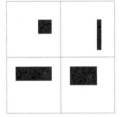

Figure 13: Rotating the two larger figures and mirroring their position shrinks the bounded center and suggests horizontal emphasis.

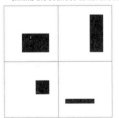

Figure 14: Arranging the figures in a pinwheel simultaneously enlarges the perimeter and maintains a discreet bounded center.

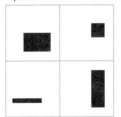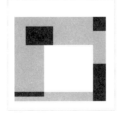

Figure 15: An alternate pinwheel arrangement moves individual elements toward the perimeter and isolates the square.

Looking at the groups

Having generated multiple variations, we begin our analysis by arranging groups of four examples as if a series of compositions. There are several useful MOTIFS for constructing any group. Our first motif arranges four compositions as a single series organized by their sequence of development. Depending on the eight variations, the results can appear obvious or uneven and certain steps in any sequence may evoke quite different features among the variations. For that reason, our example begins with a fictional sequence that is just that – uneven. Their development may follow a sequence, but they do not appear obviously sequential (10 left). By observing the boundary lines, we can diagram an external perimeter and speculate on its internal courtyard space (10 right).

As we continue to amend the first arrangement, we look for features emerging within the figure group (11–17). Scale or relative size, orientation, proportion and placement all suggest themselves. Furthermore, we can observe figures that interact or stand apart. At this point, several questions suggest themselves. Can we group elements by similarities or differences? Do some of these sub-groups serve within multiple arrangements?

These questions should prompt further variations, and those should prompt further questions. This ongoing process illustrates the SYNERGY between gestalt pattern recognition and the importance of developing a strategic vocabulary for description. When we diagram the individual figure compositions by adding boundary figures, we help clarify the visual aspect of the organizational form. Viewing those images as diagrams expands the basis for analysis to include the sequences and their descriptions.

In addition, their roots in gestalt readings prompt a sense of the interplay between figures and ground, manifesting order and allowing for any additional elements to fit within the compositional whole.

Selecting & analyzing an aggregate composition

After completing eight iterations, we make a final composition for further observation and analysis. This prompts another series of diagrams, each aimed at demonstrating particular and possible interpretations for individual quadrants and affinity groups, as well as the composition as a whole. For the

Figure 16: A variation on the pinwheel arranged to create the smallest bounded center.

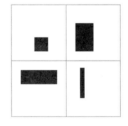

Figure 17: A final pinwheel arrangement, moving figures to the outer perimeter, creates the largest bounded center.

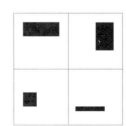

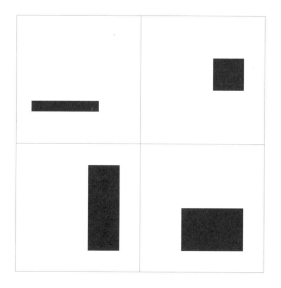

Figure 18: The four figures shown with the borders of their quadrants.

Diagram 18·1: The more probable boundary and courtyard emphasizes the isolated state of the upper left quadrant's figure.

Diagram 18·2: Extending the interior perimeter to include the upper left figure creates an irregular central area.

purpose of our discussion, we use a composition that resists simple visual resolution. This allows a broader range of observations as the project moves forward.

Our first diagram shows the four figures and their quadrants (18). Even in this simple diagram, we can recognize that the general demeanor is somewhat peripatetic. While the four figures all cluster around an off-center courtyard, the upper figures have a weaker visual relationship to that space (18·1–2). In addition, the upper-left figure displays an indecisive presence toward the whole, orienting its two broader faces toward areas outside the group. The ambiguity of the square ameliorates this somewhat, serving as an external anchor for the whole, while only its corner touches the interior perimeter.

The second large illustration reveals the boundary lines and center lines of each figure within its quadrant (19). The resulting diagram makes the previous comments concerning the composition visible as they apply to individual figures. It also renders the aggregate visual gesture of each figure within the collective.

By extending the boundary lines of each figure across the entire ground, we reveal the place and measure of possible defined fields for the figures in composition (20). The diagram also makes note of alignments found within the arrangement. These boundary lines allow us to generate yet another diagram – to visualize the dynamics of the composition – that suggests greater unity overall (20·1). This particular diagram reminds us that the purpose of gestalt exercises such as these can extend beyond analysis to include generative ideas for further development.

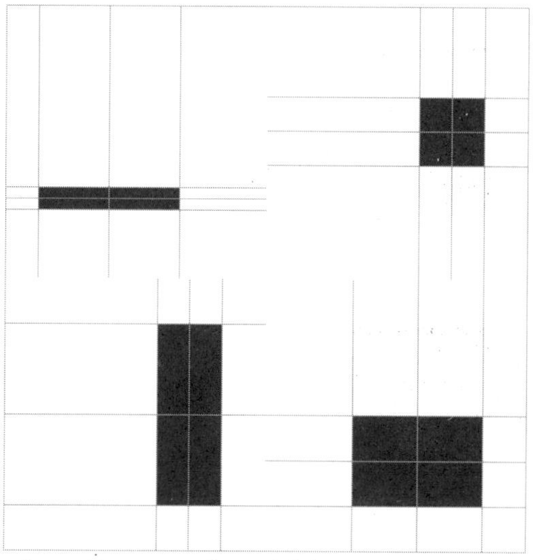

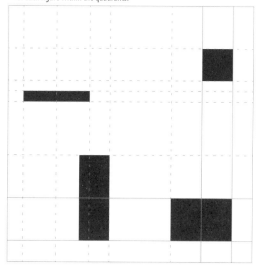

Figure 19: The composition shown with the boundary lines and centerlines of each figure within the quadrants.

Diagram 20·1: Shrinking the interior perimeter to exclude the upper figures defines a square central area.

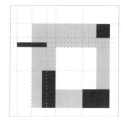

Figure 20: Extended boundary lines that mark defined fields. The solid lines show edges and centers that align.

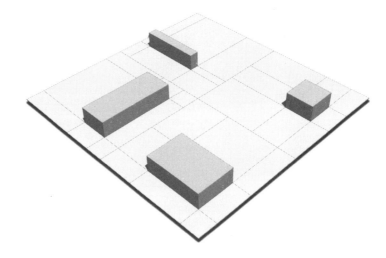

Figure 21: A model of the composition thus far. The figure height is a formal fiction for the exercise. Premised on a 4" square quadrant, the figures are 1.25" in height and penetrate the ground plane by 0.25". The ground plane shows both quadrant borders and boundary lines.

Figure 22: Diagram showing exaggerated boundary lines extended within each quadrant and overlying the previously observed courtyard scheme.

Figure 23: The same figure boundaries shown as graduated fields overlying the previous courtyard field.

Adding to the quadrants

Thus far in the project, we have defined rectangular figures on a ground and composed four quadrants chosen from the exercise. The composition offers several distinct advantages for further exploration. In particular, the dynamic of the group composition allows an exploration of figures whose sizes, shapes and placements resist easy formal resolution (22–23). To enhance the interplay of the quadrant and groups, we proceed to develop each quadrant independently, adding to their individual complexity before moving on to further resolving the whole.

This pattern embodies an underlying classroom logic. In design, complexity arises from PROGRAM, the components of a real project. Those demands define and shape the elements that comprise any design. The descriptions of large and small components – their formal relationships, their differences and similarities, orientation, size and place, as well as their rough hierarchy – form the threads of any project. Weaving those threads into a coherent fabric is the central formal task facing the designer. That some parts resist easy inclusion comes with the territory.

This project sequence reflects that weave as part of its makeup. It 'chunks out' a hierarchy of formal challenges to mimic a version of generalized complexity, reflecting the architectural task. Each step in the procedure adds components, creating demands that imitate the intricacies of the design process. This allows the project to conjure a sense of architecture while remaining appropriately abstract, as befits a first-semester assignment.

Two elements

Having determined the overall arrangement of figures and ground, we proceed to add two elements – a HALF-WALL and a FIELD – to each quadrant. The exercise continues in the mode of plan-based diagrams, with the deliberate intention of altering the balance of each individual quadrant's composition.

We represent the half-wall as an outlined figure – it is half-height and, therefore, not shown in section. We use a transparent gray area to mark the field, remaining consistent with the formal language of the previous project group. The general intention that should guide these additions is two-fold. Both additions should relate to the existing figure, as well as adjust its

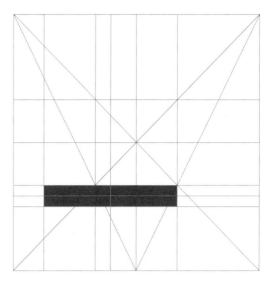

Figure 24: A diagram of the figure from quadrant one shown with construction lines and primary axis and boundary lines.

general condition in the quadrant. Other formal guidelines act as general rules of engagement for both elements. They are as follows:

· Both the half-wall and added field are orthogonal in form and placement.
· The half-wall does not touch the figure.
· The half-wall is thin (≈0.0625" in proportion to a 4" quadrant).
· The field may be larger, smaller or equal in size to the figure.
· Unlike the original figure, the field may touch one edge of the quadrant.
· The field may also overlap or pass under the figure.

Recalling that the initial figure – using the language of gestalt – acts formally as a field within a larger field that is the ground, the placement of the added elements should both enhance the original figure and amplify its relationship to the ground. In the end, the composition should be clearer and more emphatic because of the additions.

Looking to the right, we observe three two-part adjustments in response to the first quadrant (25·1–3). Each diagram pair shows a half-wall and then an added field to complete the response, although in practice they may develop concurrently or in the reverse order, depending on the idea behind their evolution.

In the first diagram pair, the two combined elements extend the presence of the figure vertically and horizontally (25·1a&b). The overall result stabilizes the figure by creating a larger visual zone of occupation. The combined vertical boundaries, being longer and more numerous, counteract the extreme horizontality of the original figure, as does the negative space.

The lower edge of the half-wall in the second example occurs symmetrically, across the horizontal center from the upper edge of the figure (25·2a). It is half the figure's width, aligns rightward and spans the vertical center. In response, the field occupies the area immediately below the centerline, aligns leftward with the half-wall and extends beyond the rightward shared edge (25·2b). The complexity of the resulting negative space also helps shift the focus to the vertical center shared by all three elements.

In the final variation, the half-wall establishes a new vertical boundary that the added field then uses for its own rightward edge (25·3a&b). The vertical height of the field derives from the centerpoint of the ground. Its width reflects the negative space to its right, and together they construe a square center third of the entire composition. The entire grouping, inclusive of the negative space, defines an even larger square area that is a stable fit within the whole.

This process of addition and analysis continues to include all four quadrants, each generating multiple examples (26–28). After observing their individual visual demeanor, we select one for each quadrant and re-assemble them as a single composition. The goal at this point in the project is to select a combination that presents the clearest prospect for further development. This may seem an obvious step – simply choosing examples that result in simpler for-

Figure 25: Below, three pairs of adjustments to the quadrant show added half-wall and related field. Each diagram demonstrates an alternate compositional tactic. The half-wall diagrams (a) include regulating lines for the quadrant; the adjacent diagrams (b) feature the resulting boundary and axis lines.

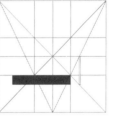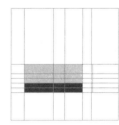

Diagram 25·1a&b: An extending half-wall and a corresponding defined field create a clear negative space and simple overall composition.

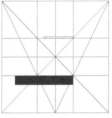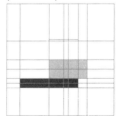

Diagram 25·2a&b: A responding half-wall and a related extending implied field stagger the resulting configuration and space.

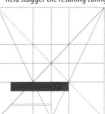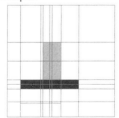

Diagram 25·3a&b: An alternate responding half-wall and a related extending implied field add cross-grain gesture and negative space.

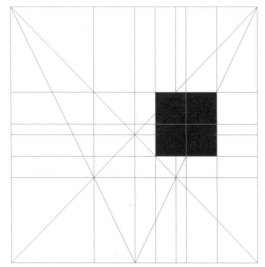

Figure 26: The figure from quadrant two shown with construction geometry as well as boundary and axis lines.

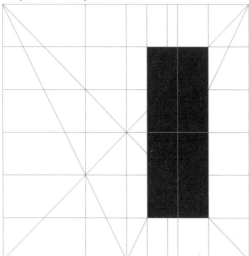

Figure 27: The figure from quadrant three shown with construction geometry as well as boundary and axis lines.

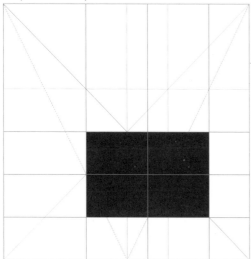

Figure 28: The figure from quadrant four shown with construction geometry as well as boundary and axis lines.

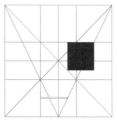

Diagram 26·1a: An added extending half-wall.

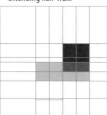

Diagram 26·1b: Extending implied field added.

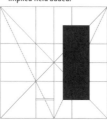

Diagram 27·1a: An added responding, extending half-wall.

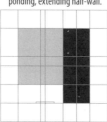

Diagram 27·1b: Extending implied field added.

Diagram 28·1a: An added responding half-wall.

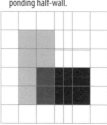

Diagram 28·1b: Extending implied field added.

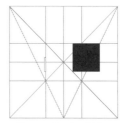

Diagram 26·2a: An added responding half-wall.

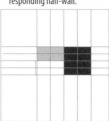

Diagram 26·2b: Extending implied field added.

Diagram 27·2a: An added responding half-wall.

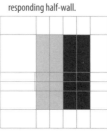

Diagram 27·2b: Corresponding defined field added.

Diagram 28·2a: An added spanning half-wall.

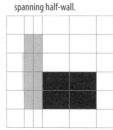

Diagram 28·2b: Extending implied field added.

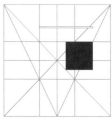

Diagram 26·3a: An added spanning half-wall.

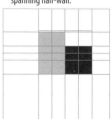

Diagram 26·3b: Corresponding defined field added.

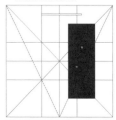

Diagram 27·3a: An added spanning half-wall.

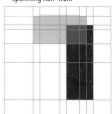

Diagram 27·3b: Corresponding implied field added.

Diagram 28·3a: An added responding half-wall.

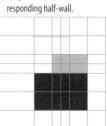

Diagram 28·3b: Corresponding implied field added.

Figure 29: The chosen variations of each quadrant with fields and half-walls shown with boundary and axis lines.

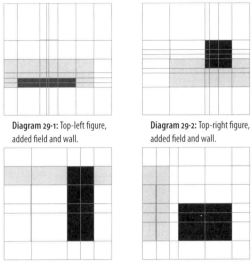

Diagram 29·1: Top-left figure, added field and wall.

Diagram 29·2: Top-right figure, added field and wall.

Diagram 29·3: Lower-left figure, added field and wall.

Diagram 29·4: Lower-right figure, added field and wall.

Figure 30: The composition with fields and half-walls added to the fields.

mal harmony. However, that choice may not always prove the richest gambit. To illustrate this point, the four variations of the quadrants that we use for our composition result in just such a visual conundrum.

The four quadrants shown above all feature elongated fields – thee horizontal and one vertical (29·1–4). Seen together, they reveal some shared characteristics despite comprising a scattered collective form (30). Further observation of the resulting edges, centers and alignments reveals an orderly underpinning to the composition. The combined directionality of the figures, fields and half-walls begins to suggest a richer formal environment (31). The nexus of alignments – the solid lines – and unanswered boundaries and axes – the dashed lines – represent the density of spatial structure that begins to characterize the directionality emerging within the composition.

We can also observe that vertical and horizontal lines – referring to the orientation relative to the page – traverse the area we noted earlier as a probable center. Similarly, the left portion of the ensemble now exhibits a more structured sense of movement along its vertical axis. What was formerly an

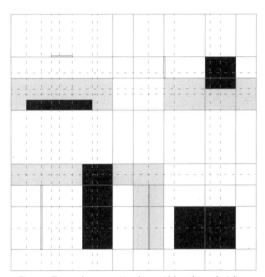

Figure 31: The complete composition shown with boundary and axis lines for all elements.

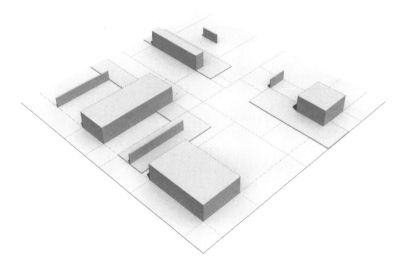

Figure 32: A model of the composition including figures, fields and half-walls. The figure height is as before. The half-walls are mid-height. Shallow relief elements represent the fields superimposed on quadrant borders and figure boundary lines.

Single-ply museum board is the usual material, being white as well as easy to cut as befits a first model exercise.

indeterminate or residual space within the composition appears less static or empty. It implies direction.

The term that best describes dominant visual direction in a field is GRAIN. Borrowed from woodworking, where grain identifies the longitudinal pattern of fiber in wood – its apparent direction – it is a common term in formal design discourse. In general, grain runs parallel to the dominant direction a figure. Thus, absent any other visual input, we attribute horizontal grain to a horizontal rectangle and vertical grain to a vertical rectangle. A square will seem ambiguous as to direction, while a linear array of squares will likely affect the sense of grain. We perceive circular forms either as absent of direction or as embodying concentric grain – again context will affect us.

Conversely, CROSS-GRAIN identifies movement across the surface, or counter to the general direction exhibited by a field or figure. If we perceive a circle as having concentric grain, then any radial motion will seem as moving across that grain. In any instance of multiple figures, part of the task of a designer is to orchestrate the visual sense of direction within a diagram.

Refining the figures

In order to refine the composition, we begin with a simple articulation of the original figures in response to the additions of half-walls and fields. For this exercise, we focus on responding to our observations concerning grain. As a learning tactic, each figure transforms into two parallel walls, a floor plate and a connecting cross wall (33&34). The goal of this construction is to articulate the space of the original figure, thus expanding the spatial implication of the whole. It proposes the next evolution in design judgment.

The form chosen for the figures' construction is purposely rudimentary, although it is not without nuance. The parallel wall construction allows the figure to articulate visual grain either parallel or perpendicular to the direction of the figure's own geometry. Taking inspiration from the primitive temple form seen at the start of CHAPTER 1 (p. 1), it allows for subdivision of the interior in response to existing geometries. The floor plate add the possibility of experimenting with vertical placement relative to the emerging shallow relief found in the ground plane. In addition, the absence of an overhead plane – a roof – maintains the visual link with the plan view, supporting the spatial development of the composition as a whole.

The exercise begins with two-dimensional plan diagrams. These are generally the same size as the accompanying model. The primary learning outcome is to draw attention to the difference between the experience of analyzing a diagram/drawing and viewing a three-dimensional artifact. This is in keeping with an overall recognition that seeing space in an orthographic drawing is distinct from recognizing size, shape and location while making the image. This distinction sponsors meaningful discussion during in-class critiques.

Observing the new figures

Drawing the individual quadrants before constructing the model allows students to observe the additions at a local level. That is, they proceed by making choices that address four individual compositions before assessing and adjusting them to the larger context.

This follows the general goal of addressing architecture – the planning and construction of articulate space – and bypasses any untutored presuppositions about what buildings are supposed to be. In this, we engage in a simple fiction to illustrate the evolution of order in design thinking. The configura-

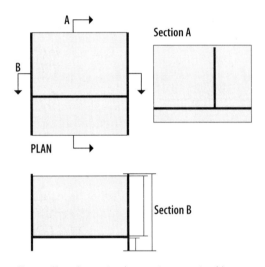

Figure 33: Plan and two sections demonstrating construction of the new figures.

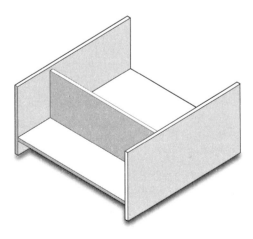

Figure 34: Isometric view of new constructed figure.

tion of the interior spaces – their general H-shape – allows each figure to orient itself proportionately to the site, and adds to the overall complexity with its visual grain as well as its internal structure – including the cross-grain divider. The four plan diagrams to the right show the combined impact of these additions, through the use of center-axis and boundary lines from all the elements in each quadrant (35–38).

In the first quadrant, we observe that the parallel walls follow the grain of the surrounding field (35). The cross-grain partition aligns with the right edge of the half-wall, creating an interior space on the right that mirrors that wall's horizontal dimension. In addition, the overall matrix of the lines subdivides the composition in a pattern that suggests an emerging order for further development.

In the next diagram we see that the field implies a square anchored in the upper right area of the quadrant (36). The cross-grain element aligns with the horizontal center of that quadrant, balancing the spaces defined to its left and right. Vertical equilibrium remains dependent on the placement of the field and half-wall. Their point of contact occurs on the horizontal centerline of the quadrant.

The figure in quadrant three uses its cross-grain element to radically counter its formal grain toward the horizontal (37). Placed at the leftward extreme, it creates a single C-shaped space oriented to the right. This tactic produces no new boundary or axis, and reflects the intent to relate directly to its quadrant boundary, and what lies beyond. Such judgment deliberately skirts the directive to develop each quadrant independently. This should prompt a discussion on the flexibility of rules of engagement in the design process, a deliberate purpose of these examples.

The horizontal disposition of the figure's parallel walls in quadrant four serves as a direct foil to the strong verticality of the field and half-wall directly to its left (38). The cross-grain wall provides a static figure – a square – anchored at its lower right boundary, in a larger square whose upper left corner occurs at the intersection of the quadrant's edge and the field. This is consistent with the generally stable geometries of the quadrant

Observing the new group

Having observed the individual figures, we direct our attention to the aggregate composition, first in two-dimensional form and later as a three-dimensional model. We begin by viewing a plan diagram of the elements, absent any reference to internal geometry (39). This view sponsors the question of whether all the design thinking described above is visible, without the connecting tissue of added boundaries and axes.

Our first observation shows that without any overlays, some alignments between components recede from the forefront while others remain visually strong. Given their color, the fields dominate more than they might in reality. The visual balance throughout is distinct from any accurate visual representation, a reminder that our use of the term *diagram* throughout the text is not an affectation. The elements that any diagram brings into play hew ardently to the truth. They may be precise and visually coherent, however, their role is to represent *ideas* about design. Therefore, they absolutely require intelligent judgment and interpretation. As we proceed with our observations, we turn to a group of illustrations and diagrams that focus on the multiple readings that the attach themselves to the group composition

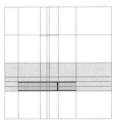

Figure 35: The figure in quadrant one follows the grain of the field while its interior wall reasserts the rightward boundary of the half-wall.

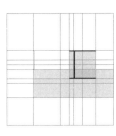

Figure 36: Both interior spaces of the square figure in quadrant two follow the grain of the field, while its dividing wall echoes the field's center axis.

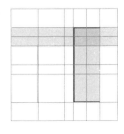

Figure 37: The construction of the figure directs its interior space toward quadrant three's right edge. This gesture also partially counters the formal grain of the figure.

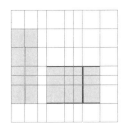

Figure 38: The new figure in the fourth quarter continues to weave a balanced fabric of geometric subdivision.

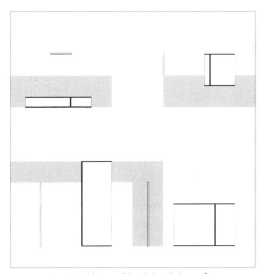

Figure 39: A combined diagram of the whole with the new figures, assembled as a group and shown without boundaries or axes.

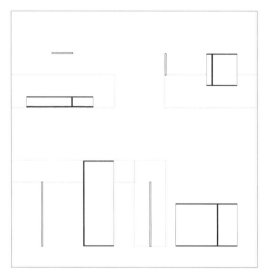

Figure 40: A diagram of the whole with the new figures fashioned as a more conventional plan drawing.

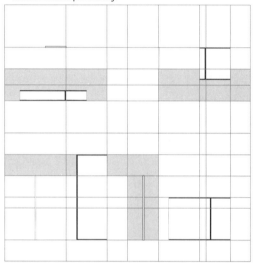

Figure 41: This diagram again uses tonal planes for the fields and includes relevant boundary and axis lines.

Figure 42: A speculative diagram exaggerating spatial grain and cross grain of the new figures.

Our first diagram attempts to represent the elements more in keeping with the visual demeanor of the model (40). This rendition simulates an artifact constructed of white museum board. The hierarchy of the diagram follows the visual hierarchy of the composition – walled figures, half-walls, floor plate and fields. Compared to the previous diagram, its subtle contrast – its gestalt – submits more easily to interpretation as a spatial composition. Suggestions of alignment emerge as a function of the judicious use of line weight and *poché*, and we begin to perceive the illusion of a third dimension 'popping' into view.

If that diagram reveals the qualities of a good architectural plan drawing, the next illustration reminds us that more abstract diagrams appeal to the imagination in other ways. The grid of lines in this instance shows only those boundaries and axes that are shared by two or more elements. The diagram helps to locate areas of visual congruence as a pattern in the weave of space and form. It also helps identify opportunities for further reference within the spatial fabric.

The last diagram is a speculative response to viewing the model (42&43). As we can view the model from multiple perspectives, we should record our observations accordingly. Traditional perspective – especially accompanied by commentary – is a useful tool. However, interpretive diagrams provide excellent alternatives. This particular image attempts to capture the sense of spatial grain associated with the figures within the model. The principal means used is variable line weight.

Thus far, we have used various two-dimensional diagrams to generate and study a multi-figured composition in plan. With internal spaces and variable heights, we are now able to introduce diagrams with other vantage points. This subject begins our next chapter.

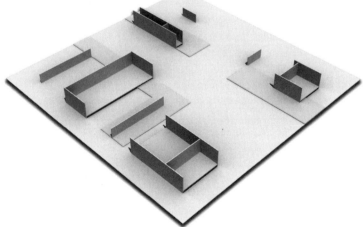

Figure 43: Model of the group composition. Once again, the material is single-ply museum board.

GLOSSARY OF TERMS

BALANCE: A condition in which different elements are equal or in the correct proportions; harmony or equilibrium of composition.

DUCK and DECORATED SHED: Terms used by Robert Venturi and Denise Scott-Brown in *Learning from Las Vegas*. One of two strategic categories for architectural form. The term 'duck' identifies any building whose function manifests in a particular form. In contrast, a unified volume that denotes function through ornament or tectonic expression results in a 'decorated shed'.

GRAIN: Term used in design to describe apparent formal direction or orientation of objects and space.

· CROSS-GRAIN: Describes the orientation or implied movement of figure, field or element that runs counter to its context's apparent direction.

HALF-WALL: A wall roughly half as high as a full-height partition.

INTENTION: Reference to a plan or aim. Intentions may directly reflect the central idea or may serve to define an element's relationship to that end, including being distinct in method or form.

ORIENTATION: The particular placement of an element, form or building in relationship to something else. In architecture the something often relates to site constraints including, but not limited to, the sun, topography, adjacencies and boundaries.

PLACEMENT: Putting something in a particular place. In design placement generally reflects particular reasoning and formal logic in combination.

PROGRAM: The list of functional and spatial requirements that guides the development of a building's design.

SYNERGY: An interaction of two or more substances that yields a combined effect greater than the sum of the parts. The term has a shady life in the language of corporate aspirations, but in design it succinctly describes gestalt laws at work.

DESCRIPTION 5
Figures & fields

Objects & space

Previously we examined the fundamental figure-ground relationship of the
courtyard building – essentially a solid volume impaled by a central void.
Beyond this simple combination, buildings engage in a range of additional
spatial relationships, particularly in urban settings. Here, the built environment will often display an intricate play of figures and fields, weaving solids
within voids, and defining spaces with framing volumes. The examples that
follow provide a brief sampling of the rich possibilities of the composition of
figures and fields.

Roman & Imperial fora

APOLLODORUS *et al.*

The heart of the ancient city of Rome had inauspicious origins: a low-lying
marsh, prone to flooding, it lay between bronze-age villages atop the Capitoline and Palatine hills, and served as both cemetery and garbage dump. As the
hilltop settlements grew and merged, the construction of a sewer, the *Cloaca
Maxima*, drained the marshy field, rendering it fit for permanent inhabitation.

The *Forum Romanun* (1A) housed the principal civic institutions of the
fledgling Republic, including the College of the Vestals, whose chaste priest-
esses maintained the sacred flame of the city; the *Curia*, meeting place of
the Roman Senate; and two *Basilicas*, large colonnaded halls that supported
a dense mix of judicial, commercial, and bureaucratic functions. The figure-
ground of the *Forum* was simple but effective: a tightly-packed ring of public
buildings facing a central, roughly orthogonal, common space. The configuration of solid to void was of the courtyard building-type, with the distinction
that here, as with the public *agorae* of Greek cities, the solid volume of the
perimeter was more porous, providing the fluid circulation necessary at the
heart of the burgeoning city.

As Rome approached its Imperial destiny, the *Forum Romanun* could no longer contain the growth of its political and commercial infrastructure. Julius
Caesar laid out plans for a second forum, to accommodate the expansion of
the city's – and his own – political fortunes. The *Forum Iulium* (1B) was completed by his successor, the emperor Augustus, who added a third, adjacent,
complex, the *Forum Augustum* (1C). As with subsequent additions to this enormous civic cluster (the *Fora* of Nerva, Vespasian and Trajan – 1D, E and F), this
followed the figure-ground relationship of the *Forum Romanum*, each more
tightly ordered than the original. The *Fora Iulium, Augustum* and *Transitorium*
each comprised an elongated paved quadrangle, bounded by colonnades and
dominated by a temple dedicated to a deity of special significance to its patron

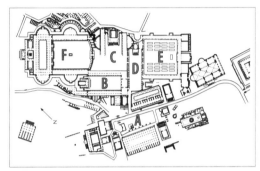

Figure 44: Plan of *Forum Romanum* and *Imperial Fora*, Rome.

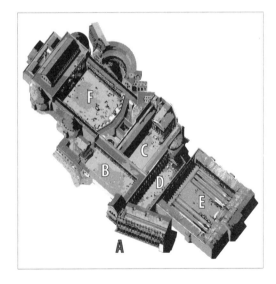

Figure 45: Plan oblique of *Imperial Fora* comprising: **A** *Forum Romanum* (partial), **B** *Forum of Julius Caesar,* **C** *Forum of Augustus,* **D** *Forum of Nerva (Forum
Transitorium),* **E** *Forum of Vespasian (Temple of Peace),* **F** *Forum of Trajan.*

Figure 46: *Campo Marzio, Ichnographia* (detail), Giambattista Piranesi.

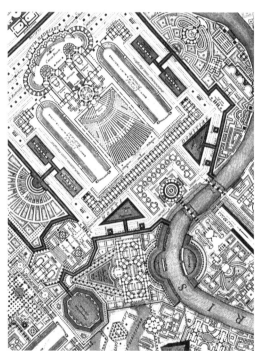

Figure 47: *Campo Marzio, Ichnographia* (detail), Giambattista Piranesi.

(*Venus Genetrix*, *Mars Ultor* and *Minerva*, respectively). The larger *Fora* of Vespasian and Trajan relaxed this script somewhat to accommodate a wider range of building types, but the essential figure-ground formula remained: an ample public (though largely ceremonial) commons bordered seamlessly by porticoes. Clustered tightly, the *Fora* were nevertheless individually self-contained spatial entities. Although each accommodated a dense mix of symbolic and bureaucratic functions, they all abide by the governing formula of a framed quadrangle – essentially the courtyard type – at the scale of the city.

Campo Marzio

GIOVANNI BATTISTA PIRANESI

An avid student of Rome, Piranesi ostensibly re-created the Imperial district of the ancient city in his ambitious publication, *Campo Marzio dell' Antica Roma*. Its centerpiece, the *Ichnographia*, appears to map the ancient *Campus Martius* in an enormous, exquisitely labyrinthine six-panel etching (3&4). Though this version of the ancient city contains remarkably accurate depictions of ancient landmarks – the stadium of Domitian, the theater of Marcellus and the sundial of Augustus (3) – most of the structures and spaces delineated by Piranesi are the wholesale product of his fevered imagination.

An architect by training, Piranesi lived in Rome during a period that saw little in the way of actual construction. To channel his creative production, Piranesi's primary *opus* was the sum of more than a thousand extraordinarily rendered etchings. Some, like commercially successful views of contemporary Rome (the *Vedute*), provided travellers with vivid souvenirs of the city. Others, like the four-volume *Antichità Romane*, combined Piranesi's skilled delineation with hard-headed archeological research. Still others, like the *Campo Marzio* and the dream-like tableaux of the *Carceri d'Invenzione*, provided fertile ground for Piranesi's prolific imaginings, while advancing his case for the supreme inventiveness of Roman architecture.

The *Campo Marzio* is phantasmagoric formal excess, a universe of form, space and order run amok (4). Elaborately nested figure-ground relationships spawn constellations of spatial riddles, wrapped in volumetric mysteries, inside an urban enigma. While the solid-void properties of the Imperial *Fora* may have served as a point of departure, the exuberance of the *Ichnographia*, with its intricacies of lace-like spatial *poché*, suggest that Piranesi's baroque predecessors – Borromini in particular – served as primary inspiration. Rendered as a single planimetric section, any clear distinctions between figure and field, interior and exterior – even block and street – give way to a fecund, delirious *assemblage*, its fractal-like scalar shifts revealing near-infinite regress, all fulfilling its author's firm conviction that 'more is more'.

Toronto-Dominion Centre

LUDWIG MIES VAN DER ROHE & JOHN B. PARKIN ASSOCIATES

Toward the other end of our spectrum of exuberance is Mies van der Rohe's solemn grammar of form and space, which speaks of a bespoke minimalism. And yet, within each of his realized projects, despite the immediate simplicity of their figure-ground relationships, despite the apparent austerity of their formal order and their strict means of expression, Mies brings forth a universe every bit as vivid, distinct and self-similar as Piranesi's.

Nowhere is this paradox more evident than with the *Toronto-Dominion Centre*, the culmination of Mies' large-scale urban projects, completed in 1969, the year of the architect's death. As with his first office tower, the Seagram building, Mies' obtained the Toronto-Dominion project via the enlightened intervention of Phyllis Lambert, scion of Seagram's Bronfman family. Comprising two towers of fifty-six and forty-six storeys, and a single-storey, single-span banking hall, the original complex shared a full city block with the existing Toronto Stock Exchange in the heart of city's financial district (5).

Like its predecessors in Manhattan and Chicago, the project in Toronto hinges upon the then unprecedented liberation of the building footprints from the surrounding street edge, permitting Mies' prismatic volumes to be arranged freely atop a granite-clad plinth that spans the full extent of the site. The deceptively simple relationship of three rectilinear figures within the gridded ground creates a pair of spaces defined by their adjacencies to the two towers (south plaza) and to all three buildings (north plaza), as well as the shallow setbacks along each of the buildings primary entrances (6).

Precise yet subtle proportions govern the entire composition of the project, at every scale. The tower footprints form double-square and golden rectangles, respectively, and the banking hall comprises a perfect 150-foot square. The doubly-defined 3:1 field that separates the two towers generates a concise, dynamic parallax effect as visitors traverse the plinth, its granite surface extending seamlessly across plaza spaces and lobbies alike, blurring distinctions between interior and exterior components of the site.

IIT Campus

LUDWIG MIES VAN DER ROHE & ALFRED CALDWELL

Mies' first major project in North America was the master plan for the Illinois Institute of Technology – IIT – in Chicago. Upon assuming his position as head of the Department of Architecture in 1938, Mies proposed a new model for the campus, one that would project the institution's emphasis on innovation in engineering and the sciences. This aim was at odds with conventional models that served to guide the planning of college campuses across North America throughout the nineteenth century, and well into the 1930s and '40s. This formula borrowed heavily from Neo-gothic and Beaux-Arts tradition, with its Oxbridge palette of chunky limestone masonry, leaded glass, intimate cloisters, and interlocking, tightly framed quadrangles, all abundant in the nearby campus of the University of Chicago (7).

As we might expect, the former Bauhaus director dispensed with the entire historicist pattern book: in lieu of tidily contained quadrangles, Mies developed an overtly Modernist spatial strategy, one that solicits the fluid interplay of figures and fields throughout the eight-block extent of the campus. Against a backdrop of dense urban fabric, Mies figures the campus as a clean slate. Then, within this voided ground, the crisp orthogonal and uniformly low-slung campus buildings are inserted, producing a striking resemblance to matte-black microprocessors, arrayed precisely across a sprawling green motherboard (8).

Mies' master plan was never fully realized. Yet, with fully twenty campus buildings completed by his office, the essential DNA of the design is self-evident. Often characterized as uninspiring and flawed in execution, when we examine the original master plan a fundamental condition of the current state of the campus becomes clear. Unlike Mies' subsequent multi-building projects in New York, Toronto and the Chicago Loop, where the effect of his *tabula rasa* planning is optimized by the crisp contrast of densely-built site boundaries, the deeply eroded edges of IIT's southside urban fabric can no longer contain

Figure 48: *Toronto-Dominion Centre,* Ludwig Mies van der Rohe.

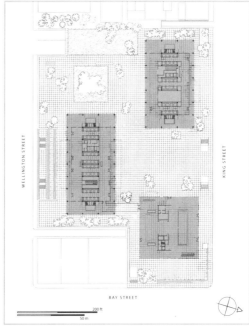

Figure 49: *Toronto-Dominion Centre,* Ludwig Mies van der Rohe.

the campus as envisioned. The figure of the campus – a planned void – leaks into a now-frayed field . Planned additions to the campus, including OMA's recent Campus Center, aim to rectify this figure-ground problem, gradually restoring the contiguously-built boundary upon which the original intent of Mies' plan depends.

Figure 50: *University of Chicago campus,* view toward Hutchinson Hall.

Figure 51: *Illinois Institute of Technology campus* plan, Ludwig Mies van der Rohe.

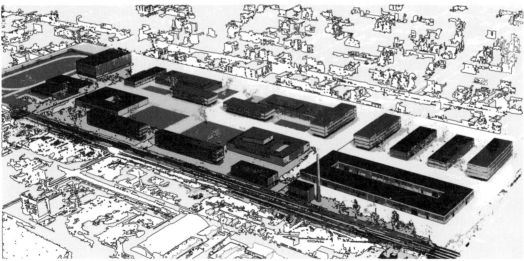

Figure 52: *Illinois Institute of Technology campus* photomontage with model, Ludwig Mies van der Rohe.

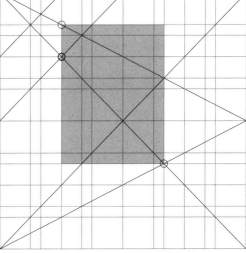

Figure 53: Example of figure determined using regulating lines.

DEMONSTRATION 5·1
Regulating lines dividing space

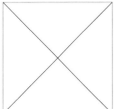 

Step 1a: Define center.

Step 1b: Extend centerlines in both axes.

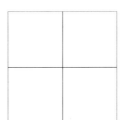

Result 1: Quartered grid.

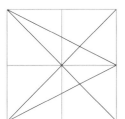

Step 2a: Define thirds by intersection.

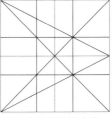

Step 2b: Mark thirds in both axes.

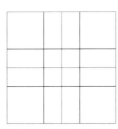

Result 2: Grid with added ninths.

Method for dividing space

Illustrations on the left demonstrate steps for deviding a square with regulating lines. The method uses diagonals to measure and orthogonal lines to mark intervals. The sequence begins with halves and thirds and thereafter subdivides the grid into finer intervals.

The figure above shows a gray figure/field within the grid that uses the regulating lines for both placement and size (1). The small, darker circle marks the origin, the lighter circles locate the terminal points.

The figure below shows the result as gridded ground with the figure in black (2). On the pages following there are further examples of fields located by this method of measurement.

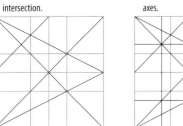

Step 3a: Subdivide halves into quarter measures.

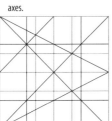

Step 3b: Extend lines from intersections in both axes.

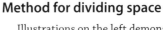
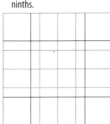

Result 3: Grid with added sixteenths.

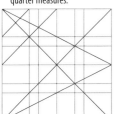

Step 4a: Subdivide quarter measure into eighths.

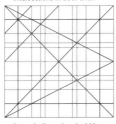

Step 4b: Extend and add lines from intersections in both axes.

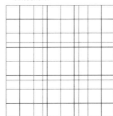

Result 4: Grid with added eighths.

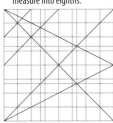

Step 5a: The same diagonal defines the sixth measure.

Step 5b: Extend lines from intersections in both axes.

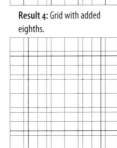

Result 5: Grid with added twelfths.

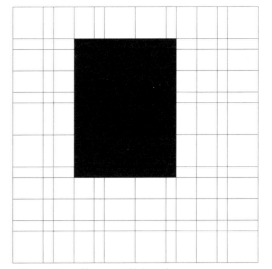

Figure 54: Image of figure on a gridded ground.

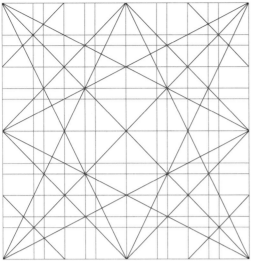

Figure 55: Redundant sets of regulating lines mark the entire relational grid.

Variations in orienting regulating lines

In practice, deciding which regulating lines to draw is a matter of intent. The arrangement and sequence vary with the probable goal. In the text and demonstrations we vary the starting point according to the needs of the illustration.

In generating a workable relational grid, one begins from the center and subdivides from there. Once the grid is on the page, it does the majority of the work. When needed, additional subdivisions and measures follow easily from the general framework.

The five illustrations on this page show the same initial sequence rotated about and reflected toward the cardinal points, as well as an example that combines the four (3&4). In this and later demonstrations, the reasons for the variations should yield to the briefest of scrutiny. As you become familiar with the process, this will become second nature.

Figure 56: Four alternate orientation diagrams of the same regulating lines along all four cardinal axes generate identical relational grids.

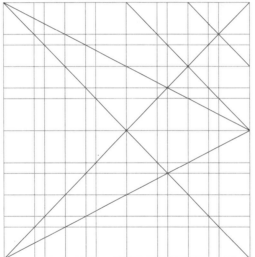

Diagram 4·1: The version used on the previous page.

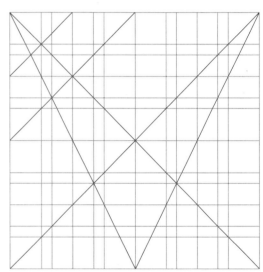

Diagram 4·2: Rotating the lines ninety degrees clockwise results in this variation, used in some examples.

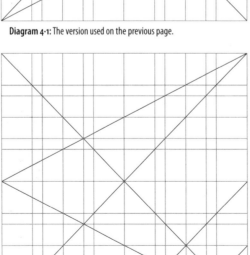

Diagram 4·3: Reflecting the original along the vertical axis yields this result.

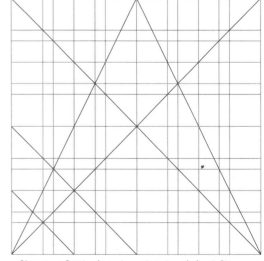

Diagram 4·4: Rotating the previous variant mirrors the lines in Diagram 4·2.

DEMONSTRATION 5·2
Figures & their construction

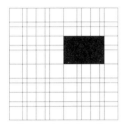

Figure 57: First horizontal figure.

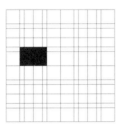

Figure 58: Second, smaller horizontal figure variant.

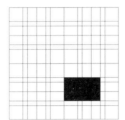

Figure 59: Intermediate third horizontal variant.

Diagram 1·1: Figure touches center point at corner.

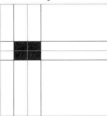

Diagram 2·1: Figure touches centerline with lower edge.

Diagram 3·1: Figure abuts centerline with left edge.

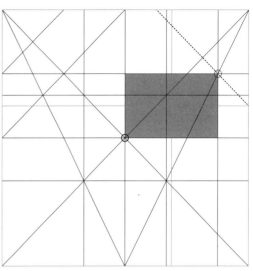

Diagram 1·2: Tall horizontal figure generated from the field center toward upper right quadrant third.

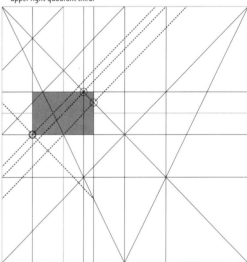

Diagram 2·2: Smaller horizontal figure generated along the horizontal centerline using sequential regulating lines.

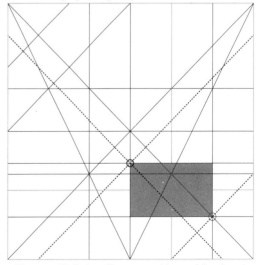

Diagram 3·2: Third horizontal figure generated downward along the vertical centerline using shifted center and corner third as references.

Criteria for the grid

Within the context of a relational grid, placement, orientation and proportions of the figure and the resulting negative space can reflect several approaches to the underlying geometry. Holding to lines and intersections with its edges and corners, the figure can manifest several means of determining its aspect either exclusively or in combination.

Extending the bounding lines and center of the figure can make the general formal order of the composition apparent. The resulting diagram reveals any overall spatial correlation to the underlying structures of quarters and centerline or thirds and center space (1·1, 2·1 and 3·1). It manifests the terms of balance within the overall organization.

Regulating lines, the method of constructing the grid, can also help determine the overall demeanor of compositional order. Because they define subdivision in sequence from large to small, they can identify intersections and their place in the formal hierarchy and thus help clarify formal intent. The fewer the number of reference points and the more directly they relate to the larger subdivisions, the more obvious they appear. As defining a form begins to require additional regulating structure, it also initiates a less obvious presence. Both tactics are of equal value. One tactic is not superior to the other. However, the character of the figure does have an impact on moving toward complexity. This page and the following pages show multiple sets of three figures, illustrating some of the subtleties of the process.

FURTHER GRID EXAMPLES

Within the context of a relational grid, placement, orientation and proportions of both the figure and the resulting negative space can embody multiple interactions with the underlying geometry. Even limited to grid lines and intersections for its edges and corners, a figure still manifests origins and relations within several tactical operations.

Regulating lines define a dynamic, directional means of measurement. As engines of ratio, they proceed from proportion and toward placement.

In comparison, counting along intervals of the grid emphasizes orthogonal partitions of both ground and figure simultaneously. Thus they solve first for place, then move toward measure.

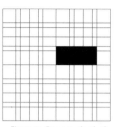

Figure 60: Figure touches both centerlines at corner.

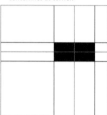

Diagram 4·1: Bounding lines sequence the quadrants.

Figure 61: Figure occupies extreme upper left quadrant.

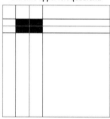

Diagram 5·1: Bounding lines subdivide from corner.

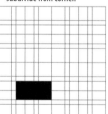

Figure 62: Figure touches centerline at corner.

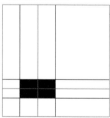

Diagram 6·1: Bounding lines privilege thirds.

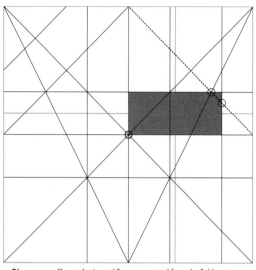

Diagram 4·2: Shorter horizontal figure generated from the field center toward upper right quadrant third and hybrid point.

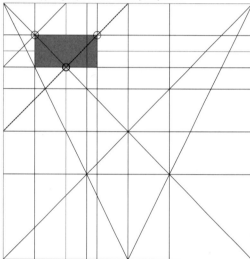

Diagram 5·2: Smaller horizontal figure generated from the center of upper-left quadrant half and quarter diagonals.

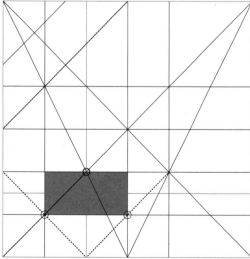

Diagram 6·2: One by two horizontal figure generated from the thirds-based subdivisions and vertical center axis.

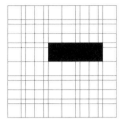

Figure 63: Figure touches one centerline and crosses the other.

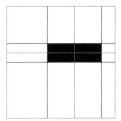

Diagram 7·1: Bounding lines identify complex dynamics.

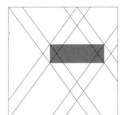

Diagram 7·2: Regulating lines reveal order.

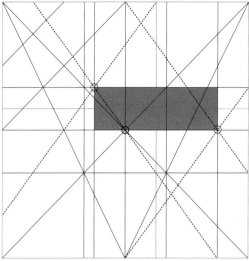

Diagram 7·3: Figure relies on horizontal centerline to balance the complexity of its secondary measurements, rooted in the field center.

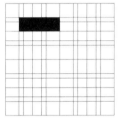

Figure 64: Figure is an elongated version of Figure 5.

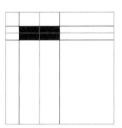

Diagram 8·1: Bounding lines move from corner to center.

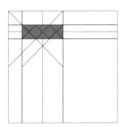

Diagram 8·2: Regulating lines reveal strict proportion.

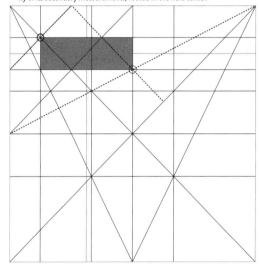

Diagram 8·3: Longer horizontal figure generated from the center of upper left quadrant half and quarter diagonals and vertical centerline.

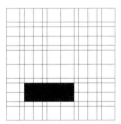

Figure 65: Figure is an elongation of Figure 6.

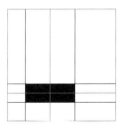

Diagram 9·1: Bounding lines emphasize asymmetry.

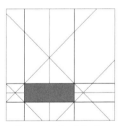

Diagram 9·2: Regulating lines reveal axial dynamic.

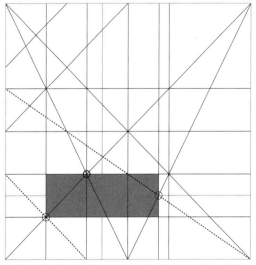

Diagram 8·3: Horizontal figure generated from the center of lower-right third, and both thirds-dividing diagonals.

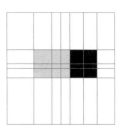

Figure 1: Fields can extend.

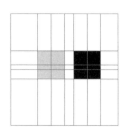

Figure 2: Fields can reflect.

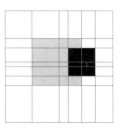

Figure 3: Fields can envelop or surround.

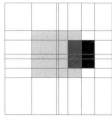

Figure 4: Fields can overlap.

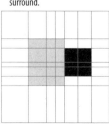

Figure 5: Fields can balance.

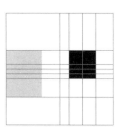

Figure 6: Fields can define.

DEMONSTRATION 5·3
Field, grain, & path

This section presents an overview of some characteristics of the compositional stature of field, grain and path in figure-ground compositions. Each represents additions to the ground that act in concert with a figure or grouping to define and imply an overall compositional strategy.

Field examples

Fields in figure-ground compositions can sponsor multiple formal events. In these examples, a second visual field represents a discrete horizontal plane in relationship to the existing figure-ground composition. In that role, it interacts with the existing figure in a compositional strategy that by convention represents a vertical element.

These added field examples operate within two limits:

· They touch only one boundary edge of the ground.
· Their general scale remains similar to that of the figure.

Within those restrictions, several formal terms describe the relationships shown between field and figure. The examples illustrate three simple groups of interactions that show the possibilities. Those groupings are:

· Extend and reflect: both conditions assume a symbiotic relationship to the figure generally along a single axis and two parallel edges (1&2).
· Envelop, surround and overlap: these conditions imply volumetric relationships about more than one edge and generally involve more than one axis (3&4).
· Balance and define: both conditions imply compound interdependence and often result in a strong gestalt presence of negative space (5&6).

These groupings neither illustrate hard and fast rules nor are they exclusive. Instead, they exhibit ways of describing the formal relationship that a limited field may have to a figure.

Grain examples

In these examples, the added visual field represents distinct horizontal planes that subdivide the ground and modify the existing figure-ground relationship. A grain field supports and reifies the dominant interpretation or intent of the designer.

Grain defines the direction of any field, in this instance that field is the ground. In this sense, it modifies the setting for the figure-ground composition. As a separate element acting directly within the ground, it shifts the inherent gestalt of the entire composition. It makes and takes sides.

Defined grain elements – like those shown here – augment, subdivide, or alter the ground condition. In these demonstrations, the elements cross the entire ground either horizontally and vertically, touching either two or three edges of the composition.

Some basic grain tactics appear in the examples. Once again they represent intentional formal groups. In this instance the four groupings show:

· Balance: the grain field modifies the ground condition to lessen the area occupied by the figure toward lesser contrast (7).
· Subdivide and bound: the field isolates the ground from the figure and, if sharing an edge, suggests attachment (8).
· Border and reapportion: as a distinct variation of balance, extremes of proximity alter the sense of weight in the figure-ground relationship (9&10).
· Surround and extend: the grain field can interact directly with the figure isolating it from the ground and either reinforcing or canceling its directional gesture (11&12).

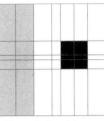

Figure 7: Grain can balance.

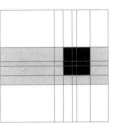

Figure 8: Grain can subdivide and bound.

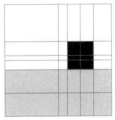

Figure 9: Grain can border.

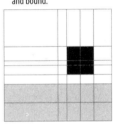

Figure 10: Grain can reapportion.

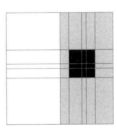

Figure 11: Grain can surround.

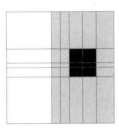

Figure 12: Grain can extend.

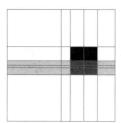

Figure 13: Path can transit through.

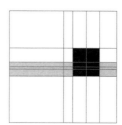

Figure 14: Path can transit under.

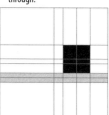

Figure 15: Path can align and pass by.

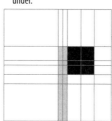

Figure 16: Path can align and halt.

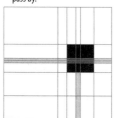

Figure 17: Path can emphasize complex grain.

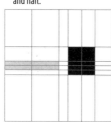

Figure 18: Path can approach and create balance.

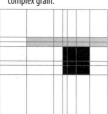

Figure 19: Path can bound and redefine.

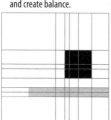

Figure 20: Path can frame and imply.

Path examples

Path is an ally of axis. Aside from sponsoring visual movement, it acts as a field and interacts with other fields. In particular, because it is a directional concept it can augment grain or add cross-grain.

In addition, paths can enter or cross figures and other fields, subdividing their form or modifying their spatial character. Thus we find that the categories of path tactics include both motion and stasis (a condition of inactivity or equilibrium). The set of path tactics begins with motion or movement and proceeds to more static roles. They are:

· Transit: the path moves over, under or through a figure and its ground (13&14).
· Align, pass by and halt: the path moves parallel to the edge of a figure. It may continue on or pause at the figure's edge (15&16).
· Emphasize: the path's direction may reinforce or counter the direction of a figure (17).
· Approach and create balance: the path moves toward a figure and or by its disposition as a field create a sense of equilibrium. The general from of the path approaches the actions of a static field (18).
· Bound and redefine: The path can emphasize movement along a figure's edge and also redefine a boundary within the ground (19).
· Frame and imply: The path can use proximity to a figure's edge and alter the apparent gestalt of the ground condition (20).

As before, these groupings do not exclude more subtle combinations. Instead, they provide a beginning structure for describing the formal relationships that a path field may have to a figure.

Combinations

The images to the right present a few examples of controlled complexity of interacting fields. Seen in combination, static field, grain and path fields alter spatial density, shift balance and symmetry and affect visual complexity. In this way they manifest spatial intention of a solid figure and suggest a nuanced ground for development of the figure's construction.

In the first example, the figure, static field and path run perpendicular to the grain field as a group (21). The figure appears as horizontally centered in the residual negative space. The overall effect of the composition suggests gesture and counter-gesture accumulating in a dynamic whole.

In contrast, the second example appears relatively tranquil (22). The figure and static field balance each other adjacent to the overlapped path and grain fields on which they rest. The space between the figure and its field display the sole sense of tension, emphasizing the off-center position of the figure on the horizontal axis.

In the third example the figure rests within a dominant grain field, surrounded by the static field and adjacent to the path (23). The elements accrue in a stable axial organization with the exception of the path whose position lends a distinct dynamic to the overall composition.

A single element in the combined composition can have a dramatic effect. The next two examples demonstrate the importance of axial gesture to the overall visual character – shown here without boundary and axis lines (24&25). In both examples, the figure, static field and grain field are arrayed about the horizontal axis. In the fist example, the path transits through the figure horizontally. The resulting composition exhibits a dense and subtle interplay of spaces and forms along the horizontal axis. In the second example, the path extends from the figure at a right angle to the other elements. This simple counter-gesture dramatically influences our perception of the whole, directing our attention to the cross-axial disposition of the static field and suggesting a bilateral center to the composition.

Our final example combines elements more openly and draws our attention to the negative space as an equal partner (26). The grain field surrounds the figure, the static field sits opposite and edge-aligned and the path connects those two fields separated from the figure. The resulting composition arranges itself in a sequence from figure to static field, balanced left and right by the grain field.

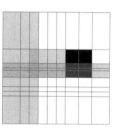

Figure 21: The figure with adjacent static field.

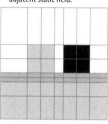

Figure 22: The figure separate from an equal static field.

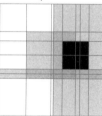

Figure 23: The figure surrounded by the static field.

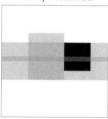

Figure 24: Figure and fields bisected by a horizontal path.

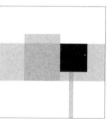

Figure 25: The same composition with a contrasting path.

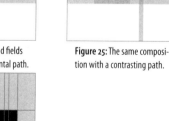

Figure 26: The figure distant from a larger static field.

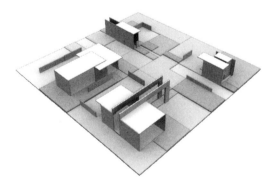

OVERVIEW
The second project continues

In this chapter, we present the completion of PROJECT 2. The exercises shown build on the figure-ground language explored previously, and broaden the base for understanding both composition and formal logic. This phase of the project aims to foster an understanding of the breadth of possible relationships between two-dimensional design and three-dimensional realities.

Good design is never a matter of adding features for their own sake, however tempting. Determining just how intricate a building becomes is a matter of judgment, and a response to intention. Within the fiction of this project, growing complexity follows specific learning objectives. We introduce multiple tools to beginning designers, and each tool leads toward further design development.

These tools also demonstrate clearly the relationship of the diagram to design thinking and design drawing. We choose them individually for their continued usefulness in studying architecture. The issues that they bring into the foreground determine their order in the sequence. In class, we promote discussion not only of the evolution of design, but also of the diagrammatic understanding that emerges while pursuing the path of the project.

CHAPTER 6
Conventions in design

Drawing in the third dimension

Having articulated basic architectural forms within four quadrants – our site – we turn our attention to observing and refining those patterns in three dimensions. In everyday terms, this is where our project turns from abstract boxes toward articulated forms suggestive of buildings. The goal is to extend pattern-making to include additions and subtractions, decisions that will define interior spaces and the paths through those spaces. In turn, the project connects notions of interior and exterior, and grounds the figures more richly within the site.

The next development follows our remarks about the spatial quality of good design drawings. In a successful drawing, line weights follow the rules of visual structure that we first described in the discussion on gestalt. Without attention to appropriate contrast, any image will be spatially ambiguous, regardless of the accuracy of configuration. To make that point, we turn to projective drawing as a tool for analysis (1).

The simplest examples of this sort of constructed three-dimensional image are common paraline conventions. Either the PLAN OBLIQUE or the ISOMETRIC

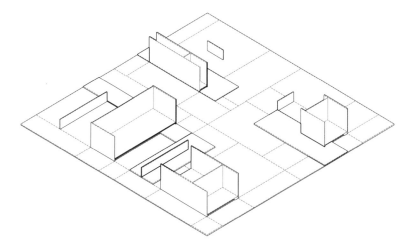

Figure 1: Isometric drawing of the project at this point of its development. This is a simple expression with three line weights. Interior edges are lightest, followed by outlines of the figures, half-walls and fields. The heaviest weight is reserved for the outline of the entire construction, including those small apertures where figures pierce the ground.

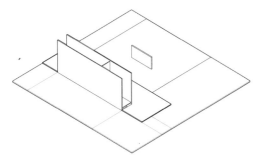

Figure 2: Isometric drawing of the first quadrant showing figure, field, half-wall and figure bounding lines.

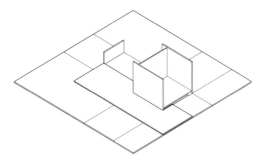

Figure 3: Isometric drawing of the second quadrant showing figure, field, half-wall and figure bounding lines.

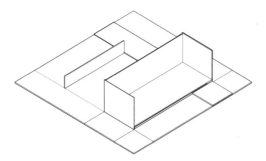

Figure 4: Isometric drawing of the third quadrant showing figure, field, half-wall and figure bounding lines.

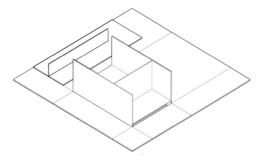

Figure 5: Isometric drawing of the fourth quadrant showing figure, field, half-wall and figure bounding lines.

drawing will serve the purpose. Both offer the simple expedience of consistent scale for all linear measurements. The plan oblique drawing – often referred to as an AXONOMETRIC in architectural parlance – has the benefit of using true angular measurement. The isometric drawing – shown here and throughout this project – is, in turn, less visually distorted.

In keeping with the pattern thus far, we examine each quadrant independently (2-5). Isolating the quadrants has the benefit of reducing the complexity of individual drawings, while also prompting increased practice in making four examples. Comparing the model, the paraline drawings and the plan diagrams, prompts a discussion of intent. In this instance, both types of drawings serve as the platform for the next stage of development.

Drawn with the proper edge-contrast, we can observe the isometric images as diagrams. The examples to the left use four line weights to differentiate appropriate edges. The figures, half-walls and fields exhibit lighter lines along their interior edges and heavier lines at their perimeters. A darker edge surrounds each composition's outline, while still lighter lines mark the bounding lines. The visible result of these tactics gives a distinct emphasis to the axial interplay of figures against a ground.

The visual character of each quadrant is quite distinct. In the first quadrant, we notice that the wall stands as a lone sentinel opposite the figure sitting along the edge of its field (2). The elements in the second quadrant, in contrast, presents a more unified configuration, defining a courtyard space between the figure and half-wall, as well as a companion space to the opposite side (3). The grouping in the third quadrant shares some similarities to that of the first. Its principal differences reflect the severe spatial orientation of the figure away from the half-wall. The fact that the field continues past the wall implies a division in the rear court (4). In the fourth quadrant, we find the half-wall combining with the field and both running in a direction counter to the figure. The result is less spatial than the other quadrants, while seeming slightly more kinetic (5).

These interpretations are admittedly brief, but they make an important point. Orchestrating a good design drawing relies on the rules of visual gestalt, and meaning follows observations that are inherently diagrammatic. Beyond presenting a design, they also prompt analysis, from which inference can lead to further refinement in the design.

Adding fields & overhead planes

In the continuing narrative of the project, we move to adding complexity to the ground in the form of two new fields. The intent that motivates the first additional field is to increase the complexity of the emerging shallow relief. The purpose of the exercise is deliberately formal – it enriches the link to two-dimensional visualization. At the same time, it provides a mechanism for reactivating the underlying relational grid that began with the first phase of the project.

In the absence of a real site, the further development of the shallow relief also helps to generate a richer context for the spatial exercise. Built architecture has the luxury and possibility of responding to an interpretation of context in the physical world. In response, our educational fiction includes the creation and management of the ground as a means of moving beyond a sterile flat plane.

The intention for the new field is to improve the presence of visual grain for the ground. As in previous stages, the procedure begins with four diagrams that precede constructing shallow reliefs as sites for the figures and walls. The position and shape of this field responds to existing edge and axis lines. We use these lines – products of the original grid and figure – to identify opportunities to enhance the condition of grain within each composition. This enhancement takes the form of a grain dominant gesture overlaid as a transparent field in each quadrant. Where fields overlap, the tone darkens appropriately.

This addition requires an evaluation of the conditions of order present in each composition. As they stand, the REGULATING LINES play a dominant role in determining the size and placement of both figure and field. It follows, therefore, that subsequent manipulations of the compositions first include an examination of those regulating lines.

The rules of engagement for the grain field are simple:

· The new field divides each quadrant into two or three distinct areas or subdivisions.
· Each field spans the quadrant either horizontally or vertically.
· Each field is orthogonal.

There are several potential visual results in placing the grain field. The field can simply amplify each quadrant as an individual composition. It might also modify the quadrant composition, as it benefits the overall group of four quadrants. The objective of the analysis is to determine a synthesis responsive to both the individual quadrant and the overall scheme. When we view all four fields as an ensemble, therefore, they should also enrich the texture and complexity of the ground, appropriate to the individual elements and the whole composition.

The four diagrams to the right demonstrate an array of responses to the particular dynamics of the four quadrants (6–9). The two fields, rendered as transparent, interact with one another. The addition of the grain field in each instance generates broad spatial structure and overall direction. In all four examples, there are also areas of overlap that define a distinct sub-field of greater visual weight. The diagram below shows the visual character across the boundaries (10). The overall result continues to structure the center of the composition.

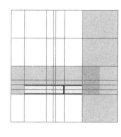
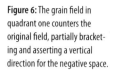

Figure 6: The grain field in quadrant one counters the original field, partially bracketing and asserting a vertical direction for the negative space.

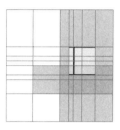

Figure 7: In quadrant two the grain field follows the grain of the field and its interior wall echoes the field's center axis.

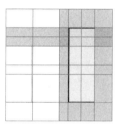

Figure 8: The grain field in surrounds the figure, crosses the original field and divides quadrant three at its center. The result asserts a stronger visual equivalence between the two halves.

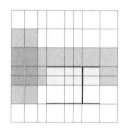

Figure 9: The new field in quadrant four provides a horizontal center that strengthens the balance between the wall and figure in the fourth quadrant.

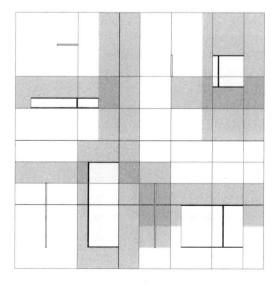

Figure 10: The complete composition with added grain fields and showing those boundary lines and axes that cross reference two or more edges or centers. Thus far the elements best structure the area shared by four original figures.

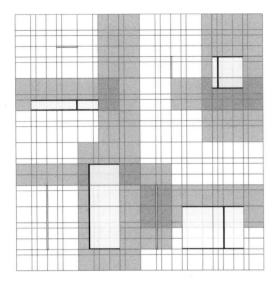

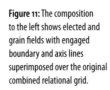

Figure 11: The composition to the left shows elected and grain fields with engaged boundary and axis lines superimposed over the original combined relational grid.

Figure 12: This virtual plan view of the quadrant one model demonstrates the result of subdividing the shallow relief. The fields and ground plane, responding to the original grid, exhibit three levels of height, adjusting the compositional elements. The half–wall has changed in response as well.

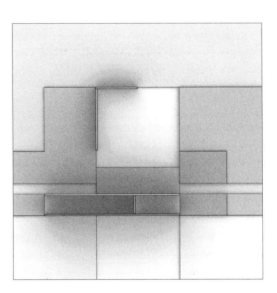

Figure 13: Virtual plan view shows the entire four-quadrant composition with subdivided shallow relief shaded for emphasis.

The suggestion of deep complexity, implied by the areas of overlap, prompts the next investigation. When we reintroduce the original relational grid, we also introduce a means of articulating a greater sub-division within the shallow relief (11). Reintroducing the grid provides a relevant filter through which it is possible to amend the visual texture, to reflect both the overlaps in the fields and the originating order. The model for this change offers the opportunity to further elaborate the structure of the shallow relief. A plan view of quadrant one serves to demonstrate the general results. The illustration highlights the four levels of the relief with hierarchical shades of gray (12).

The results of these additions remind us that the project began as a diagrammatic enterprise. In architecture, there is an important boundary between formal concept and phenomena. Designers and alert viewers traverse that border back and forth. A courtyard space – a purposeful enclosure – gains meaning and nuance exactly at the moment that we recognize it as a courtyard of particular form. That recognition can direct the design process towards greater clarity and articulation of purpose.

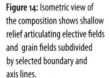

Figure 14: Isometric view of the composition shows shallow relief articulating elective fields and grain fields subdivided by selected boundary and axis lines.

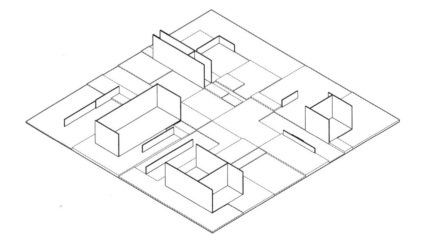

Viewing the latest field addition as a shallow relief leads us to our next proposition. The simple figures, even with minor additions to the surrounding half-wall schemes, do not share a similar level of complexity. Within the arc of the project, this serves as a prompt for further development. While our pattern of using orthographic drawings or physical models might serve the purpose, for illustrating fundamental practices in design thinking, this provides an opportunity to introduce one of the designer's best tools for exploring spatial structure: the section.

The SECTION as drawing convention makes visible a structural reality. Slicing through any object reveals its cross-section, and when that object is hollow, the result exposes the internal space and its relationship to the substance – a self-contained image of figure-ground (15). As noted earlier, the architectural plan itself is a horizontal section, a fictional slice through a building – usually at eye level. Seen as a diagram, the section allows for analysis.

Vertical sections, commonly oriented with or across the compositional grain, can both support analysis and determine rhetorical bias. That is to say, choosing a particular location for a section reflects an assessment of where important design decisions occur. In that sense, the designer sorts through her intentions for a particular space to examine and emphasize one axis by locating a significant point for design development.

Working in section also counters the inherent bias of designing in plan. As an example, a plan may show three identical spaces in succession. The section, in contrast, may reveal that the spaces and doorways have different heights or that the windows do not align on the vertical (16). In multi-storied projects, section is the visual tool that reveals relationships among plan levels.

In our project sequence, we introduce section to reflect plan geometries along a vertical axis. While this is not a routine procedure in architectural practice, it follows from the use of relational geometries as an organizing principle. Furthermore, it serves to demonstrate relational logic between plan and section, a strategy with origins in the Italian Renaissance. We conflate elevation with section, as it also lies on the vertical plane. It is, therefore, what we see as the parallel plane behind the literal section (17). Thus it fosters a comparison between the faces along a path or axis and the encountered mass or *poché* that defines the space.

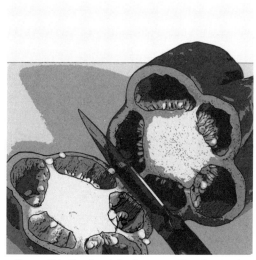

Figure 15: Slicing through any hollow figure exposes the section cut, as in the case of this pepper.

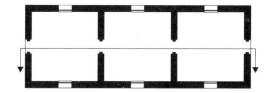

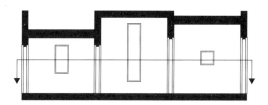

Figure 16: Three spaces that appear equal in plan view show important differences in section. Arrows mark direction and location of section cuts.

Figure 17: A section cut at the central axis of quadrant one. Thin vertical lines mark key boundaries of the composition as well as the center axis of the figure. Horizontal lines call out only the major, dominant cross-boundaries.

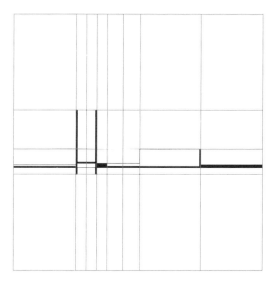

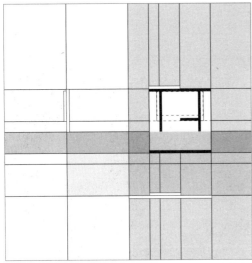

Diagram 18·1: Plan drawing of quadrant two shows alignments of added elements including enclosure, half-walls and fields.

Figure 18: Plan drawing of subject quadrant shows measuring lines and path as toned field (18·1).

West and south section drawings of the subject quadrant show key measuring lines (18·2&3).

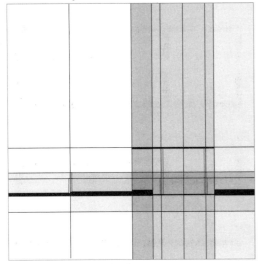

Diagram 18·2: West section of quadrant two.

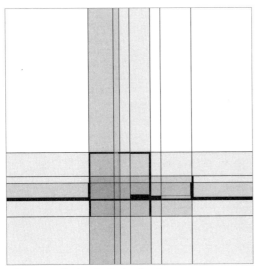

Diagram 18·3: South section drawing of quadrant two.

As an extension of our ongoing discussion of gestalt, it is appropriate to point out that studying and working from these drawings forms an appropriate object lesson in visual balance across the axis of the ground plane. As most sites are not flat planes, the visual proportions continue as implied proportions through the ground, and manipulations of level using our field additions allow us to bring this aspect into our design fiction.

Turning the grid

To make the concept of section clearer, we examine two sections drawn for each quadrant to isolate and refine the vertical and spatial elements in each. We orient each section pair from directions facing the center of the four quadrant composition – one from north or south, the other from east or west, depending on the quadrant's location. This places focus on the individual figure but permits comparison to the whole. Heavier lines mark all visible planes and black *poché* defines the section cut. We also frame the drawings in a bounding rectangle and overlay the drawings with bounding lines and center axes

The resulting diagrams should reveal proportional relationships between the figure, its constituent parts, the half-walls and the shallow relief of the quadrant. The drawings should also highlight the formal hierarchy of the composition.

Coherent hierarchy is a quality found in pattern. The section pattern should relate to that of the plan. Therefore a successful drawing will capture the spatial hierarchy and proportional relationships, as well as demonstrate axial sequence in section. The result should reveal design intent with visual clarity. It should be obvious.

Reading the section

The sections to the left demonstrate the result of design thinking applied in three dimensions. Order that began in plan now extends across all three axes. This is the role of any architecture worthy of the name. Even in a simple schematic construction, such as our quadrant models, it is possible to observe coherent form. The fiction of the fields applied to the site reflects principles

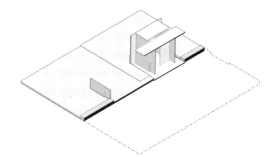

Figure 19: Isometric showing the section cut through the quadrant to reveal Diagram 18·2.

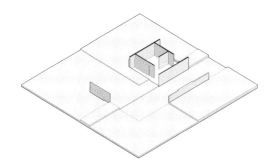

Figure 20: Isometric view of quadrant two showing the section cut represented by Diagram of 18·1.

and decisions that sponsor articulated organization throughout the small constructed figure placed within.

The overlapping gray fields of the plan diagrams have their counterpart in the sections (18·1–3). The exact disposition of the field elements in section is neither automatic nor formulaic. Instead, the designer's task is to search for a solution in section that seems related to the general visual balance of the original diagrammatic drawing. The conclusion reflects judgment and intent.

In the plan diagram, we can generalize the fields simply. The grain field divides the composition into two equal parts. The path field crosses the site and grain field as a narrow shape near the center. The responding field descends from the path halfway to the site perimeter.

In the plan, we note that wall and half-wall elements now further articulate this arrangement (18·1). The boundary and axis lines of the earlier iteration propose the placement and dimension of these additions. The most noticeable changes begin with the addition of a second cross-grain wall that mirrors the first. From this, openings follow that allow the path to cross the now defined interior space. The east-west axis sponsors a crossing interior wall while the north-south axis defines both one of its boundaries and the innermost opening.

The combined axis and boundary points of these figural elements extend orthographically, providing alignments and measure for half-walls within the field. The half-walls reflect the figure's vertical planes as they define exterior space, their placement in keeping with surrounding surface topography – that is, the articulated fields.

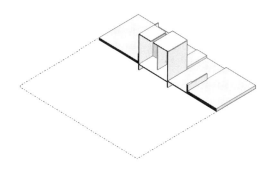

Figure 21: Isometric showing the section cut through the quadrant to reveal Diagram 18·3.

Whereas the diagrams map these relationships on a flat plane, isometric section drawings illustrate them in a volumetric context. This important idea often eludes designers as they turn from orthographic drawing to three-dimensional models. Beyond its practical use as a design drawing, viewed as a diagram, section becomes part of a narrative. It pictures the open and closed spaces of experience. It can walk us through a project, showing us both where we go and what surrounds us.

Up to now AXIS has been a little abstract. When we view it as a conceptual path that crosses through multiple sections, we also begin to test for the reality of a unified composition shared by all four quadrants. Six sections cut from

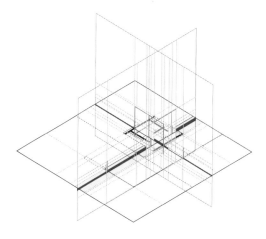

Figure 22: Composite isometric view of quadrant two with both section elevations intersecting plan.

east to west (23) have a narrative purpose. They record a sequence of spatial hierarchy encountered along the north-south center axis. The arrows and lines call out the extent of the active space encountered along the centerline when traversing the quadrants. Two additional images provide other views of section 23.5. The isometric diagram illustrates the forms shown within section. The plan view provides the context of the entire composition.

Drawn sections are formal diagrams. Given the complexity of the overall arrangement, drawing more would capture a more complete spatial narrative. Additional arrows would show the constitution of other defined spaces – behind and in front of the figures. Moreover, another sequence might traverse the cross-axis to encounter the quadrants and figures at ninety degrees to this sequence.

However, the purpose is not to generate infinite section drawings. The intent is to identify what a section reveals and to observe the model more completely with that knowledge. Looking at a model of all four quadrants

Figure 23: Six sections cut parallel to the east-west axis and moving south to north demonstrate the combined results of articulating the bounding geometries of each quadrant.

Arrows illustrate an interpretation of each encounter as it relates to the visible along the central axis. The gray surfaces identify relevant interior planes, black areas indicate sectioned *poché*.

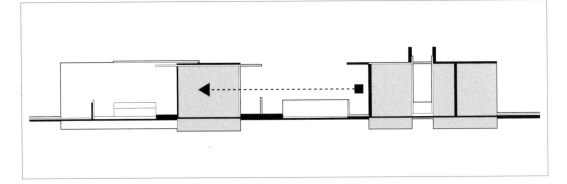

Section 23·1: The first section in the sequence shows the initial spatial relationship between opposing figures in quadrants three and four. Note that the figure in quadrant one functions as a backdrop for the figure to the left of the centerline.

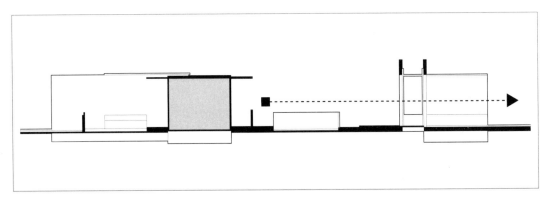

Section 23·2: Moving the section further north, the open and closed relationship reverses for the two figures. Note also the bracketed exterior spaces formed by the half-walls in quadrant three and the overhead featured in quadrant four.

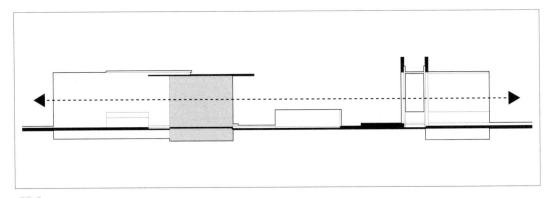

Section 23·3: Deeper into the site, quadrant three's figure opens to allows passage through itself and quadrant four's overhead extension. At this point the composition opens completely to its edges.

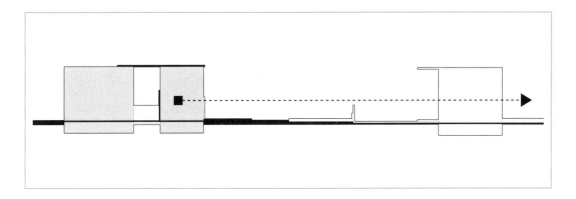

Section 23·4: The section through the figure in quadrant one shows its continuous visual link across quadrant two, and bypassing its figure. The visible half-walls subdivide the transition space.

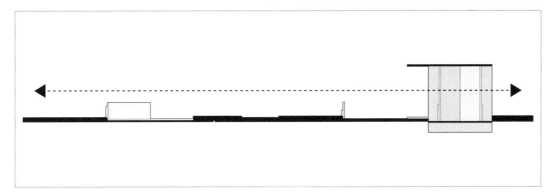

Section 23·5: The figure in quadrant two has a commanding view as well. Along its continuum, vertical elements and the fields modulate the visual path.

Below, an isometric view of the same section – left – and a simplified plan – both showing the path arrow in context.

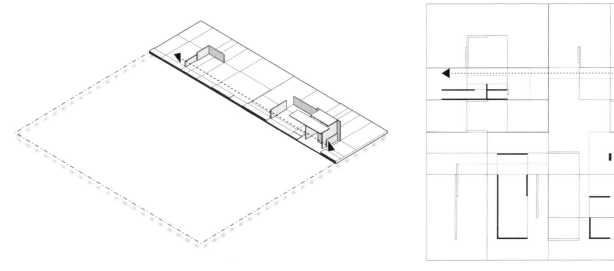

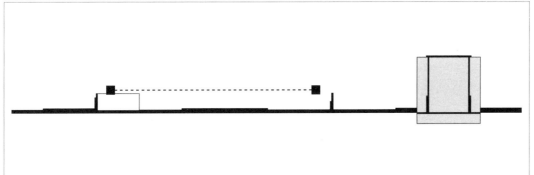

Section 23·6: The final section in the sequence identifies the space defined by exterior half-walls in quadrants one and two. A similar condition defines a forecourt for quadrant two's figure on the right.

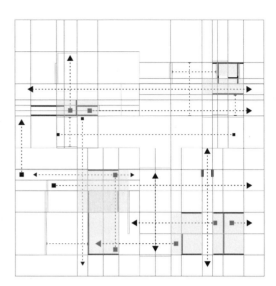

Figure 24: Plan view of digital model (left) showing all four quadrants examined in the previous section (23).

Figure 25: Arrows illustrate in plan (right) some of the spatial relationships within the model – including some of those encountered in the previous sequence (23). The ensemble shows those relationships that frame the next round of refinements.

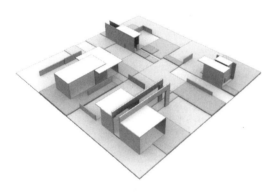

Figure 26: Isometric view of digital model shown above in plan. Tonal variation of the ground emphasizes the height variation.

together should prompt analysis and critique. This prompts yet another set of drawings and a final model for the exercise.

A final model

The design of the four quadrants thus far accounts for movement through the ground. The development of both the figures and other vertical elements show only variation in size – planar profiles remain rectilinear. Compared to the articulation of the ground, they remain more homogeneous as surfaces.

For the final iteration, we allow these surfaces to take on some of the character of the field, extending the procedure of adding half-walls to add variation in the *poché* in plan and section to include additions and subtractions to the surfaces of the figures. Moreover, in response to the analysis, existing *poché* is also open to modification.

The result – shown on the facing page – is more highly articulated form throughout the composition. As seen in the rendered plan views, figures that began as unaligned at the outset now display articulations and extensions interweave across the bounding lines (27). The space shared amongst the four quadrants – the courtyard – exists as a shifting group of defined spaces intersected by expressions of the fields that first emerged in the project, as can be observed in the corner aerial perspective (28). Study of that view confirms that, by responding to diagrammatic analysis, the final model achieves a kind of peripatetic balance. As our view moves around the model, the cadence of form in space – figures in a visual field – confirms that experience mirrors organizational principles developed throughout the process in orthographic diagrams (30–33).

As to the subject of diagramming, this project has shown one way in which three-dimensional structure can emerge from two-dimensional ideas beyond simple extrusion. It also demonstrates that seeing into an image can go well beyond the extraction of information from a document. If we review the project's arc, we should recognize the presence of gestalt principle throughout the process.

In one way, the larger lesson is that judgment is paramount in design. Furthermore, the subject of that judgment is not just the architectural artifact of building, it includes the whole of the design process. The choreography of

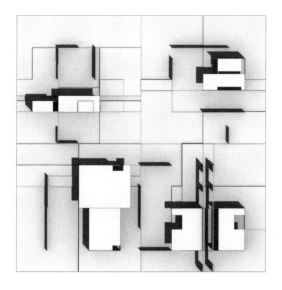

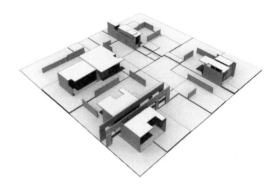

Figure 27: The more obvious alterations to the scheme show up clearly in this virtual plan view (left). Elements of each form – both large and small – exhibit visual correspondence across the composition.

Figure 28: In the near-isometric perspective (right) the correspondences between the vertical planes lend dynamism to the entire field.

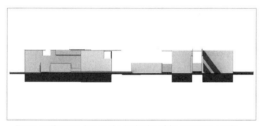

Figure 29: Elevation showing the south edge of the composition as the result of careful proportions that tie together unequal figures.

Figure 30: The perspective from the south confirms the visual result is consistent with the elevation.

Figure 31: From the west the cross-axis appears weighted to the south even as similarities in visual structure remain constant.

Figure 32: Where the south exhibits a planar bluntness, the north shows density of articulated volumes.

Figure 33: In the view from the east the fundamental disparities between large and small figures is most visible.

development from plan drawing to model creates a particular role for diagrams. It gives precedence to three-dimensional relationships that begin in two-dimensional visual explorations. When an originating relational grid combines with gestalt interpretation of figures and fields, the process privileges an orthographic bias. This is its appeal as a teaching vehicle. It allows an understanding of design thinking wherein axis and boundary dominate intent. It prompts an architecture in which spatial order manifests the experience of physical movement through space.

The inherent prejudice of this project is that this traditional role for architecture – sorting through what the poet e.e. cummings labeled 'everywhereishness' – opens the door to understanding how architects help define the spatial tissue for their audience. Judgments made during the design process require a particular capacity for sorting through representations of objects and space and articulating a clear framework for experience.

In the next project, we present alternatives within the process, enlarging both the definition and sequence of grids, diagrams and models.

GLOSSARY OF TERMS

AXIS: An imaginary straight line that divides any space or figure into two portions. Axes in diagrams take a cue from their mathematical use as reference line for coordinate hierarchies of cause and effect. Thus, in diagrams, multiple axes can identify the interrelationships of movement, SPATIAL HIERARCHY and grain.

AXONOMETRIC: A type of PARALINE DRAWING; an orthographic projection of an object – such as a building – on a plane inclined all three principal axes. Alludes to the three-dimensional but without perspective. Architects often use the term in referring to the PLAN OBLIQUE convention.

CROSS-SECTION: The surface or shape exposed by making a straight cut through something, occurring usually at right angles to an axis. Also refers to any diagram or drawing illustrating what the cut would reveal. See also SECTION.

ISOMETRIC: A technical or architectural drawing that incorporates a visual projection representing the three principal dimensions along three axes set at 120° to one another. Isometric drawings display consistent scale for all linear measurements.

PARALINE DRAWING: A method of representing three-dimensional objects in which all parallel lines remain parallel, vertical lines remain vertical, and all elements stay true to scale.

PLAN OBLIQUE: An axonometric projection on an inclined plane – most often rotated 30°, 45° or 60° – with both true measure and true angle maintained in plan. Vertical edges remain vertical.
- In cavalier projection, lengths along the vertical axis remains unscaled.
- A cabinet projection scales the receding axis to seem less distorted.

REGULATING LINES: In drawing, this indicates any guide line that aids in determining placement or dimension of an element or figure in a defined area. Typically attributed to the diagonal lines drawn across any geometric field and used to determine proportion or dimension within a relational grid.

SECTION: A general term used in architecture to refer to viewing the CROSS-SECTION of a building or object in the context of parallel surfaces behind the section cut. Plan drawings are usually devised to include horizontal surfaces such as floors, doors and windowsills that are below the cut line.

SPATIAL HIERARCHY: Term used to identify the formal pattern in architecture wherein constructed space manifests a sequence of importance.

DESCRIPTION 6
Axis & path

Figure 1: Path, defined here by spatial properties of *enfilade*.

Lines, planes & volumes

Students newly introduced to design will often equate axis with path. The reasons for this are understandable: both are terms of connection, providing physical or visual linkages among two or more elements in space. Both also suggest movement, defined or implied, between and through the space linking those same elements. Yet there are some significant distinctions between the two terms, as we define them.

With its origins in mathematics, 'axis' is an abstract notion: it can serve to describe and organize the physical environment, yet remains untouched by it. Devoid of physical properties, axes lack any true dimensionality. As such, they represent a purely motivic force. Like vectors, they suggest direction, alignment and a subtle form of potential energy. Used to divide entities into two parts, an axis denotes movement, grain or spatial hierarchy.

'Path', on the other hand, is intrinsically physical, and entirely contingent upon tangible dimensionality. Moreover, although it may parallel the linearity of an axis, a path is both planar and volumetric as well. In other words, though it may exist solely in our footfalls, bringing to mind the artfully placed path stones of a traditional Japanese garden, a path may just as likely incorporate two- and three-dimensional spatial properties. For clarity, we distinguish these as path surface and path volume. We can observe both, for example, in the spatial properties of *enfilade* – the alignment of doorways across a parallel series of rooms – shown here within the *Palazzo Cenci-Bolognetti*, Rome (1).

Hadrian's Villa

HADRIAN, APOLLODORUS, *et al.*

Over more than 250 acres, the ruins of Hadrian's sprawling imperial residence provide a unique window onto the architecture of classical antiquity, an immensely more daring and inventive legacy than the staid formulae recited by Vitruvius. Arguably conceived as a microcosm of his exhaustive travels throughout the Mediterranean world, Hadrian's penchant for innovative architecture – he likely played a pivotal role in the design of the *Pantheon* – was matched by his capacity, as Emperor, to build (2).

Hadrian probably chose the site for its relative proximity to Rome, and its ability to furnish copious quantities of running water – courtesy of nearby aqueducts – to supply the myriad pools, fountains and bathing facilities found throughout the villa complex. In scope and purpose, *Hadrian's Villa* bears comparison to the royal palace and gardens at Versailles, outside Paris. Both were ex-urban palatial complexes realized by autocratic fiat. Both layouts accommo-

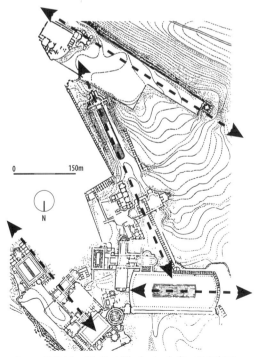

Figure 2: Partial plan of *Hadrian's Villa,* showing the four principal axes governing planimetric alignments across the main complex.

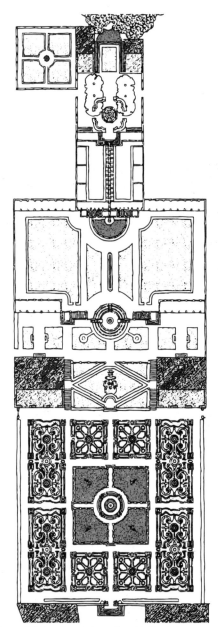

Figure 3: *Villa Lante,* Bagnaia, Jacopo Barozzi da Vignola, begun 1566.

date the extensive retinue of an imperial court, and both incorporated magnificent gardens, replete with a superabundance of pools and statuary.

For our purposes, though, the two projects demonstrate a significant distinction. The Big Idea embodied by André Le Nôtre's landscape plan for Versailles relies on a singular, overarching axis, one that nullifies or masks any pre-existing topography that stood in its way. The buildings and gardens of Hadrian's Villa, though axially coordinated, do not adhere to a single, unifying axis. Instead, four primary axes organize the overall complex, each determined by localized conditions of the site's topography. A series of architectural 'hinges' accommodate axial shifts, including the so-called *Maritime Theater,* whose circular geometry facilitates a pivot between the *Piazza d'Oro/ Libraries* axis, and that of the *Poikile/Garden Stadium.*

Villa Lante at Bagnaia

JACOPO BAROZZI DA VIGNOLA

The axial exuberance of French Baroque gardens, like Le Nôtre's designs for Versailles and Vaux-le-Vicomte, appears to have descended from the equally rigorous – though relatively more restrained – geometry of the Italian Renaissance garden. *Villa Lante* at Bagnaia, approximately eighty kilometers north of Rome, is a consummate surviving example of late Renaissance garden design.

True to type, a single, longitudinal axis that steps down along a sequence of horizontal plateaux dominates Vignola's design for the garden. Gravity provides the motive force for the garden's waters, which cascade through a series of fountains, channels and pools. At its base, we find a large sixteen-square terrace, arranged as an intricately patterned parterre surrounding a central fountain. An ironwork gate at the far end continues the longitudinal visual path, connecting the garden with the public square alongside the historic center of Bagnaia, beyond (3).

Unlike most of its Renaissance predecessors, in which the centerline of a single, dominant villa establishes the primary axis, at Bagnaia the principal visual path travels across the length of the gently sloped site, uninterrupted by an axially-centered building. In its stead, the garden relegates the architecture to its periphery, placing a symmetrical pair of comparatively modest pavilions, one to either side of the site. Vignola's scheme thereby preserved pride of place for the subtle choreography of *Villa Lante's* unfolding series of spaces, drawing visitors gently, if inexorably, along the garden's centrally aligned promenade.

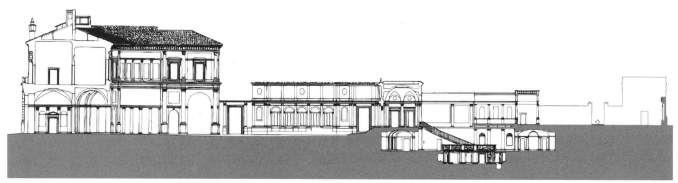

Figure 4: *Villa Giulia,* Vignola, with Bartolomeo Ammanati, Giorgio Vasari and Michelangelo, begun 1550, longitudinal section.

Farnese Gardens, Palatine Hill

JACOPO BAROZZI DA VIGNOLA

The serene equilibrium that characterizes the experience of the *Villa Lante* is deceptive. So too is the apparent simplicity of its plan. Both rely on the cumulative experience that Vignola accrued over a lifetime, designing some of the most significant projects of the mid-sixteenth century. Two of those projects, both begun in 1550, both in Rome, provided many of the lessons subsequently gathered at Bagnaia: the *Villa Giulia*, commissioned by Pope Julius III (4); and the *Farnese Gardens*, which overlooked the ruins of the Roman Forum (5-7).

The entrance to the *Farnese Gardens* lays along and within the steeply inclined slope of the Palatine Hill. To alleviate the ascent, Vignola arranged for a nested sequence of parallel and perpendicular switchbacks, multiplying and lengthening the sequence of paths necessary to arrive at twinned aviaries perched along the crest of the hill above. Though some have suggested that the splay of the pavilions mimics the plan of Michelangelo's recently completed project on the neighboring Capitoline hill, the arrangement of the aviaries allowed Vignola cleverly to integrate the otherwise errant angle of an existing cross-axis directly below (5).

Vignola's design demonstrates the related but distinct attributes of axis and path. A single dominant axis governs the overall layout, as with his designs for the *Villas Giulia* and *Lante*. This axis aligns with a path volume, a visual connection between the top and bottom endpoints of the entrance ascent. Portions of the path volume are accompanied by path surfaces – the stairs and stepped ramp centered along the axis. Yet, given the necessity for switchbacks to alleviate the slope of the hill, there are multiple paths that supplement those found along the main axis. These include the stairs, stepped ramps, trellises and grottoes that beguile visitors as they sequentially move along, against, and at tangents to the primary axis; a choreographic notion of promenade that characterizes the Italian Renaissance garden.

Salk Institute, La Jolla

LOUIS KAHN

Schooled in the traditions of the École des Beaux-Arts, it should come as no surprise to recognize the singular significance of axis and path in the work of Louis Kahn. Despite their outward appearance – the robustly unadorned, elementally formal grammar that identifies them as products of the third quarter of the twentieth century – Kahn's buildings embody a resolutely hierarchical spatial order that is traditionally characteristic of nineteenth-century Beaux-Arts principles. Nowhere is this more evident than in the serenely ordered spaces of Kahn's *Salk Institute*, near La Jolla, California.

Adjacent to a bluff overlooking the Pacific coast, Kahn arranged the laboratories, private studies and library spaces symmetrically, forming the north and south edges of a broad, paved court. Along the east-facing edge, a eucalyptus grove separated the court from entrance parking. A reflecting pool lies to the west, its surface appearing to merge with that of the ocean beyond. Kahn initially planned to fill this court with a second grove of trees. The landscape architect for the Salk project, sculptor Isamu Noguchi, convinced Kahn to leave the court empty, save for the slender thread of water that emerges from the travertine paving and flows westward toward the distant horizon.

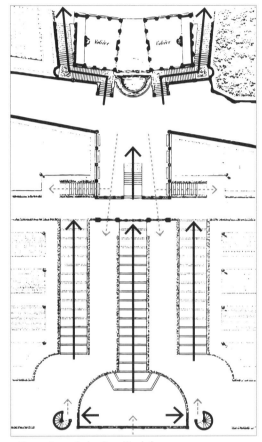

Figure 5: *Farnese Gardens,* Rome, Vignola, begun 1550.

Figure 6: *Farnese Gardens,* Rome, Vignola.

Figure 7: *Farnese Gardens,* Rome, Vignola.

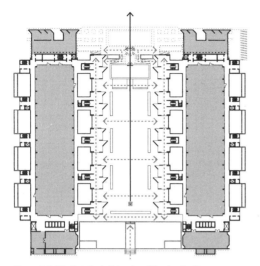

Figure 8: *Salk Institute,* Louis Kahn; plan of the plaza level.

Figure 9: *Salk Institute,* Louis Kahn; view toward the Pacific Ocean.

Figure 10: *Salk Institute,* Louis Kahn; view of the plaza level *enfilade*.

The sublime emptiness of the Salk's central court provides another lucid case study in relations between axis and path: the water, compelled to reach its own level, embodies the emphatic thrust of the primary axis toward the western horizon. Serrated vertical flanks frame the project's primary path volume, which in turn serves to amplify the exquisite desolation of the plaza's travertine surface. A series of low bench-plinths along either side of the court establishes a rhythmic array of cross-axes joining the two wings of the complex. These position a concomitant set of implied path volumes that cross both the central axis and a parallel pair of secondary axes within the court's longitudinal edges.

These secondary axes align with the open-air *enfilades* that occupy the plaza-edging spaces beneath the stacks of private studies. The alternating pattern of light and dark along these visual paths ties these spaces with that of the central court. Path and axis relations then engage the third dimension of this ensemble: the exterior stair towers, which establish a series of overt vertical axes, flank voids that join deep light wells to the sky above, voids that behave as path volumes in their own right.

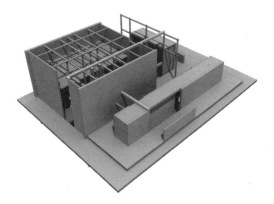

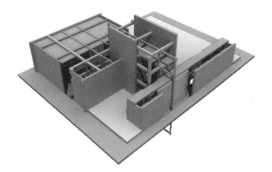

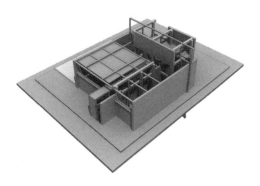

OVERVIEW
The third project

This chapter follows the complete arc of PROJECT 3. The exercises depend on our familiar figure-ground language while focusing on a broader range of represented artifacts. The design tasks continue to enliven the conceptual dialogue between two-dimensional composition and three-dimensional construction.

To that end, models take the lead in visualizing the design process while drawings frequently sustain design progress. As a consequence, we propose and examine more speculative forms of diagramming. Adding to formal interpretation and prediction in drawn diagrams, construction exercises include conjectural, interpretive diagrammatic models. The entire modeling sequence also introduces students to several material choices. In this we expand on ideas of contrast in a visual field that build on the collage techniques used in earlier projects.

The project introduces comprehensive, simple language for understanding the grid in three dimensions. This is part of developing a more volumetric and spatial understanding of section, as means of analysis and design generation.

CHAPTER 7
Starting in three dimensions

Design on a grid

Students often raise their eyebrows – and their hands – when we show them how to generate proportional objects using a compass and a straight-edge. They ask us, 'Can't you just do this on the computer?' In fact, diagonal lines often give rise to irrational numbers – something that computers do only approximately. The reason for this limit is structural. The logic of the computer – its language and its method of visualization – has as its framework rational numbers and the rational grid.

We mention this because the ubiquity of the rational grid as part of contemporary life often obscures both its Modernism and its brilliance. The imposition of the even, infinite and regular structure of the grid is no mere coincidence. It is a singular and important manifestation of a belief in the possibility of a rational life. What makes it Modernist is the philosophical proposition that rationality and its methods will lead to a final evolutionary state of humanity and that the struggle between opposites will eventually resolve itself into a better world. These sorts of post-Enlightenment beliefs underscore the idea that invoking the Modernist grid is not a neutral act. It aligns the grid with an emerging sense of progress, as well as rationality.

However, one does not have to agree with this view of destiny to use a rational grid. In this project, we use this grid as the basis for our investigations because the forms that are probable, as well as the means for developing them, alter when the rational grid replaces the proportional scheme of PROJECT 2. The differences prompt meaningful formal discussion. In addition, the ubiquity of the 'universal grid' is an important matter for beginning design students to consider.

A number of architects have worked at the interface between proportionality and whole-number thought. Although the grid as we know it may be modern, its underlying logic is ancient – recall the plan of Chengzhou (p. 46). However, interest in resolving the difference between the rational and irrational emerges most fully in the West with the onset of the Renaissance. This predates the Cartesian grid of the Enlightenment, arising as an important idea for architects such as Alberti, in his attempt to reconcile Greek measure with whole number geometries.

Later, modern architects such as Mies van der Rohe and Terragni revisited the proportions of the golden ratio – an irrational number – in the context of whole number measurements and grids. In the case of Terragni, he utilized in his *Danteum* the Fibonacci series, a system of whole numbers that approximate the golden section.*

*TERRAGNI AND THE *DANTEUM*

This famous project – the work of Giuseppe Terragni with Pietro Lingeri and Mario Sironi in 1938 – exists only as drawings and models. In the *Danteum,* ideal geometry underwrites both symbolic and compositional expression. In CHAPTER 8 we examine the project as a significant example of combined rational and irrational geometries.

The structure that we use for PROJECT 3 borrows Terragni's approach. We measure the ground using the universal Cartesian grid, while the figures gain their size and scale from the earliest part of the Fibonacci series.

The site

The most apparent formal issue that arrives with the universal grid is the reliance on constant intervals. Different measures are largely additive and orthogonal. Simply put, we measure by counting. To facilitate that approach, the 'site' for this project is an 8"×10" grid, drawn within a 9"×12" field. The grid defines the smaller rectangle centered on the larger page (1). The instructions for making the grid follow simple guidelines:

· Draw the base grid as light lines set at half-inch intervals.
· Extend each line one-quarter inch beyond the 8"×10" space on all sides as shown in the example (2).

For the project, we generally stipulate some practical matters:

· Draw all lines lightly in pencil.
· Make three copies.

Three figures

On each of the drawn grids we place three figures. Each is cut from yellow trace – for transparency – and attached with small strips of drafting tape to a 9"×12" sheet of white transparent vellum that covers the original grid. The three figures are each a specific size:

· The largest is a 5" square.
· The next is an 8"×1" rectangle.
· The third is a smaller, 2"×3" rectangle.

In placing the figures, all edges align exactly with the drawn grid lines. In addition, using the small strips of tape can have a profound effect on viewing the composition.

There are three composition strategies used in this exercise – one for each drawn grid. For each strategy, we arrange the three figures according to corresponding criteria. These are:

· The figures are separate – none touches another.
· One figure bridges to a second figure using the third – the connecting figure touches one figure and intersects the other.
· All figures overlap – each figure intersects both of the other figures.

To refer to the three strategies, we use the terms SEPARATE, BRIDGED and OVERLAPPED. The goal is to discover arrangements that exhibit distinct spatial dynamics reflecting each specific compositional character.

The use of cut paper forms allows for fluid movement across the grid, adjusting positions and observing effects. The regularity of the grid and its correspondence to the figures allows a particular form of relationship, as all forms align with the principal grid lines. In particular, issues of grain, field and axis – encountered previously – are more important than overall resulting shapes. This favors tactics for visual balance that give prominence to axis over those that focus on defining the white space. This bias represents part of the learning narrative for the project. It also provides a theme for discussing the ongoing contrast to the previous project.

Despite any seeming confinement because of the requirements and the grid, the project readily supplies a large set of variables that make themselves visible as the exercise progresses. Observing the diagrammatic examples for the three tactics, certain general issues readily make themselves visible. Observed

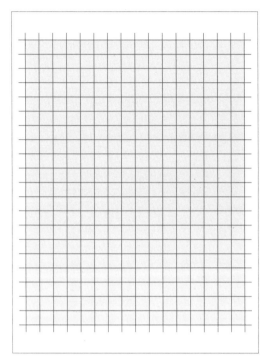

Figure 1: The base-centered grid as it appears on the 9"×12" page. The light gray color provides contrast in viewing the example.

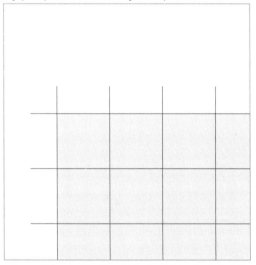

Figure 2: Enlarged portion of the grid showing the interval and extended lines at the upper left corner.

Figure 3: The three strategies shown as diagrams to the right. They are – left to right – separate, bridged and overlapped. The small tabs appended to the corners of the figures represent the drafting tape used to attach the figures.

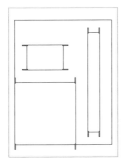

Diagram 3·1: Separate forms.   **Diagram 3·2:** Bridged forms.   **Diagram 3·3:** Overlapped forms.

together as a group and through the filter of axis, they display a sequence that reflects the procedure of moving the forms around as a means of visualization (3·1–3). All three examples also exhibit some form of buried symmetry.

The separate example places the square in the lower left corner and aligned to the center axis of the ground field (3·1). The slender figure to its right centers vertically on that same axis and occupies the middle portion of the residual space. The vertical axis of the smaller rectangle aligns with that of the square while it also centers on the defined horizontal field it occupies. These local symmetries represent a rudimentary response to grain and axis.

Examining the bridged composition (3·2), we note clear similarities with the previous diagram. The square's placement is identical. The tall figure has moved to the extreme right, maintaining its horizontal edge-to-axis relationship with the square. The lower edge of the bridging figure aligns with the horizontal center of the square, while its left edge aligns with the compositional field's vertical centerline. In this way, the bridge connects the other two figures and the horizontal extremes of the field.

The arrangement of the overlapped composition (3·3) distinguishes itself by virtue of its point of origin. The lower left corner of the two-by-three rectangle sits at the exact center of the grid. It shares its vertical axis with that of the slender figure. In turn, that element's left edge runs along the center vertical axis of the square. There are proportional correspondences present, however, it is the axial structure that interests us at this point.

Observing the same composition illustrated with transparencies and on the grid, gives us a sense of the true exercise represented by the diagrams. The areas of overlap exhibit a stronger visual sense of layered space, while the tape forms seem less present. In addition, the grid allows us to see the shared proportions that result from the overlap.

Spatial models

For the next link in the project's chain, we use the trace compositions as the basis for three simple half-scale massing models. We find that thin corrugated cardboard lends itself well to this phase. It introduces students to a new material that presents distinct construction issues and opens an interesting dialogue concerning the use of a grained material.

The exercise extrudes each form as a perimeter volume and assigns three different directions to the construction of the perimeter. Each volume also

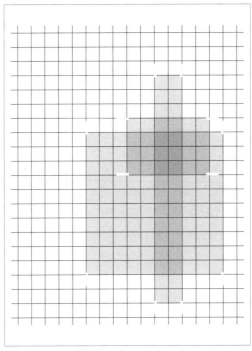

Figure 4: The example of strategy three – overlapped forms – shown as transparent fields with tape elements.

Figure 5: Two alternate examples showing overlapped figures as diagrams. Both exhibit variant flavors of symmetrical tactics in composition.
The example on the left derives from 3·2, while the one on the right derives from 4.

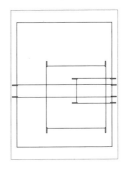 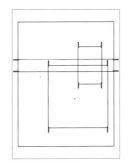

Figure 6: Examples of variations in figure height, construction and perimeter orientation.

protrudes through the base plane, resulting in a construction that counters any comfortable assumption of boxes sitting passively on a ground. This follows from the project's learning objective to approach composition equally from all three axes. It follows, therefore, that spatial grain should engage volume as early as possible.

In support of that goal, we specify that the 'site' is a fully three-dimensional space, specifically as an 8"×10"×8" spatial volume intersecting a 9"×12" planar area. The rules of engagement proceed from that premise:

· We extrude the original three shapes to either 5", 3" or 2", electing one figure for each height.
· All three figures intersect and penetrate the site plane.
· The combined figures fits within the 8"×10"×8" volume, surrounded by the site plane.
· All forms adhere to a half-inch grid as drawn in the previous exercises – now fully three-dimensional.

To facilitate timely results, we normally specify that these preliminary investigations are half-scale – 4½"×6"×4" – when we include the site plane. Aside from convenience and ease, this requirement augments the learning agenda for the exercise. Previous projects have been one-to-one, abstract investigations that might allow for speculation about scale but never address it as part of the process. Making a half-size model amplifies the issue of scale in architectural investigations to the fore.

In preparation for actual construction, we determine the volumes by drawing small-scale elevations and sections – this follows from our comments about scale. Following that, we construct each of the volumes as a perimeter form: an object with four sides closed and two sides open; a form of grained space as each perimeter orients along a different axis – x, y or z.

The construction of the volumes follows the illustrations on the left. These illustrations show variations in volume height, construction – a matter of corner detail – and orientation (6). The finished models use all three variables to articulate the compositions. The example below is one solution to the separate composition (7). In the illustration three tonal values suggest orientation of the planar surfaces, which varying line weights help bring forward construction details of the perimeter volumes.

Figure 7: First model iteration for the separate composition, showing the effects of figure height, construction and perimeter orientation.

The illustration includes a horizontal plane to mark the 8"×10" field.

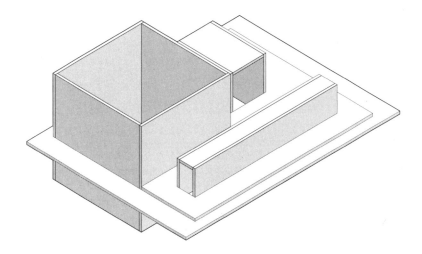

Figure 8: Three section diagrams of the separate composition demonstrate the selection of axis to characterize the spatial organization and the proposed linear elements that make it visible.

We will follow this tactic and variation through the next several stages of the project as a strategy for maintaining an uncluttered narrative. There will be occasional deviations from this practice.

Visualizing axes

In PROJECT 2, formal analysis of plan elements fostered understanding of axes and boundaries. In this exercise, we pursue a variation of that procedure and include a model in the visualization process. As the figures are already three-dimensional constructions, simple sections record their bounding and axis lines and prompt an analysis of those that capture a desired visual structure.

Using the grids as guides, we elect intersections to locate simple X·Y·Z GRID AXIS constructions. With one construction in each figure, we add linear elements to define the grid at all open faces and in the interiors (8·1–3). We draw the constructions as if made from thin basswood sticks inserted into the cardboard model (9). All elements adhere strictly to the figure grid and take into account which side each linear element falls on. Drawings explore all three of the strategies.

After reviewing the drawings, we construct physical models based on the drawings. Elaboration of the drawn grid construction includes the following possibilities:

· Extending key grid elements toward or into a second figure.
· Locating a plane of museum board within the grid construction in response to the X·Y·Z grid.
· Modify select perimeter planes to amplify the interior grid structure.

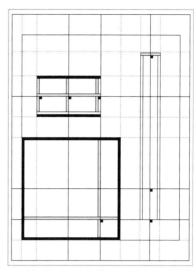

Diagram 8·1: The plan view section diagram with the proposed linear elements. Solid lines represent chosen axes.

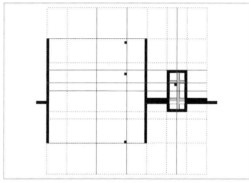

Diagram 8·2: A front view section diagram with the proposed linear elements. Solid lines again represent chosen axes.

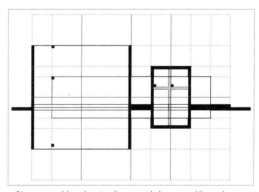

Diagram 8·3: A lateral section diagram with the proposed linear elements. Solid lines again represent chosen axes.

Figure 9: An isometric drawing of the composition with the proposed linear elements and no other modifications.

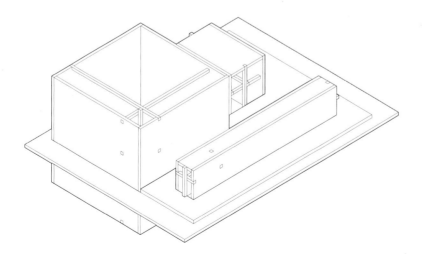

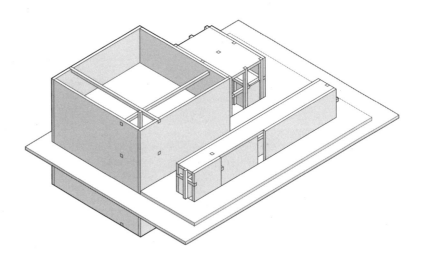

Figure 10: An isometric tonal rendering of a model showing the linear elements and selected, simple modifications to the figures' perimeters and interiors.

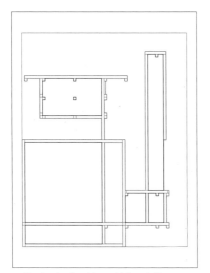

In responding to the analysis in model form, we can restrict elaboration to articulations of the perimeter and interior. In the example above, we see some possible results (10). In particular, we observe that the segregation of axial components isolates the linear gestures and amplifies the density of the individual figures. This limits visual references across the composition and lessens direct correspondence. A notable example is the perimeter break on the long, low figure. Despite sharing two edge-to-center alignments, the spatial correlations remain visually implicit.

In comparison, the more robust elaborations seen in the alternate example stretches across space, making connections among the figures visible and direct (12). In addition, the frame surrounding the rear figure draws the volume of the large cube out into the site volume, adding defined space to the composition. So too does the volumetric extension of the forward portion of the long, low figure to the cube. Although not visible in the illustration, both of these features continue below the site plane, making their effects responsive to the larger site volume. We follow this particular project into a further

Figure 12: An isometric drawing of an alternate model showing similar modifications to the figures' perimeters and interiors and including projections of linear elements to connect the volumes.

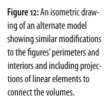

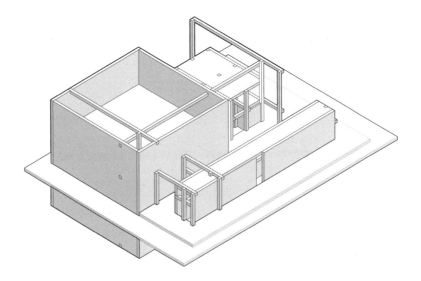

set of diagrams, revisiting some of the issues and methods from the previous project.

Spatial hierarchy: field, grain, & path

With physical models before us, we return to some earlier diagramming methods. Our two half-scale models serve to sponsor drawings that visualize the spatial hierarchy using FIELD, GRAIN and PATH as tools of analysis and development.

The site plane is of course a plan element. Therefore, we limit the investigation to plan-derived drawings. Over plans of the early axes models, we add the boundary and axis lines used earlier. Within the matrix of these lines, we use transparent fields to represent a responding field, a dominant grain field and an elective visual path that help visually to interpret that spatial hierarchy.

The transparent fields accumulate as before. The examples to the right display two interpretive sequences (13–15). The first sequence begins with identifying a responding field bordering the 2×3 figure on three sides (13 left). The field derives its boundaries from the width of the square figure, the uppermost edge of the long figure and the lower edge of the figure it surrounds. The field strengthens the connection along the vertical axis of the square.

The grain field responds to the vertical weight implied by the first field, traversing the composition horizontally across the entire site plane (14 left). As an effective counter measure, it establishes a cross-grain emphasis that links the lower half of the slender figure, bounded by the chosen horizontal linear axis. The interruptions along the way reflect the horizontal planes within the figures encountered by the field's span.

The visual path – also a field – overlays all elements of the composition save the slender figure (15 left). It defines a swath of connection that, like the grain field, spans the entire space of the site plane. The aggregate of all three fields characterizes the composition as a weave of weight and gesture, stasis and motion.

The theme that characterizes the second analytic sequence is, in contrast, connection. That process begins with the responding field surrounding the entire 2×3 figure and extending to contact the boundaries of the other two figures (13 right). The grain field likewise surrounds the narrow vertical figure while touching the boundary of the square and overlapping the first field as a go-between to link with the smaller figure (14 right). It spans the site plane vertically and reinforces its orientation.

To cement the connection the visual path repeats the vertical gesture in abbreviated form (15 right). This field spans the space between the two smaller figures, crosses the perimeter of the square and terminates at the edge of the interior site dimension. The cumulative result is a dense, weighted presence in the composition, a visual glue accreted in the shared space.

Comparing the two sequences as spatial hierarchies and gambits, we observe that the first series of diagrams proceeds towards orchestrating movement – around and through space. We can see that effect played out in the highly elaborated model that ended the previous section. The plan diagram for that example illustrates the same sort of motion-centric composition and demeanor (11). In contrast, we observe that the second hierarchy builds visual evidence of a shared domain. The diagrammatic fields together lead to the dense occupation of a communal center. However, the spatial compression is not necessarily static. The hierarchy compiles and compounds multivalent

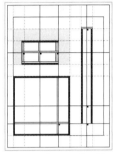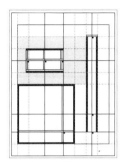

Figure 13: Two examples of the project show an elective field responding to the spatial hierarchy.

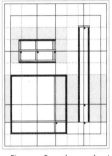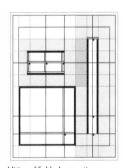

Figure 14: Examples now showing the addition of fields demarcating dominant grain within the hierarchy.

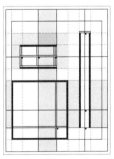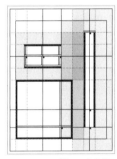

Figure 15: These examples complete the two sequences, adding path fields to the previous composites.

claims on shared area. It frames a potential for tidal motion, a repository that pushes outward as well as drawing inward.

Both of these hierarchies frame valid spatial intentions and both can lead forward towards further analysis and design.

Clarifying plan elements

The project and its artifacts now exhibit several features. The perimeters display inherent spatial orientation in the form of planar elements and surface voids. Within, and sometimes without, we observe linear constructions that suggest columns and beams. Moreover, there are planar additions within some perimeters that subdivide space. The small models, however, show their schematic limitations and seem both cramped and primitive. If we want to move the design toward a more articulate complexity we need better guidelines.

For those reasons, the next explorations expand palette of choices and begin to articulate an enriched procedure as well as an enhanced version of the underlying grid.

The new grid

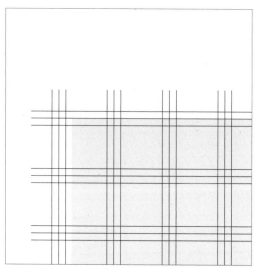

Figure 16: Example of the grid drawn with subordinate lines.

The grid remains an 8"×10" area centered on the 9"×12" site plane. However, the grid adds to the original lines at half-inch intervals a pair of flanking subordinate lines drawn one sixteenth of an inch on either side (16). As before, we show the grid lines extending one quarter inch beyond the 8"×10" field.

Strategy set

The analysis diagrams that use the new grid introduce some initial strategies for formal order. They identify roles for columns and walls that lead to refining the elements of the earlier models. As such, they introduce a basic set of guidelines for manipulating both TECTONIC elements. Taking a cue from the new grid, we explore in plan a STRATEGY set that develops and refines the previous grid models. In the process, we augment the plan logic thus far and introduce concepts that continue in the next stage of development.

Four conceptual categories define our preliminary strategy set:
- 'Envelope' governs the perimeter condition of each of the three forms.
- 'Grid elements' describes columnar placements of center and axis.
- 'Elaborations' designate added horizontal and vertical planes as well as further column deployment.
- 'Subtractions' define modifications to the perimeter wall.

The underlying grid continues to structure the dimensions and location of the elements and components. Simple examples illustrate preferred construction technique for the elements used within the figures (17). The themes describe below follow these principles using either planes, columns or both.

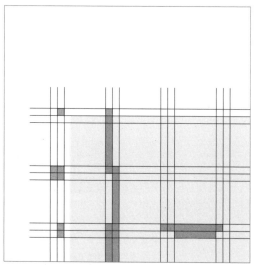

Figure 17: Examples of columnar forms – left – and wall sections – middle and right. Example forms are gray for clarity.

Tactical definitions & variations

Two themes sort through and refine our four strategies, each addressing either COLUMNS or PLANES as tactics. Each sets forth particular ways of using a single tectonic element to articulate the spatial structure within the composition. Each tactic builds on ideas that appear in diagrams throughout the text. They address three-dimensional constructive expression that is part of the language of figure and field, boundary and axis.

The tactics respond to overall form, therefore, their elements act as gestalt projections of three-dimensional form and structure. Based on forms drawn as overlays, they project observed flat pattern into volumetric elements. Beyond that, this exercise also compares patterning of columns to that of vertical and horizontal planes. The tactics for each element type are distinct according to their formal differences.

TACTICAL THEME 1: COLUMNS

Each of these three tactics governs the use of columns for each figure by describing their location either at the perimeter or within the volume. The language should be familiar:

· Columns mark the boundaries and axes of each figure. They occur at corners and centers (18·1).
· Columns mark axes of each figure and reflect boundaries and axes of other figures by locating on the perimeter (18·2).
· Columns mark and follow axes of a figure and extend axes and boundaries of other figures by their placement in the interior of each figure (18·3).

TACTICAL THEME 2: PLANES

Vertical planes can amplify similar marking gestures as do columns. In addition, planes may also appear parallel to the plan. Therefore, placement, thickness and orientation of planar elements within and surrounding each form can underscore three formal themes.

· Planes define dominant grain for the *form* (18·4).
· Planes establish spatial hierarchy for both exterior and interior space (18·5).
· Planes exhibit spatial structure both within and outside of the form (18·6).

The combined effect of these thematic elements, when used well, is order that aggregates to a clear formal demonstration. The examples to the right follow the sequences above – columns then planes. Some are obvious in their choices, other less so.

In the first image, columns overtly mark the boundaries and axes, and display an elemental pattern (18·1). Close inspection of the perimeters reveals that columns adhere to either the outer or the inner edges of the forms, reflecting one subtlety possible with the new grid.

In the second example, center columns disappear while others accrue at the perimeters of the three forms (18·2). Which columns appear reflects both judgment and intent. Multiple columns gather around the compositional center. Others follow to augment the visual connection of the three figures.

In the last variant, columns connect directly across the figures (18·3). In this example, a cruciform pattern connecting the two other figures at the upper right quadrant of the large square informs the pattern-making.

The planar tactics each result in a visual display of defined and implied figures. For that reason, observation of negative space offers the best description of their results. The dominant grain exercise gives rise to volumes with distinct direction (18·4).The smallest figure gestures horizontally, the slender figure vertically. The horizontal plane – the gray field – within the square prompts a vertical interpretation. The negative space constitutes several connecting, cross-grain spaces.

The spatial hierarchy illustration features subdivisions of space throughout the composition (18·5). This engenders a near-continuous rhythmic negative space. In contrast, the spatial structure binds the vertical planes –the darker lines – with horizontal planes acting as visual fields (18·6). The interior plane of the slender figure relates to an outer wall to its right, the square exhibits three interior zones while the smaller figure dissolves within a planar field and the remaining negative space.

Diagram 18·1: Columns mark boundaries and axes at corners and centers.

Diagram 18·2: Columns mark select boundaries and axes at perimeter.

Diagram 18·3: Columns extend select boundaries and axes in interiors.

Figure 18: Examples show the separate figures composition with additions that demonstrate the three column tactics (above) and the three planar tactics (below).

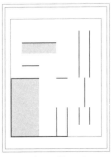

Diagram 18·4: Planar elements define dominant grain.

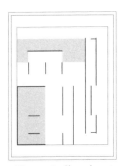

Diagram 18·5: Planar elements articulate spatial hierarchy.

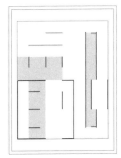

Diagram 18·6: Planar elements exhibit spatial structure.

These six diagrams demonstrate the effects of columns and planes that follow simple procedures to characterize the three figures within the composition. Recalling that these sorts of analytical diagrams have three-dimensional implications, we turn to an illustration of a hybrid diagram and its modeled form (19&20).

The patterns of the columns and planes take their cue from the prior examples. Indications of bounding lines and axes make visual the spatial connections that govern choice. The rhythm of the plan elements – columns, walls and horizontal planes – diagrams a possible tectonic outcome within a three-dimensional construction. We observe one such outcome in the model below. They both illustrate the potential for ongoing design thinking using diagrams to develop intentions in architecture.

More complex approach to strategies

Having applied diagramming as a method of simple strategic thinking, we now extend our strategies and tactical themes to consider a more nuanced and complex response to the new grid. To do so, we introduce three strategies in plan, each with three tactical variations for columns and planes – a total of nine schematic variations in plan. We use the 'bridged figures' composition for our demonstration to expand the range of compositions considered.

Strategy definitions

The three strategies exhibit some characteristics of our recent one as they still address concepts of envelope, grid elements, elaborations and subtractions. However, this time each provides a specific approach regarding subdivisions of the grid. All three sets define simple rules of engagement. They propose distinct patterns for procedure to underscore tectonic themes. To do so they invoke three tectonic criteria of increasing complexity that govern the familiar tactical menu of columns and planes leading to their combined use as seen previously in figure 19. We begin with the guidelines nearest our last venture and the most monochromatic strategy.

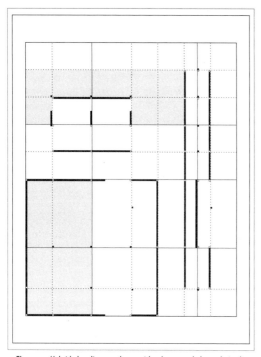

Figure 19: Hybrid plan diagram shows with columns and planes derived from the boundaries and axes – embedded columns shown as outlines.

Figure 20: Rendered model shows a simple extrusion of the forms detailed in Figure 19. The heights of the three figures remain the same as earlier phases.

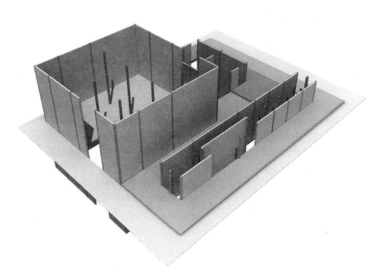

STRATEGY I

· Compositions mark and reflect axis and boundary using constant thickness. This description follows from the exercise, with minor changes. Inherently conservative, this approach aims to present the rules in action with a minimum of reinterpretation of the three figures. These are base case schemes.

STRATEGY II

· Compositions construct and clarify formal hierarchy using subordinate placement and minimal thickness variation. This description prioritizes playing one side of the center axis against the other, and requires select variation in thickness to manifest hierarchy through tectonic choices. Where the first strategy aims to conserve compositional regularity, this scheme give privilege to the expression of sequence and the connective structure among the figures. Judicious use of thick and thin elements should dominate these schemes.

STRATEGY III

· Compositions demonstrate spatial construction using articulated subordinate variation throughout. The premise behind this variation is that a gestalt reading of a plan diagram allows for a keen interpretation of contrast. Furthermore, for designers, contrast can intimate structural differences among defined and implied figures and fields in concert with resulting negative space.

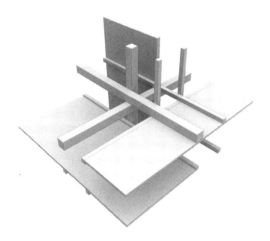

Figure 21: A three-dimensional display of X-Y-Z construction using variations of thickness and articulating subordinate variations around the axes.

Tactical themes & variations

For each of the strategic investigations, the tactical themes are given particular expression. Again, tactics address the use of columns and planes – a third includes both. These should seem familiar. However, given the emphasis of each strategy, the goal – and the underlying conceit – is that the comparative results should express each particular intention prominently. The descriptions of the tactical themes, in any case, remain simple:

· Plan diagrams include only columns.
· Plan diagrams include only horizontal planes, i.e., walls.
· Plan diagrams use both columns and walls: hybrid construction.

The underlying tartan grid governs dimensions and placement of all components. Combined variables of construction of columns and walls along all three axes follow the same underlying principles as before (17).

What follows presents the a description of each strategy together with the tactical guidelines for placing formal elements within the grid in each of nine compositions.

Figure 22: Our example of the bridged figures composition is a close relative of the separate figures example investigated with the first strategy set.

Strategies + tactics*

STRATEGY I + COLUMNS, WALLS & HYBRID

The tactics for marking and reflecting boundary and axis for all figures in each figure using constant thickness are familiar from the recent analysis:

· Columns mark the boundaries and axes of each figure – perimeter and interior (23).
· Walls define dominant grain for each figure (24).
· The base hybrid example uses corner columns and walls exhibiting parallel grain with constant thickness (25).

STRATEGY II + COLUMNS, WALLS & HYBRID

The walls define many of the same markings as columns because of their own boundaries and centers. However, wall placement together with purposeful thickness variations in each figure also brings its own potential to the tactics.

*STRATEGIES + TACTICS LIST

The diagrams described include three tactics each applied to STRATEGIES I, II and III. The strategies focus on axis & boundary, formal hierarchy and spatial construction respectively.

The three tactics employ specific elements applied to the three strategies:

· Column tactics
· Wall tactics
· Hybrid tactics – columns and walls.

The complete matrix of strategies plus tactics results in nine diagrams.

Figure 23: Strategy I with column tactic – corners and centers.

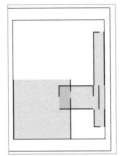

Figure 25: Strategy I with wall tactic – dominant grain.

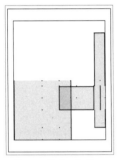

Figure 24: Strategy I with hybrid tactic – parallel grain.

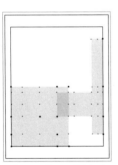

Figure 26: Strategy II with column tactic – formal hierarchy.

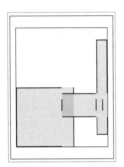

Figure 27: Strategy II with wall tactic – formal hierarchy.

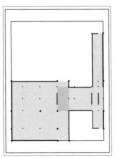

Figure 28: Strategy II with hybrid tactic – formal hierarchy.

- Columns on the perimeter mark axes of that figure and reflect boundaries and axes of other figures – the formal hierarchy (26).
- Walls establish formal hierarchy for both exterior and interior of the figures (27).
- The hybrid case modulates both columns and wall elements to express formal hierarchy using two thicknesses for each (28).

STRATEGY III + COLUMNS, WALLS & HYBRID

The tactical hybrids combine two specific, comparable variations from column and wall tactics above in concert. This provides an opportunity to amplify the overall expression of order.

- Columns placed in the interior mark and follow axes of that figure and extend boundaries and axes of other figures – the spatial construction (29).
- Walls exhibit spatial structure both within and outside of the figure (30).
- The final diagram is the most developed in complexity. The results should show columns, parallel walls and cross grain walls as a demonstration of spatial construction. The elements will also utilize subordinate variation to augment both placement and thickness (31).

Results

Each strategy and tactic results in a composition that exhibits formal and spatial order reflecting their organizational character – in the shown instances, a bridged compositions – with a variety of intentional flavors. That is, they demonstrate approaches that follow from formal ideas.

The compositions of STRATEGY I – each and all – share a central theme of focused simplicity. Both the column and wall tactics solve the spatial agenda with an emphatic economy of means. Furthermore, the tactical hybrid combines the two producing a clear and stable composition with a similar character (24).

The examples of STRATEGY II offer a more fulsome response to the three forms. They exhibit more variety in texture and emphasis. This reflects the requisite elaboration of two weights for both columns and walls (26&27). The visual patterns of both articulate a distinct hierarchy because they proceed from that requirement. In the hybrid example, a pass-through forms a shared spatial axis. In addition, as some perimeter planes recede, the bridge affects a continuous hierarchy from the large space to the elongated hall (28).

With the third set – STRATEGY III – we see the potential of added elements outside of the three figures. The column example is rife with repetition, extending the centerline and perimeter of the bridging element outward (29). A similar extension with a different flavor occurs in the walled example (30). The resolution of those two within the hybrid example shows active and

Figure 29: Strategy III with column tactic – spatial construction.

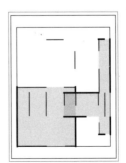

Figure 30: Strategy III with wall tactic – spatial structure.

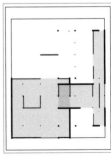

Figure 31: Strategy III with hybrid tactic – spatial structure.

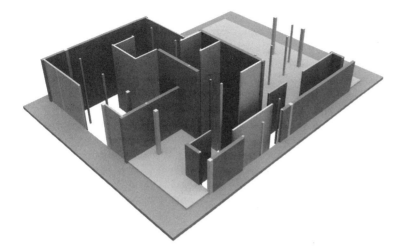

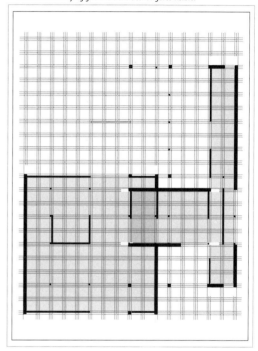

Figure 32: Model of hybrid tactic, Strategy III (31) rendered as translucent planes.

Figure 33: Complete drawing of hybrid tactic, Strategy III shown at larger scale with underlying grid and translucent figures visible.

included negative spaces surrounding the three figures (31). In model form, as pure extrusion, the spatial construction reflects the deliberate patterning of primary, secondary and tertiary forms that proofs the composition, adding density along with elaboration (32).

The presence of models for this portion of the text helps to visualize the results of decisions made in plan. In the next section we deal directly with analytical modeling as a form of diagramming in three-dimensions.

Three-dimensional diagrams

The larger scale of the drawings facilitated a more detailed exploration of the compositions. Simpler models at smaller scale suffice for our next analysis of form and space in three dimensions. The examples also return to the separate composition for the subject under scrutiny.

Four diagrammatic models serve as the media for analysis. Skirting the drawn section, the goal for each is to construct form through and around the three figural volumes as projections of the imagination. Rather than elaborate on the tectonic, the object for each model is to visualize particular concepts and render them as form. The resulting constructs invite reinterpretation of the three volumes, thereby adding to the formal arsenal available to the designer.

Diagram model #1

The first model identifies three analytic components within composition: the three figures as geometric forms, a principal path and the dominant grain. Trace overlays and pencil serve to derive the diagrammatic elements in plan (34).

Once identified, the forms, path and grain follow a simple protocol for manufacture. The model uses the three materials to identify each of the three analytic components and a fourth to construct the base.

· Thin sticks – ⅛" basswood – used in x·y·z construction map the bounding edges of each figure as linear.
· A thin gray plane – two-ply chipboard – designates the grain object as a plane.

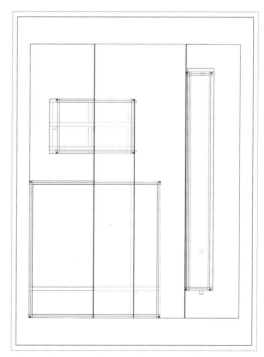

Figure 34: Plan drawing of earlier model with overlay of diagram model elements following.

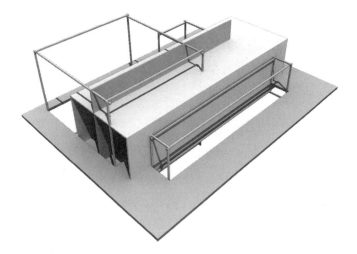

Figure 35: Virtual model of a response to the protocol showing figures, grain and path interpretations.

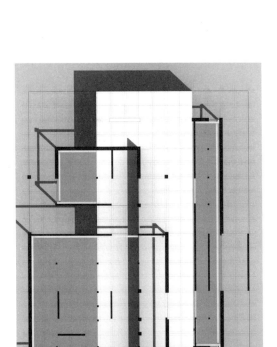

Figure 36: Plan view of the first diagram model shown as an overlay of its tactical hybrid plan.

· Thin white planes – white museum board – compose an open volume defining principal path.

· In addition, corrugated cardboard serves as the base plane within the model with removed material to define the perimeters of the figures.

The example model displays the results of the process (35). The x·y·z construction creates an open but directional depiction of the figural space – the framework for the other operations. The original spatial prejudice of each form remains visible. The vertical plane calls out the grain along the axis seen in earlier models (34). The path, now a volume, identifies a broad swath through the two figures and alongside the third. The origin for this approach derives from a plan taken from the first strategic diagram set – shown as context for the overlay (36).

The speculative diagram model presents an important opportunity to reconsider the organization of form. Our sequence for this project, as with any development scheme, proceeds from working assumptions and methods. An understanding of gestalt reminds us, however, that we tend to solve for organization from what the visual matter presents. By changing the manifestation of formal elements, we change the visual context and in turn can solve for other parameters and interpretations. This is a clear prompt for imaginative rethinking and development. Thus, we continue with three new diagram models for consideration.

Three additional diagram models

The three models that we investigate now share a similar palette of materials. The single change is the addition of thin and thick linear elements – $^1/_{16}$" and $^1/_8$" basswood sticks – still in x·y·z construction. The planar materials remain constant. The foci for the models are grain, datum and section respectively.

Diagram model 2

The first model in this new sequence illustrates the structural grain of each form independently using chipboard. It represents the cross-grain connections using the lighter museum board. There are no linear elements. The

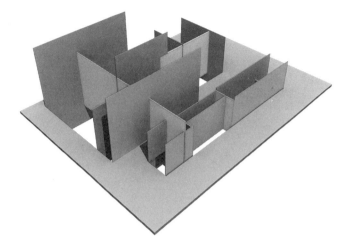

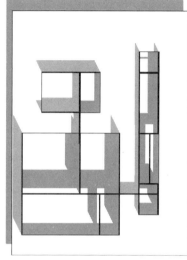

Figure 39: Plan view of model with shadows.

heavier cardboard base both provides physical connection and acts as a spatial reference – a horizontal datum (37).

In this model, the diagrammatic scheme stresses the directionality of grain along the plan. Unlike the earlier formal models, a presumption of a normative orientation of the ground plane and extrusion of planimetric elements underwrites the schematic intent. The diagram therefore lends itself to depicting a division of interior spaces pinioned to dominant axes. The formal structure of the mode shows, without surprise, directly in the plan section view (38).

Diagram model 3

In the next model of the sequence, chipboard planes demonstrate the dominant grain of the datum condition for the entire composition. The basswood sticks suggest, in contrast, tectonic frames. Again, the base plays the same role and uses the same materials (39).

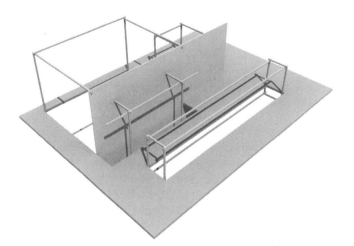

Figure 38: Model 3 shows a planar element identifying dominant grain and tectonic linear elements defining volumetric response to the grain.

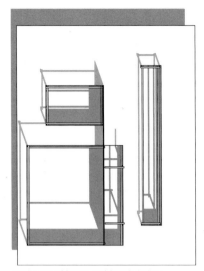

Figure 40: Plan view of diagram model 3 with shadows.

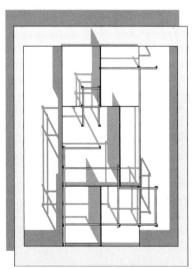

Figure 41: Plan view of diagram model 4 with shadows.

Figure 42: Model 4 uses planes to identify movement and section, and linear elements to define cross-grain section as volume.

Thus far, several of the models have aimed to demonstrate visual grain. This seems reasonable, as the idea of direction and its relationship to the interpretation of form is both central to order, and bewildering to beginning designers. As with many ideas about direction and axis, the experience of referential form resists easy explanation. Appreciation and awareness of this fundamental experience remains subliminal and, as a criteria for design, seems remote and difficult to grasp.

The intent, therefore, of this particular diagram model is to isolate a single dominant directional plane, and to distinguish form on one side from that found on the other. The plan view shows the simple gesture used to accomplish this (40).

Diagram model 4

The last model, identifies elements in the x, y, and z axes that characterize movement through the figures. Chipboard planes define movement parallel to the ground plane of the composition, museum board defines the vertical dimension and location of encountered section and basswood shows the cross-grain section as a volume (39).

The idea of path takes on its broadest expression in our example, becoming three-dimensional as it manifests across the project. The experiential references multiply and locate the experience of section – volume – through the manifestation of viewing planes. Unlike previous diagrams, the references to section do not necessarily coincide with discreet figures. They take their measure from the grid, and from subdivisions suggested by the earlier plan based drawn diagrams. As a result, the example makes several oblique references to everything that has come before. In doing so, the diagram attempts to identify the potential that resides within the more conventional construction of space that began the project.

Five tonal diagrams

All four of the diagrammatic models share one key trait: they propose an interpretation of what might exist within the perimeters of the three figures, revealing alternate intentions to the design. Re-calibrating the compo-

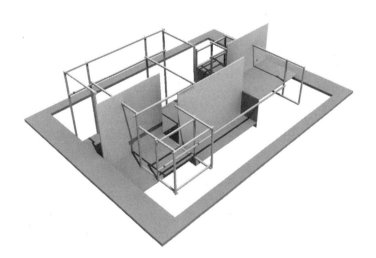

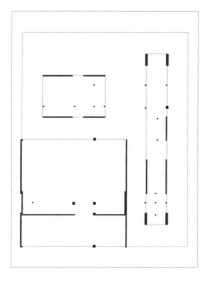

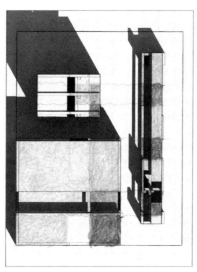

Figure 43: Reference plan for the 'separate figures' diagrams that follow.

Figure 44: Datum drawing example superimposed over a virtual model of the 'separate figures' composition.

Figure 45: Examples of the five diagrams related to the 'separate figures' composition, followed by examples of spatial hierarchy diagrams for 'bridged' and 'overlapped figures' compositions.

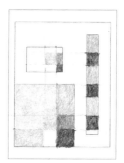

Diagram 45·1: Datum – separate figures.

sition from articulated enclosure to focus on interior expression, the models introduce forms with a high degree of permeability. They conjure themes that inform the design from a second vantage point.

Drawn diagrams, being visual artifacts, can also propose open-ended speculation. In this section, we follow five diagrams that attempt to synthesize elements of our earlier strategy sets with some of the ideas found within the four diagram models. The intent of these drawings is to represent ideas similar to those approached in the diagram models. The five drawings utilize various forms of visual cues, from elements common to planimetric representation to tonalities and transparencies that are more abstract. The resulting images reflect reality rather than depict it.

Each drawing uses line and tone in particular ways, indicated below. The examples illustrate a range of results. The first five illustrations explore the 'separate figures' composition shown above (43). The five diagram types follow four general protocols. The potential for gestalt interpretations of the results guides the selection.

- Drawings proposing datum or multiple data distinguish guiding gesture and edge, within and about the figures. Either tone or line may lead within this drawing but both should be in evidence (45·1).
- Diagrams demonstrating Grain utilize line and linear form within and about the figures (45·2).
- Cross-grain diagrams follow the same conventions as above (45·3).
- Explorations of Spatial hierarchy should exhibit a balance of line and tone as part of their intention (45·4).
- Investigations of Path will rely on tone in general and incorporate line for emphasis and measure (45·5).

The last two examples on the lower right show versions one diagram type – spatial hierarchy – drawn for the other two composition schemes as a comparison (45·6&7). All of the exploratory diagrams shown exhibit their gestural intent in their manufacture – drawn rather than constructed.

Given reasonable facility with digital tools, designers can extend the exercise and manufacture sophisticated illustrations to augment presentation with software 'tweaks' and synthetic overlays (44). However, even this simple demonstration brings to mind an important caution: the potential within

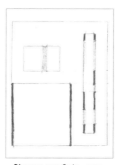

Diagram 45·2: Grain – separate figures.

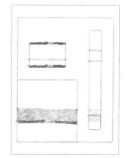

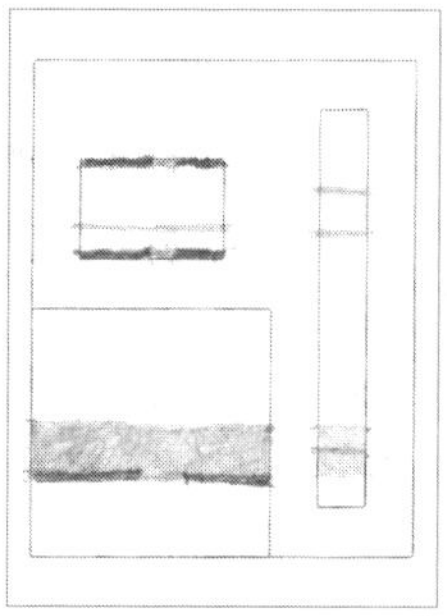

Diagram 45·3: Cross-grain – separate figures.

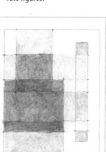

Diagram 45·4: Spatial hierarchy – separate figures.

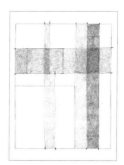

Diagram 45·5: Principal path – separate figures.

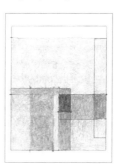

Diagram 45·6: Spatial hierarchy – bridged figures.

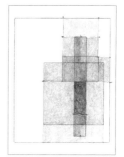

Diagram 45·7: Spatial hierarchy – overlapped figures.

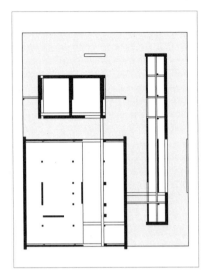

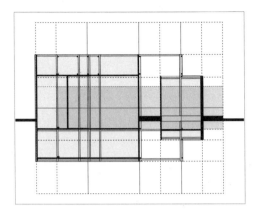

Figure 46: Plan and two sections of separated figures design.

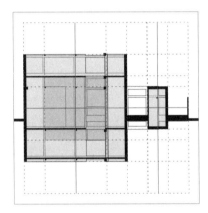

this drawing exercise comes from invoking the imagination. It brings insight, in part, from the very exercise of allowing an image to emerge. The rationale for breeding nuance through drawing lies in discovery. Clever pictures are a happy coincidence in diagrams, not their purpose.

Building the model

An end to this intense foray into diagramming leads us to the construction of a final model. Faced with this task, a practiced designer might draw from her own evolution of design thinking to arrive at a coherent expression in form. To mimic this process, we provide a speculative protocol toward a particular set of criteria.

We begin with orthographic drawings – specifically a plan and two sections – to organize the tectonic hierarchy (46). The materials used for this model includes familiar groupings and some additions.

· Thick and thin sticks: ⅛" and ¹⁄₁₆" basswood used in x·y·z construction continue to represent the linear structure.

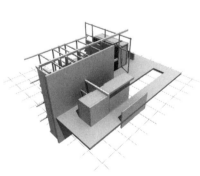

Figure 47: Fragment taken at the intersection of the three figures test the tectonic palette and construction sequence.

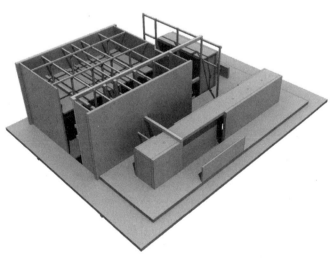

Figure 48: The final model of the separate figures composition synthesizes the lessons of the design diagrams into a comprehensive spatial structure.

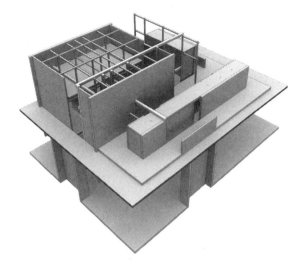

Figure 49: The final model of the separate figures composition perched on its presentation base.

· Thick and thin planes of chipboard articulate the primary and secondary planar elements.
· White museum board identify tertiary planes.
· Corrugated cardboard construes the base plane, but may also serve as an alternative surface for the figure.

In our example, we build on the diagram resulting from Strategy III, hybrid tactic, in the previous exercise for the plan (48). The development of the sections, in turn, shows the influence of the diagram models. The final appearance of the tectonic pattern likewise reflects the last diagram exercises – particularly in judging the density and final expression of the physical rhythm of the grid elements in three-dimensional form.

As a part of the tectonic development, we ask students to make a fragment of their project to test both the appearance and construction of their design (47). These fragments, properly construed, embody diagrams of the tectonic system – a structural motif that organizes the whole. The other two compositions – bridged and overlapped – following the same procedure, and at the hand of the same designer make the point: judgment follows analysis (50&51).

The project now concluded, we turn to the analysis of four buildings, analyzing their formal and tectonic logic at a larger scale. Lessons learned thus far provide a base for investigating design thinking within realized buildings. Beginning with plan logic as a two-dimensional instigator of form and moving to fully volumetric concepts, the next two chapters transform formal principles from the abstraction of studio exercises to the study of architectural precedent.

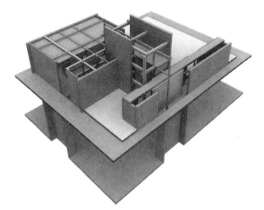

Figure 50: The final model of the 'bridged figures' composition perched on its presentation base.

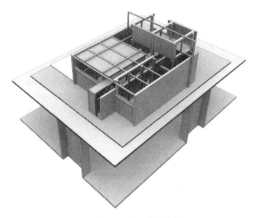

Figure 51: The final model of the 'overlapped figures' composition on its presentation base.

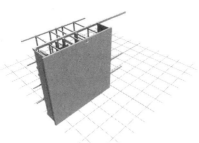

Figure 52: Fragment of the 5×5 figure.

GLOSSARY OF TERMS

BEAMS: Linear elements, positioned horizontally.

BRIDGED: A composition in which two or more elements are joined together by a single, linking element.

COLUMNS: Linear elements, positioned vertically.

DATUM: A reference point or plane against which all relative positions in a composition are measured and regarded.

OVERLAPPED: A composition of two or more superimposed elements.

PATH: Any route defined for or made by continual passage fulfils the literal, commonplace meaning. More broadly it describes the course or direction in which something moves or can move.

· A path axis is an axis aligned with the grain of a path.

· Path surface and path polume are the two- and three-dimensional attributes of a path.

PLANES: Two-dimensional elements within a three-dimensional composition.

SEPARATE: Non-contiguous elements within a composition.

TECTONIC: Short-form for architectonic, describing a clearly articulated structure, or relationships among structural and material systems.

X·Y·Z GRID AXIS: The three-dimensional network of intersections established by a universal or Cartesian grid.

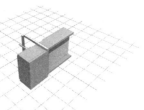

Figure 53: Fragment of the 1×8 figure.

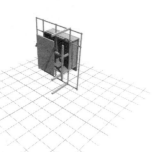

Figure 54: Fragment of the 2×3 figure.

DESCRIPTION 7
Spatial systems

Frames, planes & cells

This chapter has introduced an exploration of what we call 'spatial systems', though architects commonly refer to a set of similar categories as 'tectonic systems'. The distinction in this nomenclature arises from the issue of structure. In archi-speak, tectonics is used as a short-form of architectonics: both words refer generally to the primary system of structure employed in a given project. Given the focus of this book, spatial systems highlight the means by which typologies of form provide order and character to space.

Though there is no definitive taxonomy for architectural form, in the case-studies that follow, we focus on the three spatial systems used in the exercises throughout this chapter, defined here as frame, planar and cellular systems. Characterized by the use of linear components – columns and beams – to 'frame' space, a frame system is sometimes referred to as trabeation. A planar system is fairly self-evident, being composed primarily of vertical, horizontal and folding planes. Cellular spaces are those that resemble enclosed chambers. Today, although they are almost always constructed from multiple parts, cellular space owes its nomenclature to the largely ancient practice of creating inhabitable space through excavation – the carving out of cells or cellars from soil or bedrock.

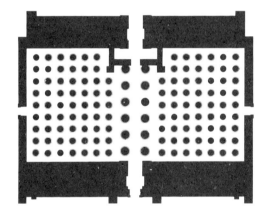

Figure 1: Great Hypostyle Hall, plan.

Figure 2: Great Hypostyle Hall, panoramic view toward central temple axis.

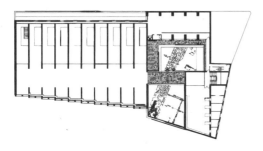

Figure 3: *Thorncrown Chapel,* Eureka Springs, Arkansas, Fay Jones, 1979.

Figure 4: *Museum of Roman Art,* Merida, Spain, Rafael Moneo, 1986.

Great Hypostyle Hall, Karnak

THEBES, EGYPT

Set amongst the largest religious site of the ancient world, the Great Hypostyle Hall of the Karnak Temple Complex is the second most visited site in Egypt, after the pyramids at Giza. Begun during the reign of Seti I in the early thirteenth century BCE, it was subsequently completed by his son, Ramses the Great. The Hypostyle array lies on the principal axis of the Precinct of Amun-Re, a sprawling temple enclosure dedicated to Amun, principal deity of the Theban Triad. Essentially a vast covered vestibule, the Great Hall preceded the inner sancta of the temple proper. Modeled to resemble both closed and splayed stalks of papyrus, the columns are thought to have symbolized the primordial marsh from which Creation arose (1).

The Great Hall now lacks the network of beams that once supported a roof, shrouding the enclosure in darkness. Today, the tightly packed array of columns stands like a densely planted sandstone forest, open to the brilliant Egyptian sky. The plan describes a simple axial arrangement, establishing primary and secondary path volumes. And yet, within such apparent simplicity, the direct experience of immersion within such a space provides for an additional, arguably more powerful effect: as with a natural forest, the phenomenon of parallax prevails. Moving among the phalanx of massive stone trunks provides an ever-shifting perspective, revealing the capacity for framed systems to provide a compellingly interactive spatial experience (2).

Frames can, of course, include horizontal – and often diagonal – members in addition to vertical columns. Because three-dimensional frames almost always act as structure, they are often masked for reasons of fire-protection and weatherproofing. When visible, though, they are capable of incredibly rich spatial articulation. The great Gothic cathedrals come to mind, with their structural embroidery of ribbed vaults, equilateral arches and flying buttresses. More modest in scale and material, though no less resplendent in their effect, the woodland chapels and pavilions of Arkansas architect Fay Jones achieve extraordinary spatial expression with patterned frames of standard dimensional lumber (3).

Figure 6: *Museum of Roman Art,* Merida, Spain, Rafael Moneo, 1986.

Figure 5: *Museum of Roman Art,* Merida, Spain, Rafael Moneo, 1986.

National Museum of Roman Art, Merida

RAFAEL MONEO

Moneo's design uses solid planes of brick-faced concrete, emblematic of construction techniques found throughout the Roman Empire, including the city of Emerita Augusta, upon which the modern city of Merida is built. The museum evokes the repetitive, almost industrial spatial rhythms of Roman *horrea* – vast public warehouses found in urban centers throughout the Empire. Its repeating bays, formed by thick, fire-proof party walls, provide the signature motif of Moneo's design (4).

The inherent insularity of this spatial system is overcome by an elegantly simple solution: Each wall is pierced by an oversize arched opening, aligned across the full span of the building. This tactic carves out an implied barrel vault against the grain of the parallel walls, a common hall linked seamlessly to the more intimate slices of space along the series of individual bays. The resulting *enfilade* of titanic arches simultaneously enhances the perception of depth across the length of the plan (5&6).

Etruscan tumuli

CERVETERI, ITALY

As its name suggests, cellular space is contained space, suggestive of a cell or room, enclosed by an encompassing set of walls and a roof overhead. Tombs are among the purest form of cellular space, in that they are designed to house the dead, with few, if any, of the allowances for the living that makes most other architecture less than hermetically-sealed. Among the most compelling collection of tombs from antiquity is that of the Etruscan *tumuli* found at the Necropoli della Banditaccia, near Cerveteri. More than a thousand tombs populate an area of over forty hectares, the largest ancient necropolis of the Mediterranean world (7–9).

The most common tomb-type at Cerveteri is the domed *tumulus*, carved into the clay-like soil of the region, volcanic tufa. Easily worked with simple tools at first, tufa subsequently hardens with exposure to the air. This property made it eminently useful both for quarrying, and for its use as a building material. The Cerveteri *tumuli*, such as the *Tomb of the Greek Vases*, are characterized by a symmetrically arranged cluster of cells, thought to reflect the

Figure 7: Cerveteri, interior of *tumulus.*

Figure 8: Cerveteri, exterior of typical domed *tumulus,* showing entrance portal.

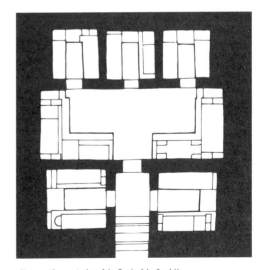

Figure 9: Cerveteri, plan of the *Tomb of the Greek Vases*.

Figure 10: *Therme Vals*, Peter Zumthor.

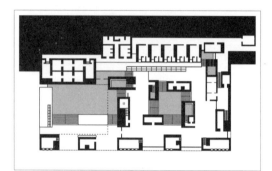

Figure 11: *Therme Vals*, Peter Zumthor.

Figure 12: *Therme Vals*, Peter Zumthor.

Figure 13: Salzburg Salt Mine.

typical plan-type of Etruscan dwelling. Typically, small 'bedrooms' feature raised platforms to either side of a central aisle, and give onto a larger common room, which in turn provides access to the surface by way of a narrow, stepped passage. Details carved into walls and ceilings mimic the features of an assembled, trabeated system of construction, consistent with dwellings built above ground, but entirely at odds with the actual process of scooping out rooms from the solid, monolithic volcanic soil – cellular space in its purest form.

Therme Vals

PETER ZUMTHOR

Shaping space through excavation was Zumthor's Big Idea for the design of the thermal baths complex at Vals, in the Swiss canton of Graubünden. Deeply embedded into the steep slope of the valley, Zumthor conceived the *parti* of the baths as a series of interlocking voids cut into the monolithic mass of the hillside, with an array of solids left intact for support overhead, in the same manner as subterranean mines are excavated (10). To a remarkable degree, the final plan stays true to this initial gesture, the continuous void given over to circu-lation and a pair of large pools. Cells carved from within the supporting solids are in turn occupied by smaller pools, saunas and service spaces (11).

The impression that the spaces of the baths are carved from living bedrock is reinforced by the ubiquitous use of the locally quarried *Valserstein*, a grey-green granite Zumthor arranges in thin horizontal bands of smooth-cut ashlar, covering the walls, floors and pools throughout the interior and exterior surfaces of the project. The compressed horizontal coursework of the stone suggests two sources simultaneously: the characteristic coursing of flat Roman brick, similar in effect to the walls of Moneo's project in Merida, and perhaps more obliquely, the horizontally striated, precision-cut vertical surfaces that one encounters in the extensive salt mines of the neighboring Salzburg region – including the tendency for ground water to accumulate in shallow pools (12&13).

The sole exception to the singular palette of *Valserstein* is found in Zumthor's arrangement of overhead concrete slabs, cantilevered from their granite supports to introduce continuous slivers of natural daylight into the crepuscular spaces within, providing further reinforcement of the sense of bathing within the precisely carved depths of the granite mountainside. This profound sense of excavation, of residing within space wrested from solid matter, is the quintessential expression of a cellular spatial system.

OVERVIEW
First precedents

In this chapter, we go beyond the sequence of projects that defines the first semester of our first-year studio. We now apply the principles underlying those exercises to the analysis of projects from exemplary works of Modernist architecture. The study of precedents traditionally fulfills a cornerstone of architectural education, part of the enduring legacy of the École des Beaux-Arts, where students acquired lessons in form and order by literally tracing plans and sections from the classical canon.

The use of precedents in this chapter and the next has a second purpose. Through the step-by-step exploration of each of the four projects, we hope to provide examples of how students might proceed through their own analysis of any given project, including their own. In the process of working through these examples, we also aim to develop something approaching a standard roster of diagram types – a definitive, if not exhaustive, set. Finally, we hope that, in revealing the proportional and modular relationships that plausibly temper these works of architecture, students acknowledge the role that such systems may play in their own practice.

CHAPTER **8**

Precedent diagrams in two dimensions

Introduction

So far, we have explored some fundamentals of visual order, building toward a basic grammar of architectural design. Along the way, we have selected some formal attributes of exemplary building projects – what architects refer to as PRECEDENTS – to demonstrate how these fundamentals of visual order dwell within actual works of architecture. In order to survey the ûbiquitous presence of order within buildings, our focus in this chapter and the next is on the diagrammatic ANALYSIS of precedents.

Precedents serve several purposes in the practice of architecture. They establish a loose CANON of exemplary projects, providing architects with a shared understanding of the traditions – and latent potential – that resides in the work of their peers. By providing insights from earlier works of architecture, precedents help to provoke innovation and invention. Rather than supply examples to merely copy, precedents provide concrete models, worthy of analysis, which can inform ideas of order.

In this chapter and the next, we will make use of precedents toward a second end: through the detailed formal analysis of a few select works of architecture, we aim to develop a toolkit of essential diagram types, a set that is in most respects definitive, if not exhaustive. Our criteria for inclusion in this set follow from the very same principles of visual order detailed in the preceding pages of this book. In this chapter, we will work through two-dimensional diagrams. In the next, we will focus on diagrams in three dimensions.

A quick review reveals three particular themes from the previous chapters:

1   PATTERN: Analysis occurs in diagrams, and those diagrams make use of gestalt strategies and tactics to identify pattern.
2   CONCEPT: Those patterns have names that reflect both geometric ideas and architectural practices.
3   EXPRESSION: From the overlap of geometric and architectural concepts, two general expressions of the design process emerge – internal division and external assemblage; that is, complexity within and complexity without or inward articulation and outward accretion.

Two concepts

Diagrams are inherently formal. As instruments of analysis, they can reveal geometric patterns providing order to a work of architecture. Frank Lloyd Wright described geometry as 'the grammar, so to speak, of the form. It is its architectural principle'. Yet architecture must also satisfy purpose: its functions must engage its form. The distinction between formal principles and

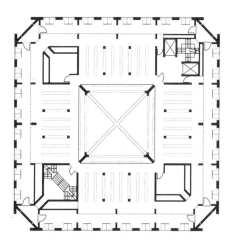

Figure 1: *Exeter Library,* typical plan, Louis Kahn.

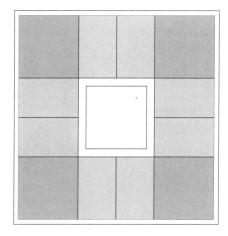

Figure 2: *Exeter Library,* Golden Corners diagram – see CHAPTER 9.

functional objectives comprises the difference between perceived pattern and architectural intent, which begins with the designer's sensitivity to the experience of inhabitation.* In turn, notions of inhabitation encompass a complex web of cultural and utilitarian aspirations that shape the spatial ordering of PROGRAM. A project's program may imply simple, generalized distinctions, such as served and service spaces, public and private spaces, or spaces of passage and assembly. In most cases, a building's program is far more explicit with respect to function.

At the outset of their studies, designers may deem diagrams to be redundant, with the assumption that a simple description pointing out activities and features is sufficient. Yet mapping OCCUPATION is not the same as diagramming buildings. The principal question is not what a diagram looks like, but rather how it interprets a building's relevant systems of order. A diagram begins with an assumption to be tested. It becomes a search for the Big Idea, the strategy by which a formal procedure manifests a functional insight.

The simple structures that we examined in CHAPTER 2 – the huts – all begin with the relationship of a hearth to an enveloping space. If we diagram the hearth and its relationship to that space, we are testing the notion that the presence of the fire was purposeful, not merely coincidental. Do we gather around the fire? Do we pass by it on our way to somewhere else? Is it a destination, or a point of reference? Similarly, acts of entry, including stepping up or down, ducking our head - all are conditions of inhabitation. Thus, the formal declaration encoded within a work of architecture that one way of inhabiting is better than another. Revealing that bias is one of the goals of the diagram.

Two expressions

The first question with which we approach an architectural precedent is whether it comprises INTERNAL DIVISION or EXTERNAL ASSEMBLAGE. These two compositional categories yield distinct differences in diagrammatic form. Another way to define this distinction is whether the composition embodies a principle articulated within a single form, or a relationship expressed between multiple forms. From that point forward, analysis engages very similar issues. In the best diagrams, however, the question of principle versus relationship determines what follows.

You will recall that in describing fields, we always return to the underlying premise that at different scales, every figure may become a field for further articulation. In practice, a design that begins from a perimeter state – a bounding figure as field – either subdivides the figure from a grid or begins with smaller figures fit within the field, also on a grid. The courtyard scheme is a paradigm, figure-as-field, as we saw with Kahn's *Exeter Library* (1&2). In contrast, Frank Lloyd Wright's *Unity Temple* expresses the dual purposes of its program – the sacred and the secular – as two figures on a field (3&4).

Two dimensions

In this chapter, we examine diagrams in two dimensions. Guided by gestalt, we approach from the domain of perception. We first perceive figure-ground, or the image. From here, we observe and articulate patterns: differences and similarities, and relationships and affinities, including some general categories that we have encountered earlier in this book, notably CONTRAST, REPETITION, ALIGNMENT and PROXIMITY.

*ON INHABITATION

We make a general distinction between merely occupying space and inhabiting space. Furniture occupies a space, as do inactive human beings. Once human activity takes place, it begins to connect to architectural space as a manifestation of dwelling or inhabitation of a locale. In philosophical terms, this is the situation in which architecture acts as the agent of human function.

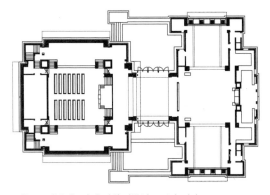

Figure 3: *Unity Temple,* Frank Lloyd Wright, main level plan.

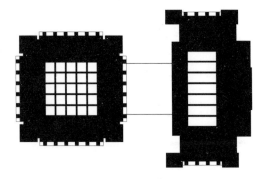

Figure 4: *Unity Temple,* figure-ground diagram – see CHAPTER 9.

We must also keep in mind that buildings represented in two dimensions usually refer to events that are three-dimensional, and to notions of inhabitation. These include AXIS, PATH, BOUNDARY and ENCLOSURE, among others. Thus, two-dimensional diagrams of architecture coexist in the space of both perception and projection – that is to say, in the formal and material properties of the building, and in the intentions implied by the arrangement of those properties.

Two projects

To demonstrate a set of fundamental diagrams in two dimensions, we will examine two exemplary works of architecture from the twentieth century: the *House with Three Courts*, 1935, by Ludwig Mies van der Rohe, and the *Danteum*, 1938, by Giuseppe Terragni with Pietro Lingeri and Mario Sironi. Generated almost entirely by planimetric geometries, both designs are therefore optimal for two-dimensional analysis. In addition, as neither design was ever constructed, both exist solely as representations, as 'mere' projects. Our knowledge of the intentions of the designers can therefore focus on the drawings and models that survive, without the supplemental evidence available when projects are realized as buildings.

House with Three Courts

LUDWIG MIES VAN DER ROHE, 1935

Mies' *House with Three Courts* is one of a series of houses, designed subsequent to his *Barcelona Pavilion* of 1929, that explore figure-ground strategies with courtyards, in conjunction with the interplay of structural grid and planar

Figure 5: *House with Three Courts,* Ludwig Mies van der Rohe, 1935.

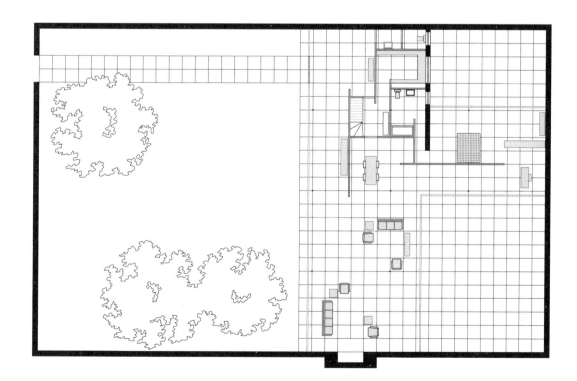

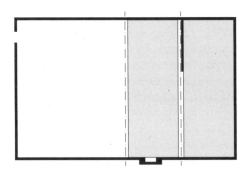

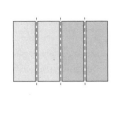

Figure 6: In its simplest form, the diagram distinguishes between the figure of the house and the field of its forecourt. The centerline indicates that the field and the figure are not quite equal in size, a by-product of the use of both rational and proportional systems of measure.

Figure 9: Our first glance at the interior organization of the house yields a two-bay division, separated by a 1 meter-wide gap defined by the interior load-bearing wall, and the offset glazed wall separating the interior from the larger of the corner courts.

Figure 7: Figure-ground can be further articulated to illustrate the position of the two inner courts of the house, which share a common dimension. The width of the main wing of the house, at ten meters, is half the width of the forecourt, and one meter wider than the two corner courts.

Figure 10: A number of possible configurations provides the makeup of the T-shaped plan of the interior. Three adjacent fields, each with the proportion of 2:3 rectangles, comprise one such possibility.

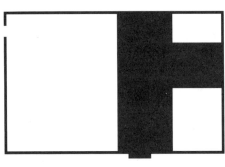

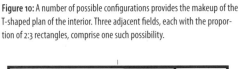

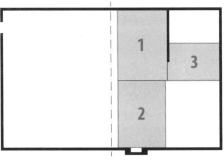

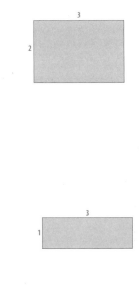

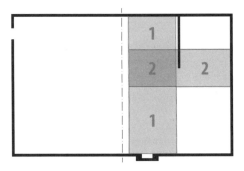

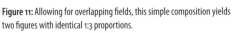

Figure 8: This figure-ground diagram reverses the tonality of the first two, to emphasize the simple rectangular figures of the three courts within the ground of the overall site, and the white boundary-wall merged with the roof plane.

Figure 11: Allowing for overlapping fields, this simple composition yields two figures with identical 1:3 proportions.

geometry that characterizes the modernist practice/notion of the FREE PLAN. As at Barcelona, distinctions between interior and exterior spaces are deliberately undermined or sublimated, characterized by the ostensible slippage and interpenetration of (solid and transparent) vertical planes.

Unlike at Barcelona and the *Tugendhat House,* designs premised on a close relationship with local site conditions, Mies' courtyard projects of the early 1930's give way to a virtual independence from specific topographic characteristics, premised as they are on complete insulation from the world beyond their walls. The enclosed courtyards provide clearly defined exterior spaces that integrate visually with the layout of the interiors. With these projecting fields, the spatial integrity of the interior remains fully preserved, in spite of the fact that the exterior walls are almost entirely transparent planes of glass.

Figure-ground diagrams

We begin our analysis with diagrams that demonstrate patterns – the fundamental gestalt principle of figures and fields. The *House with Three Courts* presents a singularly concise initial pattern, in that the figure of the house occupies the entirety of the site or ground of the project – a walled rectangular perimeter, interrupted only by the single entranceway providing access to the site, and the masonry structure enclosing the hearth.

The basic FIGURE-GROUND diagram (6) illustrates the division of this rectangular precinct into two fundamental sectors: a walled forecourt, and the domain of the house itself. The plan drawing establishes this distinction, a clear contrast between the permeable ground of the forecourt and the gridded ground-plane of the house. A slightly more articulate figure-ground diagram (7) distinguishes between a T-shaped figure, describing the house's covered interior, and the two corner courts contained within its gridded footprint. The third figure-ground diagram demonstrates the alternate reading that accompanies the inverse of the contrasting solid and voids of the composition (8).

A second set of figure-ground diagrams begins to investigate the fundamental compositional properties of the plan of the house itself. We begin by identifying a significant interstitial field, a one-meter wide divisor between bays of equal width (9). The left bay runs the full twenty-four meter width of the interior. The right bay comprises the two corner courts, and the bedroom wing that separates them. The interstitial field aligns with the interior masonry wall defining one edge of the smaller corner court. Its one-meter width also encompasses the glazed plane running the length of the larger corner court. When taken together, the interstitial field plus two bays equals the area of the forecourt, when mirrored against the vertical centerline of the site. Taken another way, we can discern the site as an array of four, twenty-four meter by nine meter fields, spaced at one meter intervals. This alternate reading nevertheless reinforces our initial gestalt reading of the site comprised of equal halves defining forecourt and house.

Universal & proportional systems of measure

The third set of diagrams illustrates the presence of both rational and proportional systems of measure that we speculate governed Mies' design process in this project. In the first, we can establish the overall dimensions of the project using the one-meter square grid, a product of the rational CARTESIAN GRID. Measuring twenty-four meters by thirty-nine meters, the proportions of this figure constitute a whole-number equivalent to the GOLDEN RATIO. The second diagram in this sequence demonstrates the allocation of a spiral generated by

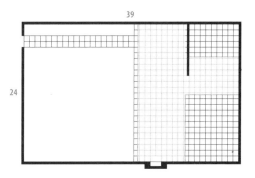

Figure 12: The one-meter square grid that defines the hard-surfaced extent of the ground plane also provides a measure of the site using rational numbers. As depicted, the hard-surfaced area of the site – comprising the house interior and the two corner courts – is the nearest whole number grid equivalent to half the surface area of the overall site.

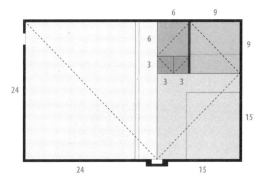

Figure 13: The overall site dimensions – 24 × 39 meters – are drawn from the Fibonacci sequence, manifesting a whole-number equivalent of the golden section. As such, the site and house are composed of an amalgam of rational and irrational systems of measure: the universal grid and the relativistic proportions of the golden section.

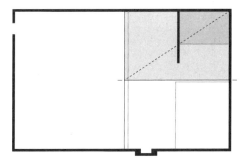

Figure 14: The golden ratio of the overall site is found again in fields generated along the diagonal – including the proportions of the smaller corner court.

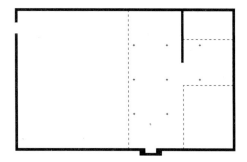

Figure 15: Structure. This simple diagram isolates the two distinct systems of structural support: load-bearing masonry constitutes the perimeter walls of the site, the hearth, and the single, opaque 'privacy' wall within the interior; and a frame of eight cruciform steel columns (enlarged here for clarity) arrayed on a six-meter squared grid. The dashed lines correspond to the overhead plane of the roof.

Figure 16: Repeating square-bay units – structural 'bays' of six meters in both vertical and horizontal directions.

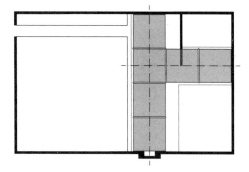

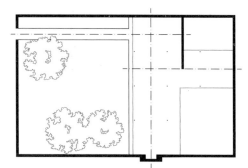

Figure 17: Axes and paths.

the sequence of squares. We arrive at the pattern of whole numbers through the FIBONACCI SEQUENCE, the numerical sequence that approximates that of the golden ratio. As the diagram demonstrates, the primary division of the site is aligned to this series of diagonals and squares. The third diagram illustrates a subset of these relationships. It demonstrates the presence of three nested golden rectangles – those of the entire site, one quadrant of the site and the smaller of the corner courts – allowing for a minor degree of inaccuracy caused by the discordance between the pure ratio, or PHI (approximately 1.62) and the whole-number Fibonacci sequence, which snap to the one-meter grid underlying the composition.

Structural grid & repetitive units

Another system of measure contributes to the compositional play of the house – that of its structural frame. The necessity for structure in the design of every building determines that it always plays a central role. As such, diagrams demonstrating the logic and disposition of structure are among the most fundamentally revealing for works of architecture.

A simplified structural diagram of the *House with Three Courts* reveals two systems: load-bearing walls and steel framing (15). Masonry walls surround the site, frame the hearth and provide privacy for the bedroom court. They also complete the grid of the steel structural frame. As with Mies' *Barcelona Pavilion* and *Tugendhat House*, the columns here are carbon steel angles – L-shaped members – assembled as a cruciform and sheathed in polished chrome. As with *Tugendhadt*, the columns array to form a six-meter square grid .

The history of the structural frame in architecture is a product of rationalization, contingent upon a number of concurrent advances in the understanding of the properties of matter, applied mathematics and the standardization that accompanied the onset of industrial modes of production. This is particularly true with steel framing, with its standardization of sections which allowed for reliably accurate, and thus optimized, material usage. Left to their own logic, structural frames of standardized materials tend toward uniform spatial distribution, i.e. grids, to maximize efficiency. For Mies and other architects of the Modernist movement, there was no greater emblem of what he called 'the will of the epoch' in architecture than the precision of a structural frame composed of standardized steel members.

The uniformity of material and arrangement in a structural frame in turn creates spatial regularity, as with the six-meter square MODULE formed by the array of columns depicted in the diagram. The spatial rhythm, or 'meter', set in motion by this grid provides a measured tempo, a regular counterpoint to the spatial fluidity of the free plan of vertical planes of glass, polished stone, and brick in the *House with Three Courts*. The column grid also creates a three-bay module that overlaps and syncopates with that of the two-bay rhythm established in the previous set of diagrams. Whereas the two-bay system results from the practice of subdivision (half of half of the width of the site) inherent in proportional methodology, the three-bay system is a product of the rational grid, with its additive system of six-meter spans (18).

Structural grids, or bays, constitute the most common example of REPETITIVE UNITS, a nearly ubiquitous constant in architectural composition. With a few notable exceptions, the combination of structural grid and its accompanying repetitive spatial unit constitutes a fundamental diagram, one that portrays the formal DNA of any given work of architecture. Such a diagram generally accomplishes several key tasks in tandem: it enhances the visibility of (one or more) structural grids, which, due to their relatively light footprint in plan, are often obscured within the complex articulation of plan drawings; it provides vivid contrast, like an x-ray, to distinctions between structural and non-structural materials. It reveals, at a glance, the fundamental play between repetitive and unique spatial units that lie at the heart of a building's formal order (19&20).

Defining axes & paths

Structural grids further our understanding of fundamental figure-ground relationships within architectural design. They also provide prompts for our understanding of the likely disposition of significant axes and paths at play in any given work of architecture.

Axes are, strictly speaking, linear. They connect two or more points along a straight line. Paths may also be linear, in that they connect two or more

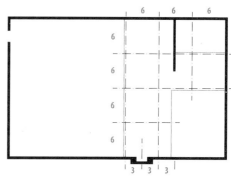

Figure 18: Six-meter square column grid. The six-meter bay is arranged symmetrically on the centerline of the hearth.

Figure 19: Repeating square bay units – structural bays of six meters in both vertical and horizontal directions within the plan.

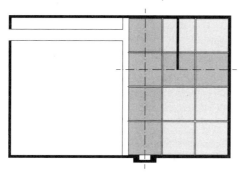

Figure 20: Repetition of the square as a motif in the composition of the plan. A nine-square and squared forecourt join the six-meter square module.

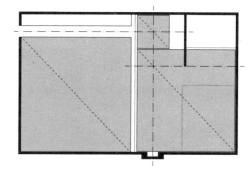

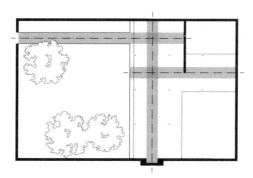

Figure 21: Axes and paths. Using the two–meter width of the entrance path as a guide, this idealizing diagram adds a pair of spatial paths defined by the centerlines of the structural grid in both directions.

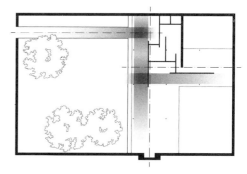

Figure 22: Axes and paths. The idealizing geometries of Figure 21 are here adjusted by the location of interior walls. Gradients record the variation in spatial charge between path intersections and endpoints.

Figure 23: Initial, fundamental bilateral symmetry – the figure of the site bifurcated into front·back, void·solid, positive·negative, exterior·interior.

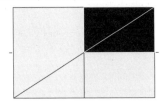

Figure 24: A sequence of incremental, counter-clockwise subdivision begins with the halving of the solid figure, bifurcating the right side of the site.

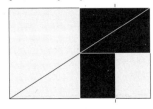

Figure 25: The next step restores half of the half, reproducing the original bifurcation in the lower right quadrant of the site.

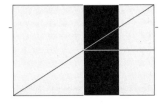

Figure 26: The subsequent step restores half of that quadrant, again reproducing the original bifurcation of the site.

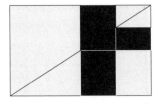

Figure 27: A final step restores half of half of half of half, reproducing the original bifurcation, now in the upper-right octant.

Figure 28: We arrive at the final footprint through four cycles of counter-clockwise rotation, bifurcation and restitution – a sequential balancing.

points. Nevertheless, paths also usually entail area and volume. For the sake of clarity, we refer to three categories: path axis, path surface and path volume.

An analysis of path and axis in the *House with Three Courts* allows us to visualize their similarities and distinctions. Three axes reveal themselves readily – one between the entrance gateway and the front door, and two aligned with the centerlines of the structural grid (17). Initially, we might diagram a set of accompanying paths centered on these axes, and with a width of two meters, determined by that of the paved approach (21). Subsequently, as we overlay this idealized pattern on a more complete plan, existing walls adjust the paths' alignments and widths (22). Despite these variances from the initial gesture, the set of path-axes describe a general sequence, a procession in three stages: entrance, public suite, private suite.

Symmetry & balance

Another pair of terms often used interchangeably when describing visual order is SYMMETRY and BALANCE, concepts which overlap yet provide clear distinctions in the analysis of formal composition.

Symmetry may affect balance, but is not intrinsic to the definition of balance. Symmetry is the mathematical identification of a relationship between a form and its axis. It identifies a center and defines its formal reference. Symmetry in composition is a product of visual parity: it thereby participates in descriptions of visual balance.

Balance, in comparison, describes a phenomenal, empirical and perceptual relationship; it is more fully accountable to gestalt principles of completion and common fate. A fuller description of any instance of balance will account for ideas of contrast (differences of form), alignment (establishment of axes and edge), repetition (the number of elements) and proximity (the active grouping). The notion of parity is more variable than balance, and more open to judgment – even between visually unlike or opposite elements.

Examining our precedent, we begin to deduce the roles that symmetry and balance may have played in the process of its design. For starters, we recall the initial figure-ground diagram (6&23), which demonstrates the most fundamental type of symmetry: bilateral, literally 'two-sided'. The site divides neatly along its centerline, half an open forecourt, the other half describing the hard-surfaced area of the house. With this diagram as a starting point, a series of geometric operations progressively repeats this bilateral division, arriving at the T-shaped figure that is the final footprint of the house. (23–28)

This sequence serves to demonstrate two fundamental principles of visual order – principles that can apply to the analysis of architectural composition. First, repetition of basic forms and relationships can yield complex geometries that belie their simple origins. We may require diagrammatic analysis to unveil, or 'reverse engineer' the processes of design, literally tracing backwards to propose the fundamental building blocks of a design.

The second principle holds that symmetry and balance are traits of visual order that can act simultaneously, in ways that are both simple and complex, singular and serial. The process of designing a building may include geometric operations that are linear and sequential, but that process will just as likely also involve patterns that act cyclically or simultaneously. Diagrams can illustrate various patterns in the final form of a work of architecture. They can also demonstrate the processes and patterns that may have led to that final form.

Unraveling the probable origins of the design process is fundamental to an analytic understanding of a work of architecture.

Two motifs

Once our diagrammatic analysis yields recurring patterns in a work of architecture, we may identify such a pattern as a MOTIF. As we have described earlier, a motif is a pattern that acts as a signature element, a motive that drives or governs the pattern of decisions inherent in any given work of design. The signature pattern that motivates the sequence shown to the left (23–28) is a primary motif of Mies' project. The simple bifurcated figure yields two equal but opposing fields. Within a network of other guises, this motif of sequential subdivision arguably governs the evolution of the composition.

In this same project, a second motif reveals itself. Like the first, it is a product of the symbiotic play of symmetry and balance. What we might refer to as TURNED PATHS, or TURNED SPACE, thread themselves throughout a broad range of work by Mies van der Rohe. In his *House with Three Courts,* we can identify this motif in two complementary but distinct diagrams. In the first instance (29), we can identify three large, angled (or L-shaped) fields set within the footprint of the plan, each defining distinct but superimposed spatial sequences: entrance to public, public to private, private to service. In the second diagram, we identify the primary instances where right-angled turns govern movement through the house (30).

Such a motif is arguably one of the signature patterns of the Modernist palette, one which set itself in distinct opposition to the formal and spatial patterns characteristic of Neoclassicism. Two iconic projects illustrate the contrast clearly: comparing the plan of Mies' project, the *Brick Villa* (31) with Palladio's *Villa Rotonda* (32), we can identify the distinction between a neoclassical expression of order via hierarchical axial alignment, and the modernist preference for angled or turned axes, a product of the Romantic penchant for effect. The notion of circulation as strict progression modeled by social hierarchy – ENFILADE – is challenged by sequential interactivity, the peripatetic path of Modernism – encounter. The history of Western garden design provides a parallel, the plan of *Villa Rotonda* representing the transparently axial arrange-

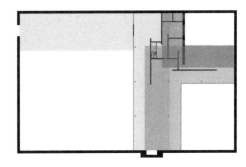

Figure 29: Turned space. Three angled fields reside within the footprint of the house, distinct yet superimpsed.

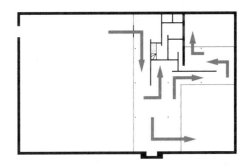

Figure 30: Turned paths.

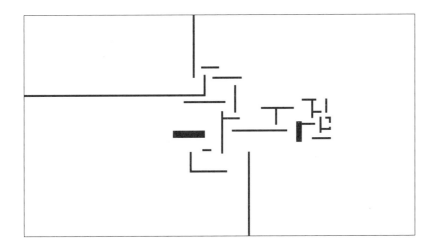

Figure 31: *Brick Villa,* ca. 1924, Ludwig Mies van der Rohe, (project).

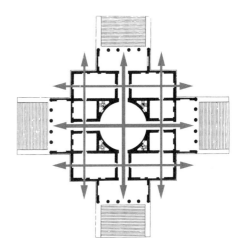

Figure 32: *Villa Rotonda,* begun 1567, Andrea Palladio.

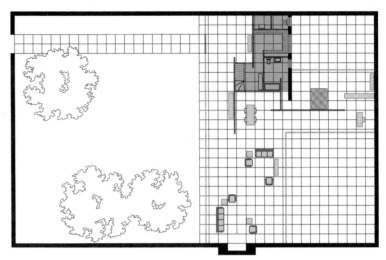

Figure 33: A compact utility core (in gray) *serves* the rest of the plan.

ment of the Italian Renaissance garden, and that of Mies' *Brick Villa* suggestive of the sequential encounter of the English landscape garden.

Served & service

One particularly revealing diagram for works of architecture is a formal hybrid, one that relies upon notions of figure and ground, axes and paths, and symmetry and balance in equal measure. What we will call the 'served and service' diagram merely reveals, in a limited sense, the location of utility spaces. It demonstrates the relationship between primary living spaces and those spaces that serve to support them.

This diagram type is inherently less ambiguous than diagrammatic distinctions between public and private, formal and informal or even primary and secondary space, relationships that are inherently subjective in their application, and which may reveal little as to the inherent compositional motives at work in the design. A served and service diagram type is better equipped to reveal characteristic strategies of an individual architect's approach to space planning. Applied broadly throughout their *oeuvre*, it may yield characteristic 'fingerprints' of an architect's working method. For the *House with Three Courts*, the shaded area reveals a densely compacted core, deftly concealed from the fluidly arranged spaces for living, dining and sleeping (33), a strategy found throughout Mies' work.

Parti

In previous chapters, we have referred to the Big Idea as that principle or concept that governs any given formal composition. Among architects, the Big Idea is most often referred to as the PARTI, a term steeped in the history of the discipline. The term originates with the École des Beaux-Arts, generally considered the first formal program of architectural education in the West. *Parti* here translates roughly as 'option' or 'course of action'. As such, for a student of the *École*, it constituted an early declaration (and commitment) to a general, characteristic, arrangement of the plan. The *parti*, a Platonic ideal, reified as a diagram in the form of an ESQUISSE, a French word derived from the Italian *schizzo*, meaning sketch or outline. Although the *esquisse* traditionally constituted the physical artifact, today when architects refer to *parti*, they describe both a building's Big Idea and its corresponding diagram.

What would constitute a representative *parti* of Mies' *House with Three Courts*? Our first take (34) would begin with the fundamental figure-ground identity of the project, a simple golden rectangle, its fore (garden) and aft (paved) halves joined by a perimeter wall. A further distinction indicating the presence of interior courts might be included. At the same time, some indication of the proportion of the rectangle ought to be unmistakably evident. In its simplest form, the unique signature of the radiant arc, arising from the midpoint of the side of a square, denotes the golden ratio.

An alternative means of denoting the same proportion may also be used, particularly because the dimensions of the project – 39×24 meters – give rise to a Fibonacci spiral. In this case (35), the straight-edged Fibonacci volute overlays on a figure-ground illustration denoting the extent of the overhead roof plane and the six-meter grid of cruciform steel columns that supports that roof while providing a Cartesian counterpoint to the proportional spiral. In particular, this grid's implied centerlines, running along the length of both 'wings' of the T-shaped interior, align with the series of turning-points that form the angular volute, while also suggesting the twin motifs of angled fields and paths (29&30)

In fairness, with a project containing the multiplicity of operations and concerns witnessed here, we ought not to limit the possibility of rival versions of the *parti*. Although an *esquisse* aims to convey the essence of a project's Big Idea, this does not suggest that there can only be one, definitive expression of any given *parti*. Both versions described above demonstrate the same fundamental premise, despite the variances employed. A third version (36) might aim to synthesize the findings of the previous two attempts. Here, the figure–ground of the first version reappears, without the intermediate gray to signal the distinction between forecourt and the two rear 'corner-courts'. The inclusion of the forecourt's tree canopy serves the same purpose, but to greater effect and with more clarity. The pairing of Fibonacci spiral and column grid is adopted from the second version, with the cruciform footprints scaled up to avoid being optically overwhelmed by the black footprint of the house's interior.

A method, not a matrix

It is tempting to imagine that, by following a one-size-fits-all set of diagrams, we could arrive at a persuasively complete analysis of any given work of architecture. Experience reveals that it is never that simple. Although we have chosen to begin our case studies with a relatively simple – yet highly refined – project, one that has yielded a correspondingly elemental series of geometric analyses, it would be a mistake to imagine that we might simply apply this same formula universally. Even when we restrict ourselves to two-dimensional analyses, the project itself determines the nature and the extent of a 'definitive set' of diagrams – a set capable of revealing and supporting the Big Idea.

Our companion project for this chapter shares several significant attributes of the *House with Three Courts,* and it shares many of the same fundamental first stages of diagrammatic analysis. Yet, as we shall see, the *Danteum* calls for an approach all its own.

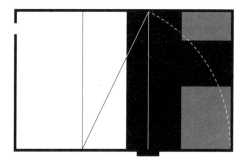

Figure 34: *Parti* diagram, demonstrating the fundamental figure-ground identity of the design within the perimeter of its golden rectangle.

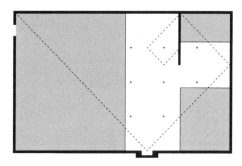

Figure 35: *Parti* diagram, illustrating the relationship between skin and structure, with a Fibonacci spiral denoting alignment of the column grid.

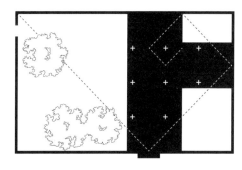

Figure 36: *Parti* diagram combining elements of two versions above.

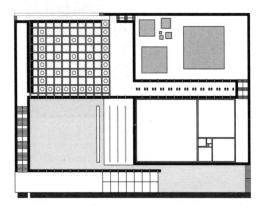

Figure 37: *Danteum, top level – Paradiso.*

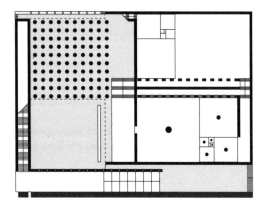

Figure 38: *Danteum, mid-level – Purgatorio.*

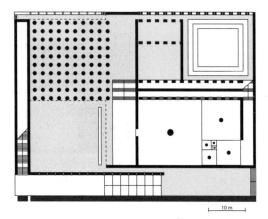

Figure 39: *Danteum, base level – Inferno.*

The Danteum

GIUSEPPE TERRAGNI, WITH PIETRO LINGERI & MARIO SIRONI, 1938
Like the *House with Three Courts*, the *Danteum* remains unbuilt. Yet, along with Mies van der Rohe's project, we recognize it as a significant milestone in the Modernist movement. Both projects combine a relatively restrained palette of form and material with a richly-layered use of ideal geometry. In the *House with Three Courts*, we might portray such geometry as playing a merely supportive role in the arrangement of the plan. With the *Danteum*, however, ideal geometry is intrinsic to the project's symbolic expression, and to the logic of its composition. And although we examine both projects as two-dimensional schema, we have placed them in a deliberate order: Mies' house is composed atop a single, horizontal plane, while Terragni's project unfolds around an ascending series of stepped tiers (37–39), a sequence that leads us into the more fully three-dimensional projects of the next chapter.

The *Danteum* was to be as a monument to Dante Alighieri. As 'father' of the Italian language, Dante's *oeuvre* was central to a nationalist mythology popularized in Italy under Fascist rule. His *Divine Comedy* was of particular significance to Benito Mussolini, for – among other things – the *Commedia* prophesied a resurrected Roman Empire, a central conceit for the Fascist leader. Giuseppe Terragni, founding member of the Rationalist *Gruppo 7*, seems a natural choice to design the *Danteum*, having previously garnered acclaim for the *Casa del Fascio* in Como. Yet, the actual commission came by way of his erstwhile collaborator, Pietro Lingeri, a college roommate of Rino Valdameri, the influential Milanese lawyer and academic who was also the principal sponsor of the *Danteum* project.

The premise for Terragni's design is an allegorical journey drawn from the story line of the *Commedia* itself, from the 'rough and stubborn forest' of its opening stanzas, through its three primary volumes: *Inferno, Purgatorio* and *Paradiso – Hell, Purgatory* and *Paradise*. Yet, apart from the program of figural reliefs that Mario Sironi designed for the otherwise blank street facades (40), Terragni chose to evoke this epic narrative with an austere kit of the most basic elements of architecture – vertical and horizontal planes, columns and apertures.

Proportional systems

This simple set of physical elements was arranged using the ordering elements provided by ideal geometry. Principally, this entailed the adoption of three rectangles: equilateral (square), $\sqrt{2}$ (ROOT 2, or the LICHTENBERG RATIO, approximately 1:1.414) and ⌀ (phi, or the golden ratio, approximately 1:1.618). With this strict set of ratios, Terragni developed a richly woven tapestry of proportional affinities. In one sense, such geometries draw from the broadest traditions of architectural composition. Although we trace their origins back to Theano of Thurii and beyond, the history of their use, from Vitruvius through Alberti and Palladio, continued well into the twentieth century. This includes Terragni (the *Casa del Fascio,* among others) and his contemporaries, Mies van der Rohe (as above) and Le Corbusier (his *Modulor* derived in part on the Fibonacci sequence).

At the same time, Terragni's reliance on the geometric properties of these rectangles was also tied to references specific to the *Danteum* project itself, drawn from the symbolic structures of the *Commedia*, and from the particularly rich context of the project's location (42). The proposed site lay along the Via dell' Impero ('Street of the Empire', now the Via dei Fori Imperiali), the broad, straight avenue that Mussolini carved through the ancient center of Rome, establishing an axis between the Colosseum and his offices in the Palazzo Venezia. Across the intersection with Via Cavour stood the *Torre dei Conte*, a medieval tower dating back to Dante's lifetime. More significantly, the *Danteum* sat at the edge of the Roman Forum, an assemblage of vast civic spaces and structures whose remnants provided the backdrop for Mussolini's own imperial ambitions, and whose architecture demonstrated the ubiquitous role of proportions found in Terragni's design. It was from the golden section nested within the *Basilica of Maxentius* – its hulking mass lies directly across the Via dell' Impero – that Terragni derived the footprint of the *Danteum* (41).

Equilateral rectangle

The square (43) not only serves to generate the proportions of the other two rectangles in play, it has a fundamental role in the geometric underpinnings of the project. In the text that Terragni composed to explain the formal logic of his proposal, he refers to the 'square constructed from the minor side' as the 'most easily perceived characteristic of the work.' A second square occurs 'where the frontal wall is displaced in front of and parallel to the major side of the golden rectangle', a shift that also creates the narrow, vertiginous passage along the front facade that serves as the entrance to the building (46). The spatial compression of this passage gives way to an expansive forecourt, bounded by high walls that yield to the open sky above.

Beyond the brilliant daylight of the court lies a densely massed square portico, ten rows of ten columns that initiate the narrative sequence. In the *Danteum*, as in the underlying structure of the *Commedia* itself, numbers carry symbolic associations. Here, the one hundred columns embody the hundred cantos of the epic, comprising thirty-three cantos for *Inferno*, *Purgatorio* and *Paradiso* alike, with one additional canto at the outset of the *Inferno* – the very place where Dante begins his journey amid the ominous shadows of the Dark Wood, manifested by this self-same forest of columns. Directly above, at the uppermost level of the *Danteum,* a crystalline array of the thirty-three columns-as-cantos of *Paradiso* fills out a squared precinct aligned with the century of columns below.

Figure 40: *Danteum*, physical scale model, courtesy of Jaymon Diaz.

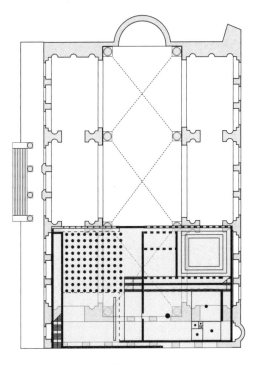

Figure 41: Nested proportions of the *Danteum* and the *Basilica of Maxentius*.

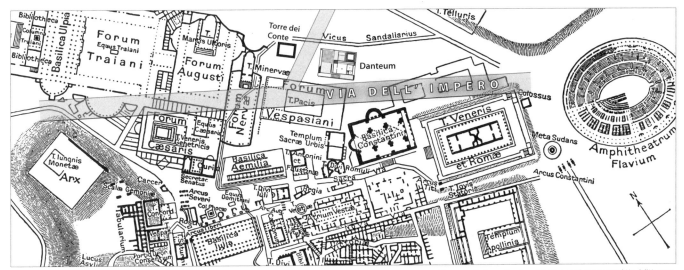

Figure 42: *Danteum* site, along the then-newly constructed *Via dell' Impero* – now *Via dei Fori Imperiali* – across from both the *Basilica of Maxentius* (here labelled *Basilica Constantini*) and the medieval *Torre dei Conte*.

Figure 43: Square – 1:1.

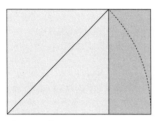

Figure 44: √2 rectangle – 1:1.414....

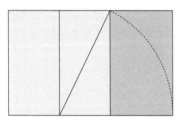

Figure 45: Golden rectangle – 1:1.618....

The square also appears in the pair of identically scaled rooms that comprise the first two volumes of the *Commedia* proper: *Inferno* features a cascading group of square ceiling slabs, each independently held aloft by a single, centered column, the diameter of which is scaled to the corresponding mass of the cantilevered slab above. *Paradiso* features a corresponding group of square apertures that pierce its ceiling to reveal framed views of the Roman sky, providing brilliant contrast to the crepuscular interior of *Inferno*. Both sets of squares derive from the geometric construction that defines the proportions of their respective rooms, each set demonstrating the distinctive infinite spiral that characterizes the irrational ratio of the golden rectangle.

√2 rectangle

While the golden rectangle produces the distinctive telltale sign of its DNA, an algorithmic spiral, the √2 rectangle (44) produces an equally distinctive signature through its capacity to infinitely split itself into self-same couplets, the geometric equivalent of mitosis. It is the same irrational ratio which provides the international paper size standard – ISO 216 – a scalable format allowing for the efficient folding of sheets to make pages that maintain their original proportions without need for trimming and waste.

If we imagine the footprint of the *Danteum* extending outward to the monolithic wall directly adjacent to the Via dell' Impero, we can identify it as a √2 rectangle (47). As such, it follows that the division of this footprint aligns precisely with the perpendicular wall dividing the plan in half, resulting in two further √2 rectangles. A further examination of the plan uncovers additional use of the √2 ratio (48). The forecourt sponsors one, which divides itself in two along the horizontal centerline of the building's footprint. The proportions of the plan of *Inferno* that extend to the same centerline in the library similarly describes a √2 rectangle, which further distinguishes the office and archives from the larger reading room.

Golden rectangle

The most significant recurring figure in the design of the *Danteum* is the golden rectangle (45). In his accompanying text, Terragni describes his search for a shape that:

> would imprint, through the happy relation of its two dimensions, that value of absolute geometric beauty onto the entire structure of the monument; this being the tendency of the exemplary architectures of the great historical epochs.... These peoples have left behind typical examples of rectangular plan temples in which the golden rectangle is used; and most often composed with numerical relationships as well.*

Terragni's myriad references to the geometric practices of ancient empires were as likely motivated by the contemporary context of Fascist rule as they were by the rich historical context of the *Danteum* site. Though tolerant of the Modernist precepts of order and efficiency, Fascist 'principle' dictated that architecture assert traditions and values native to Italic civilization, in opposition to the cosmopolitan, internationalist inclinations of Modernism. Terragni was well aware of the necessity of invoking historical precedent.

By aligning the *Danteum*'s proportions with those of civic and sacred monuments of past empires, and through numeric concordance with the structure of the *Commedia* itself, Terragni attempted to persuade Fascist authorities of the historical allusions underpinning the geometric severity of his design, without need of the overt historicist bombast that characterized much of the

* *Relazione sul Danteum*, Giuseppe Terragni; translation by Thomas Schumacher, in *The Danteum*, 1985.

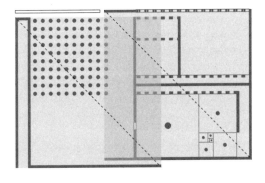

Figure 46: The primary square is dimensioned by the width of the building's footprint. Its twin is delineated by the displacement that forms the narrow entrance passage along the front facade.

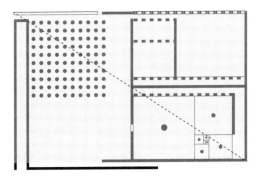

Figure 49: The primary golden rectangle. The displacement created by the entrance passage 'fractures' the rectangle into the two primary squares (46).

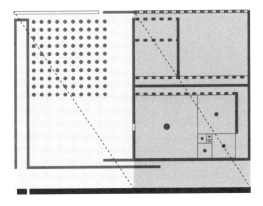

Figure 47: √2 rectangle of the site footprint, which divides itself (and the plan) equally into a pair of half-sized √2 rectangles.

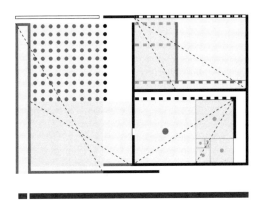

Figure 50: Nested golden rectangles, indicated by their primary diagonals.

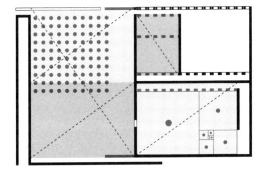

Figure 48: Subsequent √2 rectangles defining further subdivisions of the plan.

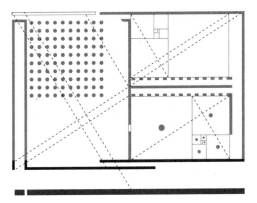

Figure 51: Further enmeshed groupings of golden rectangles.

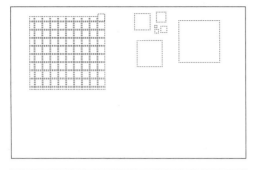

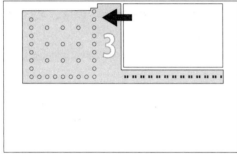

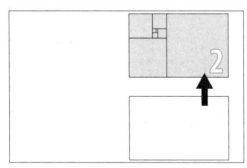

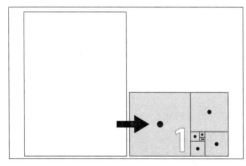

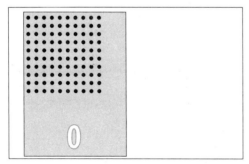

Figure 52: Flat-pack diagram illustrating the processional sequence of the tiered floor plan of *Danteum*.

work of his contemporaries. The *Danteum* is rife with proportions determined by the golden ratio, most notably in the footprint of the project itself (49). Sets of nested golden rectangles exist throughout its primary spaces (50 & 51).

Among the geometric properties intrinsic to the golden rectangle is the logarithmic spiral formed by the ratio, denoted by the Greek lowercase letter *phi*, or ⬚. For Terragni, this provided a powerful yet simple evocation of the shrinking spiral of Dante's *Inferno*, its stepped circles descending toward the abyss. Just as the coiled path ascending *Purgatorio* mirrors the downward helix of *Inferno*, the shallow spiral ascent of Terragni's *Purgatorio* is the symmetric obverse of the stepped descent of his *Inferno*. The ratio ⬚ constitutes, like its close cousin √2, an irrational number – a ready allusion for Terragni to the infinite, and to the incommensurability of the divine. The primary mathematical confirmation for irrationality is the PROOF BY INFINITE DESCENT – *discesa infinita* – a term presumably not lost on the architect of the *Danteum*.

Procession & ascent

The primary spaces of the *Danteum* follow an ascending arc, aligned with the narrative structure of the *Commedia* itself. Though it borrows from the Modernist spatial penchant that we identified in the *House with Three Courts* as turned space or turned paths, the *Danteum* differs markedly with respect to circulation. Whereas Mies' project suggests a dispersed field of implied turned axes, the narrative that provides the *Danteum* with its symbolic significance determines a linear (albeit cyclical) PROCESSION in a prescribed sequence, modeled on the 'pilgrim's progress' of the *Commedia*'s narrative arc (52).

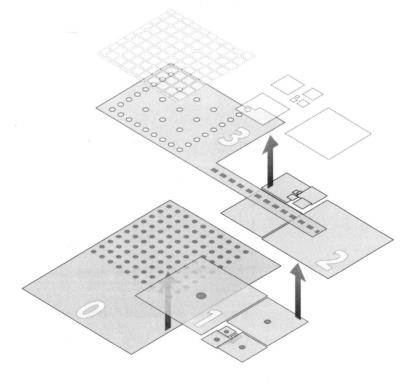

Figure 53: Isometric diagram illustrating processional sequence of tiers in *Danteum*.

For our purposes, the *Danteum* highlights another important distinction from Mies' project: his *House with Three Courts* occupies a single, flat plane. In a sense, it is a strictly two-dimensional composition, whose section is almost entirely a simple extrusion of its plan. Although the geometric tactics of the *Danteum* are primarily planimetric, the vertical axis is intrinsic to its compositional strategy (53). As such, Terragni's project occupies a distinct position between the two-dimensional diagram and the volumetric diagrams we examine in the next chapter.

Parti

Earlier, we described *parti* as a singular evocation of a project's Big Idea. We also stated that with any project containing a multiplicity of operations and concerns (as most do), this does not suggest that there can only be one, definitive, expression of the *parti*. Such is the case with the *Danteum*, even with its limited palette of formal and material means.

Adopting a simplified plan-with-overlay, our first version of the *parti* foregrounds the essential figure of the golden rectangle, which governs the basic footprint of the project (54). A pair of squares mark the rift creating the narrow entrance passages at the front and rear of the building. A second version of the *parti* distinguishes between the golden rectangle and the √2 section (55). While dashed diagonal lines denote the golden ratio in the first *parti,* here the diagonals mark the presence of a nested sequence of √2 rectangles. Golden rectangles proceed from the sequences of squares found within the quadrants associated with *Inferno* and *Purgatorio*.

A third *parti* combines the proportional relationships of all three primary figures in the composition: square, and √2 and golden rectangles (56). Here, two tactics enhance visual clarity. First, rather than using a plan-with-overlay, we opt for a simplified abstraction – the only vestige of the original plan is the freestanding wall that faced the Via dell' Impero along the lower edge of the composition. Tone is added to line to create clear distinctions among the three principal geometric figures: the primary √2 rectangles in the plan – the overall footprint defined along its lower edge by the freestanding wall, and that of the forecourt containing the forest of columns; black lines – both solid and dashed – indicate the various iterations and subdivisions of the golden rectangle; finally, a pair of thickened gray lines depicts the shifted squares derived from the first *parti* (54).

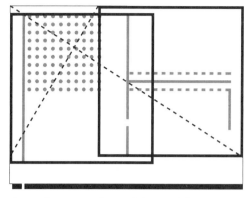

Figure 54: *Parti esquisse 1* – foregrounds the essential relationship between the golden rectangle of the building footprint, and shifted squares.

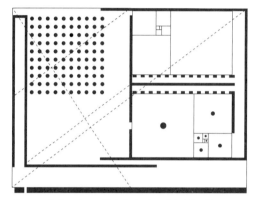

Figure 55: *Parti esquisse 2* – illustrates fundamental relationships among both √2 and golden rectangles.

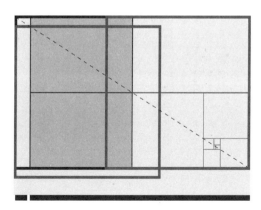

Figure 56: *Parti esquisse 3* – perhaps the simplest evocation of the three fundamental proportions governing the composition: square, and √2 and golden rectangles.

GLOSSARY OF TERMS

ASSEMBLAGE: A number of things gathered together; a collection, group, cluster.

CANON: In the sense in which we use it here, a list of literary or artistic works established by long-standing practice as being of the highest quality. More generally, the term describes a general law, rule, principle, or criterion by which something is judged.

CARTESIAN GRID: Also called a universal grid, it represents infinite lines that cross one another at right angles at regular – sometimes numbered – intervals to precisely locate and measure objects and space.

CONCEPT: An abstract idea or mental picture of a group or class of objects, formed by combining all their aspects.

CONTRAST, REPETITION, ALIGNMENT and PROXIMITY: The four fundamental attributes of visual phenomena, according to gestalt theory of perception. See main glossary for definitions of individual terms.

ENCLOSURE: That which is contained within defined boundaries.

ENFILADE: A suite of adjacent rooms with aligned doorways or other openings.

ESQUISSE: From the Italian *schizzo*, for sketch, the initial sketch or thought of a design. Used in conjunction with PARTI.

EXPRESSION: Manner or means of representation. The process of manifesting qualities by appearance or other forms of evidence.

EXTERNAL ASSEMBLAGE: One of two general expressions of the design process, the other being INTERNAL DIVISION; also defined as complexity without or outward accretion.

FIBONACCI SEQUENCE: A sequence of whole numbers in which each number is the sum of the two preceding numbers: 1, 1, 2, 3, 5, 8, etc. As the sequence continuos, the ratio of each Fibonacci number to the previous one tends toward the GOLDEN RATIO.

FIGURE: Descriptive shape or form that appears in contrast to a visual ground – as in FIGURE-GROUND. Also used to refer to any distinct element in a composition.

FREE PLAN: A floor plan with non load-bearing interior partitions. A product and conceit of Modernist architecture, wherein a structural frame relieves the exterior envelope and interior walls from supporting a building's mass.

GOLDEN RATIO: An irrational mathematical constant, approximately 1.618, its geometric expression – the golden rectangle – has traditionally been considered aesthetically pleasing since Greek mathematicians first described it. Other names and symbols frequently used for the golden ratio are the golden section, golden mean and the Greek letter PHI.

INHABIT: To dwell in, occupy as an abode. To permanently or habitually live in, to reside in.

INTERNAL DIVISION: One of two general expressions of the design process, the other being EXTERNAL ASSEMBLAGE; also defined as complexity within or inward articulation.

ISO 216: International standard for paper sizes derived from the ROOT 2 or LICHTENBERG RATIO.

MODULE: Standard unit of measure or proportion used in the design of a particular project. The module can be a unit of length, area, or volume.

OCCUPATION: The action or fact of living in or using a building or other space.

PARTI: A diagram that delineates the dominant organizational or formal concept governing an architectural scheme. From French, translates roughly as 'option' or 'course of action' – what we might call the Big Idea.

PHI: Greek letter used in modern mathematics to symbolize the GOLDEN RATIO.

PRECEDENT: An example to be followed or copied. In architecture, an exemplary project, usually influential and closely studied, and often emulated.

PROCESSION: The action of moving forward in orderly succession in a formal or ceremonial way.

PROGRAM: A project-specific list of spaces and functions created to guide and govern the subsequent design of a building.

PROOF BY INFINITE DESCENT: A type of mathematical proof used to establish the existence of irrational numbers.

REPETITIVE UNIT: Module or some other component defined by its multiple iterations.

ROOT 2 or LICHTENBERG RATIO: The positive algebraic number which, when multiplied by itself, equals the number 2; an irrational number approximately equal to 1.414. The length of a diagonal across a square with sides one unit in length.

TURNED PATH: A common MOTIF of Modernist architecture, in opposition to traditional linear axiality.

TURNED SPACE: A common MOTIF of Modernist architecture, characterized by an iterative, peripatetic, yet fluid unfolding of a building's spaces.

OVERVIEW
Further precedents

In this chapter, we go beyond the world of two dimensions, to enter the realm of volumetric diagrams. For as long as architects have drawn, two-dimensional projection has been the predominant mode of representation, for obvious reasons: such drawings have been far simpler to generate than three-dimensional views, and such diagrams have communicated more easily to a broad audience. The advent of powerful and increasingly intuitive digital tools has closed this gap, permitting the rapid and nimble generation of virtual models that generate paraline and perspective views.

Beyond this, sophisticated animation software will soon provide a widespread facility for creating robustly manipulable digital modeling, capable of supporting highly interactive and as yet unexplored modes of diagramming. None of this suggests that any of these will supplant the value of established forms of two-dimensional diagrams. Just as new modes of representation in other fields serve to supplement existing media rather than replace them, as in the case of, for example, oil painting, photography and cinema, emerging methods of ordering visual knowledge will supplement rather than supplant traditional practices.

Introduction

For as long as architects have drawn, they have relied on the principle of ORTHOGRAPHIC PROJECTION. This, the primary form of architectural representation, places the observer perpendicular to the entire surface of an imaginary picture plane. Orthographic projection underlies the triad of drawing types used most frequently in the process of designing architecture: PLAN, SECTION and ELEVATION. Because of their close, symbiotic relationship with architectural drawings, most common forms of architectural diagrams, including those used in the previous chapter, also rely upon orthographic projection.

As shapes and tones arranged on a sheet of paper or a computer screen, drawings occupy an infinitely thin surface. Orthographic drawings, in addition to their material flatness, depict a flattened universe, devoid of any semblance of depth. Most diagrams are therefore doubly two-dimensional, derived as they are from orthographic drawings. For a pursuit so fully embodied in three dimensions, the observation that we primarily conceive and describe architecture in two – as plans and sections – might strike the casual observer as absurd. Yet, their very limitations make such drawings so versatile. Their flatness preserves scalar dimensionality throughout, while their relatively simple construction makes them an efficient tool.

Historically, drawings that simulate the three-dimensional reality of buildings occur in fewer numbers, relative to plans and sections. This disparity might suggest that architects have valued other modes of drawing less, but that conclusion would be false. PARALINE DRAWINGS, like ISOMETRIC and AXONOMETRIC projections, preserve the dimensional properties of orthographic drawings, while adding a semblance of three-dimensionality (1). At the same time, since its invention – or discovery – in Renaissance Italy, linear perspective has provided architects and artists with an infinitely malleable form of ostensibly naturalistic representation.

Such forms of architectural projection have always been more time-consuming to draw. As such, they were less suitable for the purposes of construction; a process that demands a large number of highly detailed, dimensioned and notated drawings, all subject to ongoing revision. Only recently, with the arrival of sophisticated computers, have architects been able to generate three-dimensional representation as readily as plans and sections. The advent of parametric digital tools promises to take this process one step further, reversing centuries of established practice: as in the Renaissance, the MODEL – now digital – will regain its status as the primary means of conveying the

Figure 1: Detail from the *Baths of Caracalla*, from *L'Art de Bâtir chez les Romains*, Auguste Choisy.

Figure 2: *St. Peter's Basilica*, Rome. Original model of Michelangelo's design for the dome, in painted wood, 1:15 scale.

design intentions of the architectural project, with orthographic drawings relinquishing their current status.

Representing the third dimension

The relationship between two-dimensional drawing and three-dimensional reality is so intimate that we often forget that they are not the same. This is not merely a question of media, it also represents a perceptual and intellectual reality. Orthographic drawings and diagrams are highly purposed – we construct them to make a point, and exclude anything that does not serve that goal. This accounts for why they are routinely in black and white. Three-dimensional renderings and models are more generous: because of their greater illustrative capacity, they are more likely to show us things we have not anticipated. An interior perspective reveals a different, ostensibly 'naturalistic' – though equally abstracted – view of a building's interior than a section (3&4). Models provide even greater contrasts: they embody multiple points of view on a continuum, including views that are unlikely to be experienced in the full-scale reality of the building (2).

We teach our students about three-dimensional modeling using diagrams precisely because of their broad range. We have a particular interest in harnessing the suggestive power of the model's mutability, not only for its nuances, but also for the purposes of ongoing analysis. Nuance translates in many ways into ambiguity. That is, we make models with a particular purpose in mind, but we can also train ourselves to step back from the model and discover relationships we neither intended nor suspected. A schematic model held in the hand can rotate infinitely, and when it does, it acts within a luminous world of changing contrasts and emphasis.

The primary reason for the re-ascendance of the model in architectural practice is self-evident: once its inherent advantages are realizable for the purposes of construction, BIM – Building Information Modeling – provides a more fully integrated design process than the inevitably more haphazard process of coordinating sets of two-dimensional drawings. Parametric modeling is particularly advantageous with regard to the integration of a building's myriad systems – mechanical, electrical, plumbing, etc. – developed by teams

Figure 3: *St. Peter's Basilica,* Rome. Sectional perspective illustrating interior scaffolding.

Figure 4: *St. Peter's Basilica,* Rome. Longitudinal section through basilica and Piazza San Pietro, after Carlo Fontana.

of engineers and contractors in tandem with the architect's design. Historically, each team generates its own set of construction drawings, all primarily orthographic plans and sections. A unitary, jointly developed BIM model can now provide immediate feedback to all members of the design team simultaneously, coordinating their efforts and indicating potential conflicts and errors in the various building systems earlier in the design process, reducing the number of costly and time-consuming mistakes throughout the process of construction.

For diagrams, the primary advantage to incorporating the third dimension is representational. The relationship between plan and section is conceptually orthogonal. It reflects the left-right, up-down, front-back nature of our embodied experience of reality. Drawing is referential to an intrinsically understood framework. Therefore the idea of axis and path, as well as its manifestation, is distinct in three-dimensional drawings and models. An arrow is a path marker. A three-dimensional rendering of path has more possibilities. It might be a plane, horizontal or vertical. It might be a volume: a tube or I-beam. A simple arrow limits itself to direction: its three-dimensional variations can carry greater nuance.

Owing to their distinct properties, choosing optimal modes of representation form a crucial part of a designer's methodology. An example of this is the so-called 'worm's-eye view', notably adopted by nineteenth-century architectural historian, Auguste Choisy (1). His was not a lazy choice: Choisy's representational preferences emerged with his desire to best reveal the material and constructional methods of Roman architecture. Paraline drawing enabled him to combine the precise scalability of orthographic representation with a workable facsimile of the intuitive spatial representation of linear perspective. The singular importance of vaulting in Roman architecture, its complex permutations permitted by the discovery of concrete, led Choisy to adopt a worm's-eye or 'under-side' angle to best reveal the essence, the Big Idea, contained in his diagrams.

Phillips Exeter Academy Library

LOUIS KAHN

As in the previous chapter, we will use two exemplary buildings as case studies for analysis. Here, our focus will be on three-dimensional diagrams. Both buildings examined here provide us with lucid examples of architecture conceived integrally as three-dimensional volumetric and spatial compositions, rather than the more common practice of simple vertical extrusion from the plan – think of most tract housing or office towers – or lateral extrusion from a typical section.

Kahn's *Exeter Library* is an ideal project to help us pivot from two- to three-dimensional analysis. Its apparent simplicity – a square plan, cubic in volume with a smaller cubic void centered within – allows us to grasp it fully, at a glance. Its ready identification with the basic courtyard plan – as we noted in CHAPTER 4 (79&80) – places it within a fundamental formal category, or TYPE. Its identity as a library makes its program and operation easily relatable – all of us, whether architects or not – implicitly recognize and understand what a library is, and how buildings might be arranged to facilitate their role as a library. Kahn betrays his training in the principles of Beaux-Arts composition with the clear sequence of circulation between principal volumes, most notably in the curved double staircase connecting the entrance vestibule and the full-height central court (5-9).

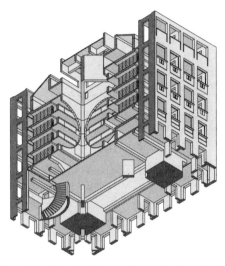

Figure 5: *Exeter Library,* Louis Kahn; worm's-eye sectional isometric in the manner of Auguste Choisy.

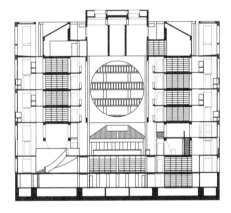

Figure 6: *Exeter Library,* section.

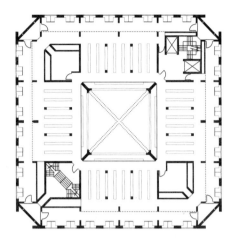

Figure 7: *Exeter Library,* typical floor, with perimeter reading carrels.

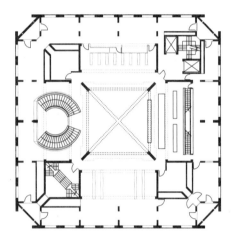

Figure 8: *Exeter Library,* main floor.

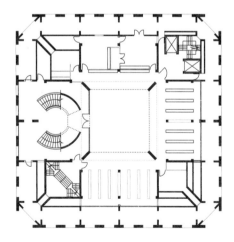

Figure 9: *Exeter Library,* ground floor.

That said, the formal clarity of Kahn's premise resonates beneath and beyond its apparent simplicity. Closer inspection and analysis with two- and three-dimensional diagrams yields a network of formal and spatial correspondences that dovetail so precisely, and reinforce one another so seamlessly, that the full extent of intentionality on the part of its designer remains exquisitely elusive to quantify. Nevertheless, a number of fundamental correlations – whether deliberate or residual – are significant enough to merit mention.

The fundamental figure-ground diagram reinforces the library's primary identity as a courtyard scheme (10). Closer analysis of the material and structural ordering of the plan reveals a cluster of concentric rings: an outer ring of brick masonry houses and supports the simple rubric of windows and open apertures found on the building's four near-identical facades (11). Discovering the 'front' of the building reveals its underlying subtlety. The entrance interrupts and encloses four bays of the ground-level ambulatory to form a foyer at the base of the curved stairs (9). Looped circulation paths occur on either side of the ring defining the building's concrete structure, coincident with the extent of the book stacks and the corner volumes containing vertical circulation and mechanical services (7, 11).

Once we identify the thirty-two foot square of the central court as a MODULE, we can easily identify two iconic diagrams, one self-evident, the other elegantly derived. Applying that square module across the plan readily yields a simple NINE-SQUARE tartan grid. The spacing of the twinned lines of the tartan grid is set by the width of the structural ring surrounding the central court and repeated by the width of the aisles separating the book stacks (12). Maintaining that same spacing, we can derive a series of squares and golden rectangles formed in sequence with one another, starting with the central square of the court, and moving outwards toward the square defined by the corner balconies (13&14). This linked pattern, a method of generating the golden ratio adopted by the École des Beaux-Arts, would have been familiar to Kahn.

The next pair of diagrams in our sequence demonstrates cruciform arrangements derived from the dimensions of the central court, which in turn reveal nested alignments throughout the geometries of the squared plan (15&16). The first reveals a pattern of doubled squares, completed by the perpendicular overlay of 1:2 rectangles. The outer edge of the resulting smaller double squares – identified here with diagonal lines – aligns with the centerline of the concrete structural ring containing the stacks (also seen in 19). The second reveals a similarly cruciform arrangement of two overlaid golden rectangles, with widths derived from the thirty-two foot module of the central court. Here, the outer perimeter of the cruciform aligns with three of the four edges defining the extent of the bookshelves in all four quadrants of the plan. Along the inner edge, it defines the centerline of the pairs of squared columns closest to the center of the plan; the flanks of the cruciform similarly align with the outer pair of bookshelves in each quadrant (16&19).

The diagram we label here as 'Cornered goldens' (17) comes closest to epitomizing the nested elegance of the plan. Here, we adjust the square module, now enlarged to include the structural perimeter of the central court. If we refer to the plan-with-overlay version of this diagram, shown in the previous chapter (8:2 p. 169), we see that the outer edges of the center square align precisely with the inner walls of the corner service volumes, as well as the outer edges of the diagonal columns supporting the courtyard roof. Light gray zones in the image describe pairs of golden rectangles (17). The common edge shared by each pair of goldens aligns with the vertical and horizontal centerlines of the plan.

Combined with one of the adjacent squares, shown in dark gray, each small rectangle forms larger golden rectangles, their width equivalent to the square center court module. The long side of each of the larger goldens defines half the width of the entire plan. Pairs of these larger rectangles overlap to share the four corner squares. The overall composition yields a nested set of eight large and eight small golden rectangles in a deceptively simple image (17). Meanwhile, the diagram we label 'Mezzanine goldens' demonstrates a related geometric relationship. Here, the golden cruciform from Figure 16 extends in the cardinal directions by an additional quartet of smaller golden rectangles, whose lengths equal the width of the original square module. The outer edge of this extended cruciform defines the square footprint of the mezzanine levels of the library, their outline indicated here by the dashed perimeter (18).

Finally, a plan-with-overlay diagram extends the original thirty-two-foot square module across a simple nine-square pattern (19). This module in turn generates a set of diagonals locating the squared quartets of concrete columns centered within each of the quadrants housing the bookshelves. The outer edge of this same nine-square figure locates the centerline of brick masonry structure identified earlier (11).

Though far from exhaustive, this set of planimetric diagrams outlines a comprehensive set of simple geometric relationships which almost certainly assisted with the evolutionary refinements of the library's plan.

Plan + section = isometric

So far, we have retraced the analytical steps laid out in the previous chapter. To allow for the transition to three-dimensional analysis, we begin by generating diagrams in section that corroborate and extend the discoveries we have made in plan. Taken together, plan and section then generate three-dimensional diagrams. Using *Exeter* to illustrate this process, we return to the most basic figures on this page (10–12). Each guides the generation of section and three-dimensional diagrams on the next two pages. To illustrate more clearly the fidelity to the actual building, we render the section diagrams as drawings-with-overlay. For greater clarity, the volumetric diagrams appear here as trans-

Figure 10: Figure-ground.

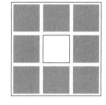
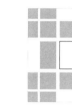

Figure 11: Concentric rings.

Figure 12: Nine-square.

Figure 13: Derived squares.

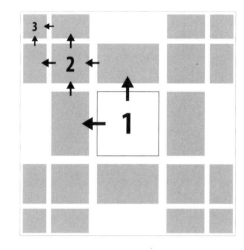

Figure 14: Derived squares, showing linked sequence of derivation.

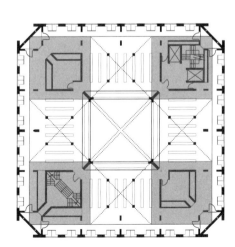

Figure 19: *Exeter Library;* plan with overlay, with thirty-two foot grid locating concrete columns and centerlines of perimeter masonry structure.

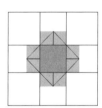

Figure 15: Doubled squares.

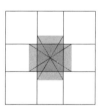

Figure 16: Golden cruciform.

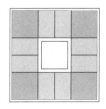

Figure 17: Cornered goldens.

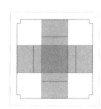

Figure 18: Mezzanine goldens.

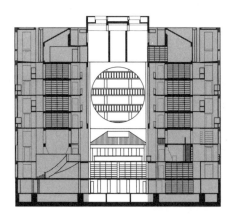

Figure 20: *Exeter Library;* section overlaid with basic figure-ground distinction.

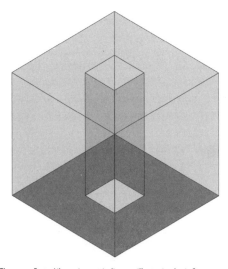

Figure 21: *Exeter Library;* isometric diagram illustrating basic figure-ground distinction.

Figure 22: Figure-ground.

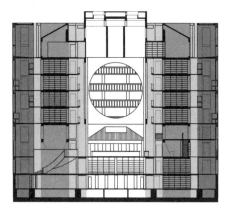

Figure 23: *Exeter Library;* section overlaid with concentric rings of structure and circulation.

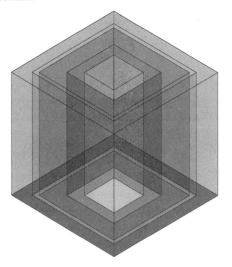

Figure 24: *Exeter Librar;* isometric diagram illustrating concentric rings of structure and circulation.

Figure 25: Concentric rings.

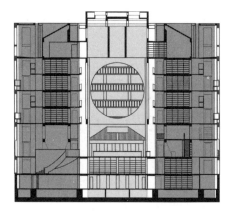

Figure 26: *Exeter Library;* section overlaid with main floor, illustrating alignments in nine-square of plan and section.

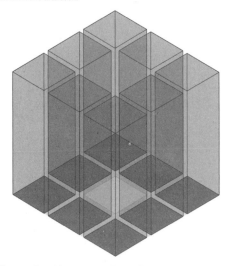

Figure 27: *Exeter Library;* isometric diagram illustrating alignments in nine-square of plan and section.

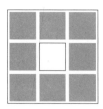

Figure 28: Nine-square.

lucent isometric images, visibly joining the three-dimensional extrusions to the underlying diagrams – from which they literally emerge.

When overlaid with the section, our basic figure-ground diagram (22) reiterates *Exeter*'s *parti* as a fundamental courtyard type (20). Extending upward from the main floor to its nine-square COFFERED CEILING, the court is distinguished by its signature circular openings. Carved from the shaft of *in-situ* concrete that defines its bounds, these apertures create an indelible visual connection between the center space and the library's collection. A pair of deep, diagonally crossed beams provide ample surface for deflecting baffled sunlight from the crown of clerestory windows into the heart of the building.

Figure 23 further illustrates the fundamental tectonic strategy articulated in the library's *parti*. Kahn defined both the central court and the inner 'ring' of book stacks and vertical circulation as communal space. Accordingly, he assigned its structure to monolithic, poured-in-place concrete. An inner peripheral path both separates and joins these two communal zones. A second looped path separates the inner ring from an outer circuit, defined throughout the library's floors by exquisitely detailed reading carrels. Kahn designed these intimate niches to emphasize this outer perimeter as space for the individual, fostering study and personal reflection. To provide emphasis for this spatial, programmatic distinction, Kahn chose load-bearing masonry to structure this outer ring, the hand-sized, aggregated units of brick perhaps representative of the shift in the scale of occupation along the library's outer walls (23–25).

As its plan makes plain, Exeter is a nine-square composition *par excellence*. Compare its array of eight squares surrounding a common open space with the city plans of Chengzhou and Albia, Iowa, in CHAPTER 3, p. 46. The nine-square figure (28) differs from the previous diagram (25) in that its paths form a simple network instead of closed loops, in a pattern reminiscent of an octothorpe (#) rather than the rings of a tree. This same form of order governs its section. Taking the thirty-two-foot width of the center space as its module, the section reveals a basic A·B·A·B·A rhythm running all the way up through the building, the interstitial space of the tartan nine-square defined by the width of the courtyard's vertical structure. Even for the two floors tucked beneath the level of the central court, the nine-square figure governs both plan and section, providing ample evidence of the thoroughness of Kahn's commitment to the library's *parti* (26–28).

Beyond the expression of *Exeter*'s section as a simple extrusion of the plan's nine-square (27), we can take the notion of this composition one step further, considering the figure vertically as well as horizontally. Superimposing plan and section, we immediately recognize that elements that appear at first glance to be discrete one-off gestures, likely link directly to one another. The most striking correspondence evident in the superimposition of plan and section is that of the entrance stair and the circular oculus of the central court, which appear to share the same diameter. The diagonal figure of the paired clerestory beams cross in the perfect center of the same oculus. Meanwhile, diagonals witnessed in the section – the entrance stair and the sawtooth roofline to either side of the central court – appear centered within one of four corner shaft spaces on the plan.

Examining the overlay, whether we agree or not on all of the possible correspondences in plan and section, we can feel confident in two observations: one, that in the design of *Exeter*, the nine-square was a thoroughly integrated compositional template, imaginatively embedded, and more than a facile gesture; second, the superimposition provides a vivid reminder of how fun-

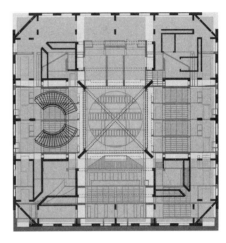

Figure 29: *Exeter Library;* section overlaid with main floor, illustrating alignments in nine-square of plan and section.

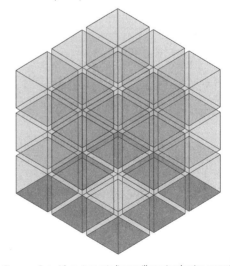

Figure 30: *Exeter Library;* isometric diagram illustrating the nine-square in cubic array.

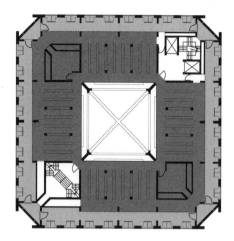 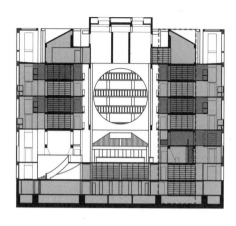

Figure 31: *Exeter Library;* plan with overlay: vertical and horizontal circulation.

Figure 32: *Exeter Library;* section with overlay: vertical and horizontal circulation. Dark tone indicates mezzanine floors.

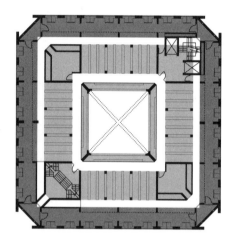 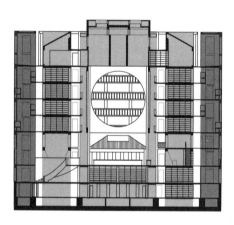

Figure 33: *Exeter Library;* plan with overlay: two rings of concrete structure with load-bearing masonry perimeter.

Figure 34: *Exeter Library;* section with overlay, illustrating concrete and masonry structural zones.

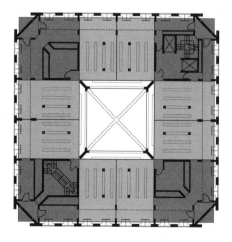 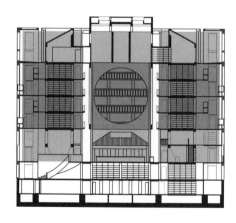

Figure 35: *Exeter Library;* plan with overlay: golden rectangles nested at corners.

Figure 36: *Exeter Library;* section with overlay: golden rectangles define the height of the central court, depth of diagonal cross-beams and thirty-two-foot cube.

damental is the practice of overlaying two or more images drawn on translucent paper – this is the reason why architects go through rolls of trace so quickly,part of the enduring legacy of the École des Beaux-Arts, the school in which Kahn's own teachers learned the discipline of design.

Three-dimensional anatomy

By adding further specificity to three-dimensional diagrams, we confront the same fundamental question raised for simpler, two-dimensional schema: when does a diagram become a drawing? Beyond the subtleties of distinction that we described in the first chapters, new issues arise with the addition of a third dimension. Most importantly, the challenge of visibility: along with the added issues for revealing what governs a design comes the difficulty of assigning priority to competing systems. The relatively new capacities of imaging software aid in these possibilities. Nevertheless the primary task remains the clear and telling image: diagrams that facilitate and demonstrate the anatomy of a Big Idea.

To demonstrate this practice, we return once again to the trio of ideograms that began our analysis of *Exeter*, this time in order to reveal some more specific attributes of the building. If we revisit our basic figure-ground diagram (22), we can add the pair of vertical circulation cores into the void of the central court (31). Further, by integrating the alternating pattern of mezzanine levels found in the section, we derive a three-dimensional image that clarifies the fundamental relationship of vertical and horizontal circulation in the design (32&37).

Continuing onto our second initial figure, concentric rings (25), adding plan-with-overlay to its companion section allows us to speculate about how a three-dimensional diagram might evolve beyond the simple extrusion shown in the previous section (33&34). Specifically, they provide the means to distill the tectonic essence of *Exeter*, isolating and revealing the structural systems embedded within each of the three primary rings of the initial ideogram. Visible at the building's core, the intersecting clerestory beams reach the ground via a quartet of slender piers set at the corners of the square court (38). Further out, our diagram reveals four pairs of concrete trusses that transfer the load borne by columns to the monolithic slabs flanking each row of bookshelves. Then, the outer ring: load-bearing masonry frames tower over the building's perimeter, its front-facing ranks omitted from the diagram to better reveal the inner workings of the concrete structure.

Finally, the nine-square: or rather, a project-specific version of this diagram-type that we call 'Cornered goldens' (17). The essence of this diagram is that it combines two compositional forms in one diagram, seamlessly integrating nested golden rectangles into a basic tartan-grid nine-square figure. As with the standard nine-square, the section-with-overlay of *Exeter* reveals a plausible role for this figure in shaping the arrangement of the section as well as the plan (35&36). More importantly, applying the geometry of the cornered goldens to a three-dimensional matrix generates a three-dimensional *parti* diagram, an elegant synopsis of the building's deceptive simplicity and a potent emblem of Kahn's formal virtuosity.

Figure 37: *Exeter Library;* isometric diagram illustrating vertical and horizontal circulation.

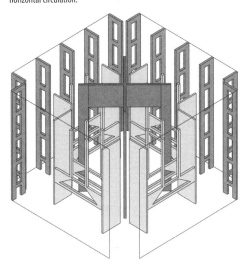

Figure 38: *Exeter Library;* isometric diagram illustrating concrete framework and load-bearing masonry piers (foreground piers omitted for clarity).

Figure 39: *Exeter Library;* isometric diagram illustrating vertical and horizontal interlocking of golden-rectangular and cubic volumes.

Figure 40: *Unity Temple,* Frank Lloyd Wright. (Below) longitudinal section.
(Bottom) main level plan.

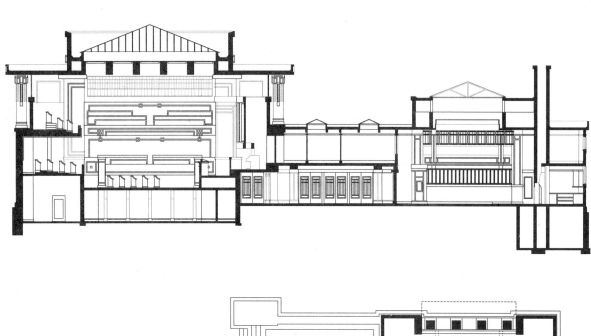

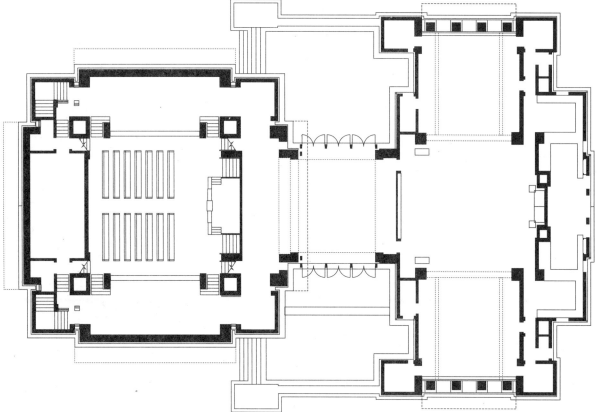

Unity Temple

FRANK LLOYD WRIGHT

With Kahn's library, we have explored strategies for three-dimensional composition within a simple geometric envelope. The lessons found in *Exeter* have relevance to a wider world of more complex forms. As an example, we now look to one of two projects by Wright underway in 1905 – a year as significant for modern architecture as it was for modern physics – the *Unitarian Universalist Church* in Oak Park, Illinois, more widely known as *Unity Temple.**

Much has been written on this building. For our purposes, we draw attention to Wright's characteristic use of a proportioning system, or module, based on simple, Platonic shapes. Use of the square governs Wright's early designs. One of his final Oak Park projects, *Unity Temple*, adopted a three-dimensional unit – the cube – as its fundamental module. Here, we note an almost uncanny connection between Kahn's library and Wright's church: at the literal and symbolic center of both buildings resides a thirty-two foot cubic volume, from which all other components and proportions appear to be derived (41).

We can trace the central presence of an identical cubic module to several potential origins. The first possibility is, as Wright scholar Robert McCarter has suggested, that of a deliberate *homage:* McCarter sees in Kahn's approach to design the abiding influence of Wright's methods for establishing order, despite the ostensibly disparate signatures that characterize their respective bodies of work. Like Wright, Kahn drew inspiration from primary Platonic volumes to establish clearly articulated spatial hierarchies, particularly in the overt distinctions both established in what Kahn referred to as served and service spaces. We see this similarity in the squared vertical extrusions placed at the corners of the central void in both *Exeter* and *Unity Temple*, which serve to combine structure, vertical circulation, and mechanical systems.

The cubic module shared by these two projects might have a more mundane explanation: thirty-two is a particularly easy-to-use multiple, its subdivision yielding whole numbers, particularly four and eight, which are well-suited to the operational arithmetic of construction and the standard dimensional units of building materials. Alternatively, it is possible that the presence of this common denominator is itself a mere coincidence, a happy accident of greater interest to geometers and numerologists than to the more sober analysis of architectural history.

Regardless of the source of the similarity, the common module for this pair of projects allows us to see how a unit, whether linear, planar or volumetric, can generate both an outwardly 'simple' composition like *Exeter*, and more complex geometric forms of *Unity Temple*. Wright's project demonstrates that even the most fundamental module – the simple cube – does not prevent the emergence of highly articulated formal invention. In fact, architects that routinely adopt the use of modules commonly argue that this practice enhances the possibility of enriched articulation precisely because it allows for such exuberance while maintaining clear relationships of parts to whole.

Fundamental diagrams

To begin our analysis of *Unity Temple*, we will retrace the process we have described in our previous precedent projects. Therefore we concentrate on the results of our analysis rather than describing methods for arriving at an appropriate set of diagrams.

*1905: ANNUS MIRABILIS

The other building was the *Larkin Administration Building* in Buffalo, New York, demolished in 1950. For physics, 1905 saw a 26-year-old Albert Einstein publish four papers, formulate the theory of special relativity and explain the photoelectric effect by quantization.

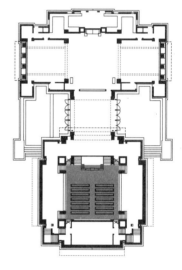

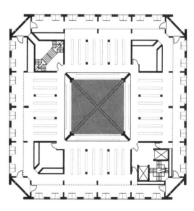

Figure 41: *Exeter Library* and *Unity Temple* at the same scale, showing identical thirty-two foot cubic volumes at the core of each project.

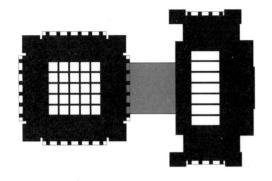
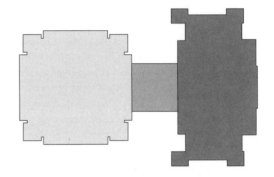

Figure 42: (Left) *Unity Temple;* figure-ground diagram.

Figure 43: (Right) *Unity Temple;* program. Left to right: Temple, loggia, Unity House.

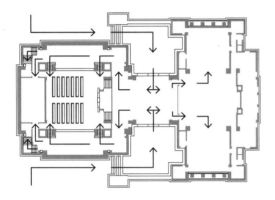
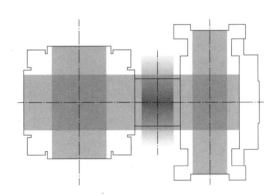

Figure 44: (Left) *Unity Temple;* turned paths.

Figure 45: (Right) *Unity Temple;* axes and paths.

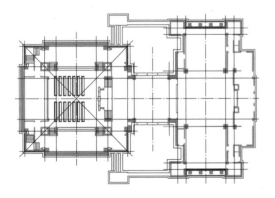
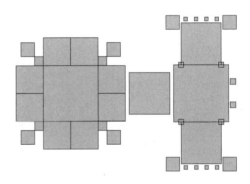

Figure 46: (Left) *Unity Temple;* regulating lines.

Figure 47: (Right) *Unity Temple;* derivation from cubic module.

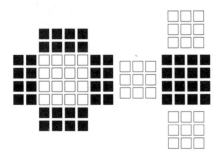
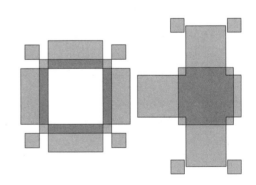

Figure 48: (Left) *Unity Temple; parti esquisse* 1.

Figure 49: (Right) *Unity Temple; parti esquisse* 2.

As before, we start with figure-ground, the fundamental condition of gestalt principles. The most basic figure-ground diagram of *Unity Temple* would reveal an essentially bipartite formal arrangement, the expression of the building's programmatic division: Unity Temple itself – the name sometimes given to the building's sanctuary space – and Unity House, containing meeting and support spaces for the congregation.

The figure-ground diagram shown here (42) includes an additional layer of information – the grid pattern of skylights and clerestory columns – to articulate the fundamental figural distinction between the cruciform of the sanctuary and the linear symmetry of Unity House. The gray tone of the entrance loggia further emphasizes the bipartite identity of the building's plan. Closely related, a program diagram establishes the clear division of defined usage or occupation within the plan, and reinforces the formal reading of the building's figure-ground relationship. Here, a simple outline suffices, with variation in tone clearly identifying *Unity Temple*'s three fundamental zones (43).

The next two diagrams reveal aspects of symmetry, balance and movement within the arrangement of the composition. The first of the pair (44) conveys patterns of circulation throughout the main level, from adjacent sidewalks, through the bilaterally symmetrical entrance to the building's loggia, and into each of its two principal spaces. The second diagram illustrates the primary axial alignments of the plan, largely matched by the path volumes therein (45). Together, what these diagrams illustrate is the presence of both classical and Modernist spatial motifs, as described in CHAPTER 8, pp. 177–8. Here, Figure 45 reveals a traditional cross-axial set of formal geometries that we characterized in our image of Palladio's *Villa Rotonda* (8:32; p. 177). At the same time, in the Turned Path diagram of *Unity Temple* (44), we see the same Modernist spatial motif that identified in Mies' *House with Three Courts* (8:29&30; p.177). This indicates that Wright's early work straddled two formal paradigms, one couched in the inherited axial traditions of Western classicism, the other expressive of an emergent modernist spatial sensibility.

Our next diagram, REGULATING LINES (46), might well be labeled 'grid lines', based on the nature of the composition's basic module. Regulating lines usually describe strictly proportional relationships – the kind we identified in both Mies' and Terragni's projects. With *Unity Temple*, relationships of parts to whole appear to derive from a universal, Cartesian grid – simple increments of the thirty-two foot square, rather than one based on relational proportions. Nevertheless, given that this module is applied primarily through subdivision, the traditional methods for deriving geometric figures usings diagonals and intersections renders the process sufficiently similar. The comparison diagram illustrates the recurrence of the square figure throughout the plan (47).

Finally, a pair of ESQUISSE diagrams describe two interpretations of the *parti* of Unity Temple. The first (48) makes use of an eight-foot square module, arrayed to demonstrate the fundamental proportional relationships of the building's two primary forms, both of which contain the primary thirty-two foot square spatial module at their centers. The four by four center of the sanctuary is flanked on its four sides by double-squared balcony spaces, while the four by four center of Unity House is flanked on three sides by nine-squares, all using the same eight-foot square module (48). The second *esquisse* diagram makes use of these same primary geometries, but adopts the use of continuous looped lines to achieve a more fluid effect, borrowing the Wrightian motif of extending lines beyond edges and around corners. This

Figure 50: *Unity Temple,* isometric solid-void diagram of Sanctuary interior: cruciform void squared by corner solids.

Figure 51: *Unity Temple,* interior view of Sanctuary, toward pulpit.

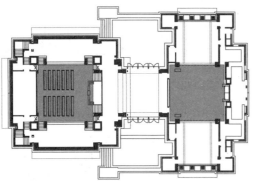

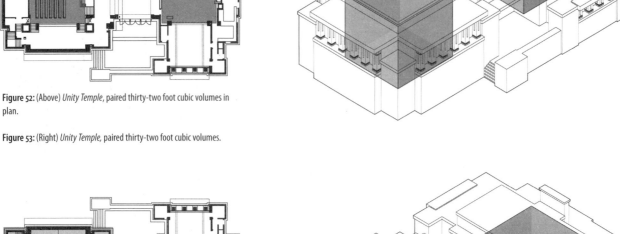

Figure 52: (Above) *Unity Temple,* paired thirty-two foot cubic volumes in plan.

Figure 53: (Right) *Unity Temple,* paired thirty-two foot cubic volumes.

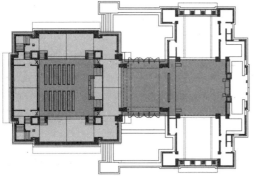

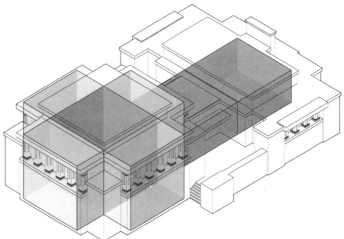

Figure 54: (Above) *Unity Temple,* thirty-two foot square and half-square volumes.

Figure 55: (Right) *Unity Temple,* thirty-two foot square and half-square volumes.

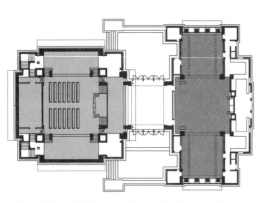

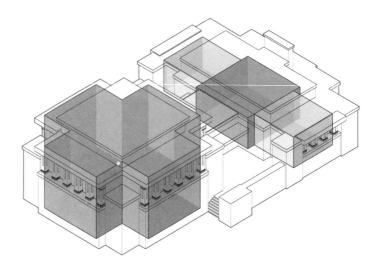

Figure 56: (Above) *Unity Temple,* cruciform and flanking squares in plan.

Figure 57: (Right) *Unity Temple,* cruciform and flanking cubic volumes

characteristic tactic aided Wright's attempts to achieve a sense of spatial continuity in his Prairie-period projects, an effect enacted at *Unity Temple* with lines of molding that perambulate across and around its interior surfaces.

Cubes in common

As we mentioned at the beginning of this section, *Unity Temple* adopts a cube as its module. As we might expect, three-dimensional diagrams lend themselves particularly well to the analysis of projects composed with volumetric units. Although the previous set of diagrams establishes the role that a square surface plays in the composition of the plan, and a similar set of sectional diagrams would achieve similar ends (58), paraline views, like the isometric diagrams on the opposite page have the obvious advantage of demonstrating the three-dimensional properties of a volumetric module more immediately.

The first in our set of three isometric diagrams establishes the doubled presence of the thirty-two foot cube in the composition (53). An equivalent section demonstrates the generally square proportions of the Unity House cross-section (58). It is, of course, significantly shorter than the entirely enclosed module inside the sanctuary; in fact, further analysis reveals that the principal ceiling height of Unity House is exactly half that of the sanctuary, thereby establishing a premise for the next diagram (55).

Here, half-modules align both vertically and horizontally, revealing two essential relationships: first, we recognize the center-edge arrangement of double-squares around the central module of the sanctuary (47&48, 54). If we add a further pair of double-square volumes, only this time laid horizontally, we generate the now self-evident role that the founding module plays in composing the connection between the building's two primary parts. The squared center of Unity House is spaced exactly one additional square from the sanctuary's cruciform perimeter.

That same cruciform provides the basis for our third diagram (57), which attempts to define a volumetric equivalent to our basic figure-ground diagram. As such, it distinguishes a second figure composed of a half-height module, flanked by squared volumes with sides three-fourths as long – twenty-four feet apiece. Here we deliberately omit defining the linking loggia, to allow for clarity of expression in the isometric view, although the addition of a third flanking volume with its matching lighter tone would yield a similar result.

In all, the images generated in this chapter demonstrate the intrinsic properties of three-dimensional diagrams. Essentially, once a designer develops the ability to generate three-dimensional representations – either manually or with digital tools – she can generate such diagrams almost as expeditiously as their orthographic counterparts. Their advantages appear obvious: they illustrate a fuller, more simultaneous impression of the volumetric properties of architecture, which is, after all, a fundamentally three-dimensional proposition.

These diagrams also have their drawbacks, particularly as long as we continue to define diagrams by their traditional, immobile media.* The peculiarities intrinsic to any form of representation that transfers three-dimensionality to the flat surface of a page – or screen – inevitably introduce their own set of biases and blind spots. Because the more overtly two-dimensional means of projection also have their own strengths and shortcomings, what constitutes the 'best' form of diagram cannot be determined simplistically. Rather than valuing one mode of diagramming above all others, optimal solutions arrive

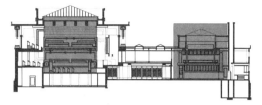

Figure 58: *Unity Temple;* paired thirty-two-foot cubic volumes in section.

Figure 59: *Unity Temple,* interior view of Sanctuary toward one of the corner piers.

*THE INTERACTIVE FUTURE

Diagrams are already frequently generated using interactive modes of representation, animating what until recently has been necessarily static and fixed. The idea that diagrams can now be made to respond to an observer's input is still so novel that it has yet to yield a general sense of their potential capacities.

on a case-by-case basis, determined exclusively by criteria attached to a specific project, and by the properties of its methods of analysis.

Diagram as generator

Over the course of CHAPTERS 8 & 9 we have analyzed a quartet of exemplary works of architecture. Precedent projects, or case studies, have a longstanding role in architectural education for several, complementary reasons. Above all, case-studies foster an active, analytical process of discovery, one that requires closer attention and yields deeper insights than mere passive observation. From these early, formative experiences, students may naturally come to associate the practice of diagramming with existing works of architecture.

While the analysis of completed projects is of enduring value to architects, the role that diagrams may play in the design process – in the development of new works of architecture – is even more important. In other words, diagrams as analytical tools are surpassed only by their capacity as generative instruments, capable of clarifying the intentions of a design, and revealing possible directions for its evolution and enhancement. The most significant lesson taught by precedent studies channels the insights gained in the analysis of existing projects in the realization of new works of design.

In *Toward an Architecture*, Le Corbusier declared that 'the plan is the generator.' We reply that the diagram is the generator. As we concluded in the first chapter of this book, the proof of architecture resides in its diagram.

GLOSSARY OF TERMS

BIM: Acronym for Building Information Modeling, a term that defines processes of generating and managing building data, generally achieved with the use of parametric modeling software.

COFFERED CEILING: A ceiling defined by an articulated relief pattern, usually conforming to an orthogonal grid determined by the spacing of primary and secondary spanning members.

ESQUISSE: From the Italian *schizzo*, for sketch, the initial sketch or thought of a design. Used in conjunction with *parti*.

MODEL: A translation of an idea or object into another medium, with particular characteristics for the purposes of study and analysis. Models place select properties into an appropriate framework.

NINE-SQUARE: A square array, three squares to each side; a common figure used in architectural composition.

ORTHOGRAPHIC PROJECTION: A drawing convention representing three-dimensional objects as two-dimensional; a form of parallel projection wherein projection lines are perpendicular to the picture plane.

PLAN, SECTION and ELEVATION: The three most common conventions employed to represent architecture, all using two-dimensional, orthographic projection. See main glossary for individual definitions.

TYPE: The general form, structure, or character distinguishing a particular kind, group, or class. In architecture, a taxonomy of buildings, using PROGRAM and function as primary criteria for classification.

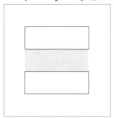  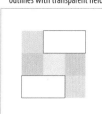 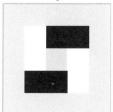 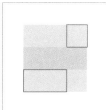  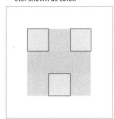 

CHAPTER **10**
Color & material in diagrams

First observations

The text thus far has relied on black and white images and diagrams. In practice, this is sufficient for effective communication. However, adding COLOR to the mix can introduce other options that are worth considering. In addition, diagrams are not always or even usually the product of either printing or design software. In an educational environment, what we now refer to as traditional media – pens, pencil, paint and collage remain the common tools for two-dimensional images. Physical models too, the utility of their virtual cousins notwithstanding, augment learning in ways unique to real materials. A desk full of made artifacts and images lends itself to conversations and shared experiences different from those found at an electronic desktop.

Three themes interweave in this chapter. The first locates and explores basic effects of material color in developing and understanding good diagrams. The second elucidates some potential benefits of materials used to present diagrams in three dimensions. The third theme guides beginning designers who read this book toward intelligent experiments in using color to make things clearer to themselves, their colleagues, students and critics.

Merging intellectual growth with relevant practical skills remains a central objective for beginning design projects. Each assignment should teach both content and means, and include relevant practice as part of its outcomes. To satisfy that criterion, our studio projects involve an integrated skill set as part of their learning sequence.

Initial encounters

The first project set, the content of CHAPTER 4, begins with drawing as a basic practice. The procedure for constructing the relational grid introduces students to careful line drawing and measurement. To render the figures in the compositions we turn to working with cut black paper. This decision brings with it a number of benefits. The results exhibit uniform visual contrast that supports the discussion of figure-ground. The use of collage also allows the introduction of measuring, cutting and adhering planar materials – modeling skills, however rudimentary.

Following that, we use cut YELLOW TRACE to represent fields within the composition. This brings with it the benefits of TRANSPARENCY and color to both the assignment and the virtual examples shown in the lectures. The practice, while not definitive in any way, allows for significant observation and discussion of the effects of material and material attributes on visual communication.

Figure 1: General diagrams of the first project with transparency and color – compare to Figure 28 (p. 65) in CHAPTER 4.

Diagram 1·1a: Figures as red outlines with transparent field.

Diagram 1·1b: Transparent field and blue ground.

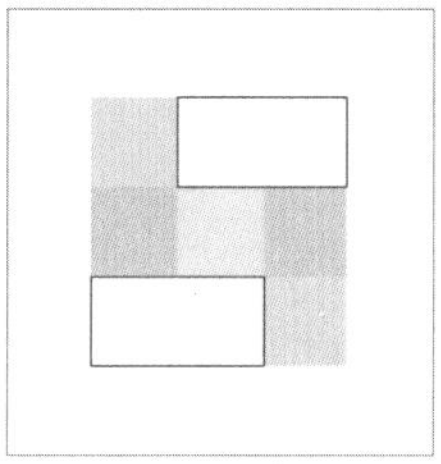

Diagram 1·2a: Transparent fields overlap.

Diagram 1·2b: Defined negative space rendered as white.

Diagram 1·3a: Defined perimeter shown as color.

Diagram 1·3b: Defined fields as overlapping transparencies.

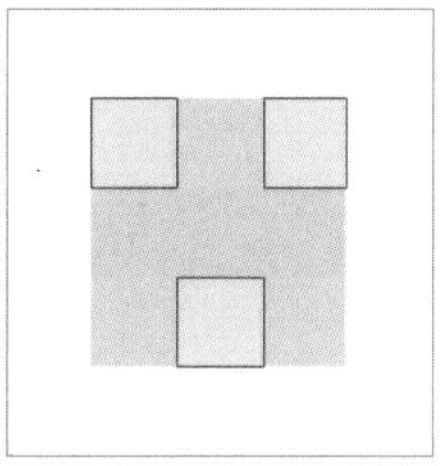

Diagram 1·4a: A different composition for comparison.

Diagram 1·4b: Defined fields overlap with negative space.

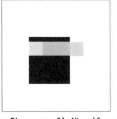 

Diagram 2·1 a&b: Aligned figures with defined and implied fields, either overlapping or discrete.

Diagram 2·2 a&b: Staggered figures with defined and implied field, either overlapping or discrete.

Diagram 2·3 a&b: Edge-aligned figures with defined and implied fields, either overlapping or discrete.

Diagram 2·4 a&b: Fitted figure example with defined and implied fields, either overlapping or discrete.

Figure 2: Diagrams show the four composition types – seen in CHAPTER 4 – with defined and implied fields rendered as transparent yellow trace.

This particular material PALETTE plays part in all of our first year projects, and is a staple for diagrams throughout the program. Observing the images to the left, the distinct character of the yellow trace harmonizes with the white ground and exhibits greater contrast with the figure due to its color (2·1–4). Aside from the relative ease of manufacture, the trace in the diagrams also has better visual affinity with the ground, acting as a filter to everything below.

In the lectures that support the assignments, color offers the potential for synthesized examples that demonstrate simple ideas pushed forward toward expressions that are more complex. In the example below, a number of defined and implied fields overlap to present a complex visual array of fields and figures (3). The intent is rhetorical, rather than practical. However, adding the red bounding lines prompts a discussion of what the project promises for future projects as well as providing a basis for summary remarks before embarking on the assignment at hand.

A first visual palette

The use of yellow trace is both part of a palette of materials and procedures and the first step in practical color. Relatively neutral in color – a result of its transparency – it also offers a basis for remarks on the choice of color in diagrams.

Beginning students, particularly those without a previous background in color or COLOR THEORY, are prone to use color in a symbolic fashion, without regard to the overall effect on visual clarity in their diagrams and illustrations. The opportunity offered by a profusion of diagram types is that the assets of good images – effectiveness and clarity – become a course-long discourse of

Figure 3: Fitted figure example with multiple defined and implied fields shown as overlapping. The fine red lines represent the bounding lines of the figures and contrast with the underlying black grid.

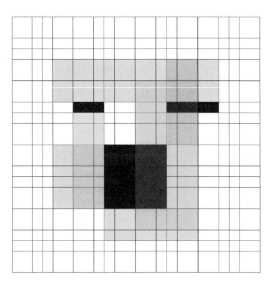

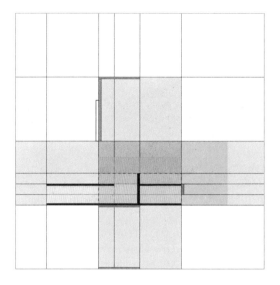

Figure 4: (Left) The plan diagram of quadrant one shows accrued fields as transparent trace overlays, horizontal planes as tonal variations and half-walls rendered as either white or gray.

Figure 5: (Right) The plan diagram of quadrant two showing the same kinds of elements as (4).

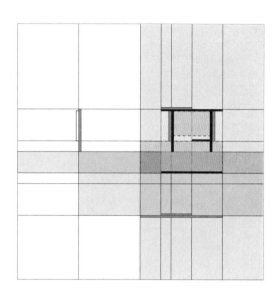

equal importance to the architectural premise of the class. Indeed, the second project overtly uses the same procedures, developing a sophisticated response to the visual field and its influence on design thinking.

The four plan diagrams shown here (4–7) use a hybrid approach to architectural representation. Aside from the continued use of yellow trace, we assign tonal grays as part of the drawing. The ground exhibits the lightest possible TONE, augmented by two transparent tones for the horizontal elements – floor and overhead – while additional half-walls receive the deepest tonal treatment. The original half-walls remain white and the *poché* is black.

The overall result is a diagram that represents process as well as design. It asserts a visual hierarchy, adding neutral tone to the emerging visual palette. The muted tones produced when the yellow overlaps gray fields – including the lightest shade of the ground – results in a sophisticated play of color. The dashed lines, marking planes overhead, correspond to tonal shifts in the overlapping planes. The entire diagram becomes visually coherent and rich as all the colors form a continuous visual pattern.

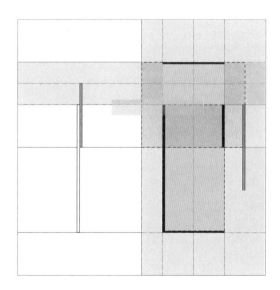

Figure 6: (Left) The plan diagram of quadrant three with similar elements types as (4&5).

Figure 7: (Right) The plan diagram of quadrant four reveals a complex use of fields, half-walls and overhead elements rendered as in (6).

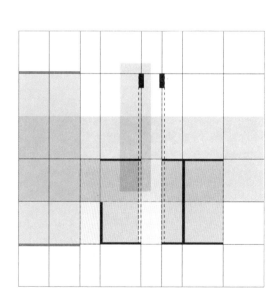

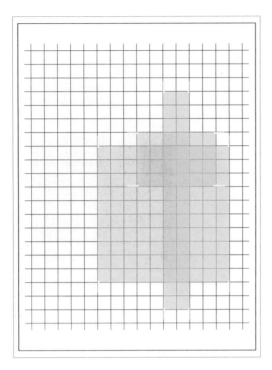

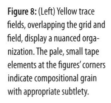

Figure 8: (Left) Yellow trace fields, overlapping the grid and field, display a nuanced organization. The pale, small tape elements at the figures' corners indicate compositional grain with appropriate subtlety.

Figure 9: (Right) Material color and shadow help clarify the illustration of perimeter orientation in the model on the right.

Color & materials

In three-dimensional work, materials can be diagrammatic as well as representational. Differences of surface and color can quickly communicate hierarchy as well as systemic design thinking. The cardboard of the model shown to the left, communicates solidity appropriate to its role in establishing volume (10). In contrast, the light-colored basswood and pale museum board play subservient roles in sorting through the resulting space.

In diagrams, lines drawn in pen or ink can render the articulated forms of a design, for example, lines of red and blue can differentiate boundaries from axes in a clear visual hierarchy (11). This of course is purely symbolic color, coded to identify different roles in a drawing or diagram. The palette of red, yellow, blue, black and white has a long history of use, dating from early scribal practice, when red ink was used to set hierarchy in text.

The original reasons for that practice are lost to us. However, it is clear that the materials – the inks – provided both means and opportunity. Both that history and our physical response to bright red – we see it first and forward of

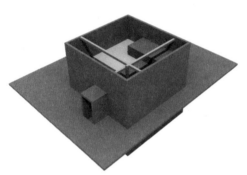

Figure 10: Virtual model representing three materials: cardboard, basswood and white museum board.

Figure 11: Elevation drawing with dashed lines in blue marking boundaries, and red solid lines indicating axes.

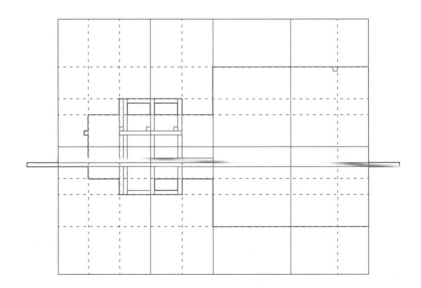

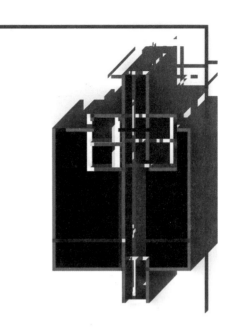

Figure 12: The red *poché* stands out in the rendered plan-section, separating the abstraction of section from the virtual reality of cast shadows.

other colors – makes it an ideal choice in denoting 'otherness' in images with diagrammatic intent. As with most *saturated* color, it tends to separate from its context and therefore works best when used for particular purposes in constructing images (12).

A plan diagram, with the usual black *poché,* is an ideal candidate for multiple overlays in analysis. Here we find real utility for the full gamut of color tactics. In the example below, we can easily separate section – solid black forms – from outline – black outline – to infer planimetric space (13). The red and blue lines easily sort out boundaries and axes without interfering with our comprehension of the design. Moreover, the yellow trace, being both planar and transparent, plays its role clearly in the form of speculations about fields, without insisting that they have actual physical presence in the composition. In this way, color is of particular merit in analytic diagrams during the design process.

This extreme form of differentiation works differently in three-dimensional models. Here color can separate elements according to purpose, and announce a quasi-rhetorical purpose behind the construction by creating visual groupings and alliances for clarifying a complex form. This strategy plays out in the work of several Modernist architects, influenced by the work of the DE STIJL group (1917–31). The connection to our discussion here is interesting, as it supports the inference that diagrammatic ideas about architectural form can survive into the actual construction. This plays out in the constructed diagrams for PROJECT 3.

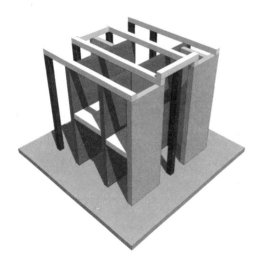

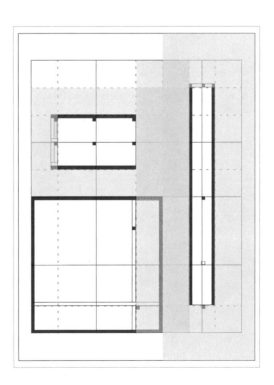

Figure 13: The black and white portions of the diagram (right) contrast with the multiple overlays of colored lines and fields.

Figure 14: Color in the diagrammatic model (left) identifies types of vertical tectonic elements: columns, parallel walls and cellular construction.

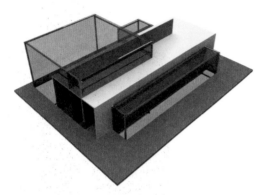

Figure 15: Diagram model #1 uses four materials – cardboard, chipboard, museum board and basswood – to identify different thematic ideas.

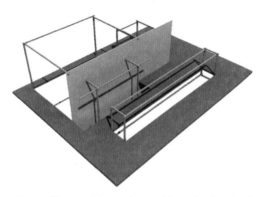

Figure 16: Diagram model #3 uses three materials – cardboard, mat board and basswood – to identify the base plane, grain and cross-grain space.

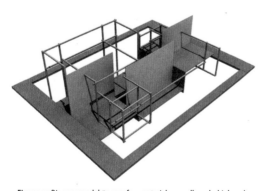

Figure 17: Diagram model #4 uses four materials – cardboard, chipboard, museum board and basswood – to identify different themes.

Color & materials in diagrams

As we have shown, color in two- and three-dimensional diagrams can follow one of two strategies. Diagrams can take their color from the materials or substitute an imposed color scheme. The advent of virtual models makes either scheme possible. Images obtained from such models therefore require serious consideration.

The models for the third project group offer ready examples of both approaches. The four models on this page (15–18) show the results of using colors that approximate those of common traditional model materials:

· White stands in for museum board.
· A pale tonal yellow – near to ochre – colors basswood elements.
· A light warm tan – a mid-tone burnt umber – approximates chipboard.
· Another mid-tone tan – slightly darker and with a touch of red – represents cardboard.

The renderings follow advanced protocol, exhibiting cast shadows from artificial sky illumination and bounced light. The results are spatially comprehensive illustrations rather than photographs of models. In the plan view, there is no perspective (18). Instead, contrived shadows provide clues of depth. In the other three models, the distinction between chipboard elements and cardboard – the base – derives distinction more from the thickness of the material than from the subtle difference in color.

As all four models represent diagrammatic analysis, the choice of a simple color scheme makes their function part of their execution. By limiting their correspondence to surface color without crossing over to complete mimicry, their rhetorical purpose becomes clearer.

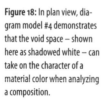

Figure 18: In plan view, diagram model #4 demonstrates that the void space – shown here as shadowed white – can take on the character of a material color when analyzing a composition.

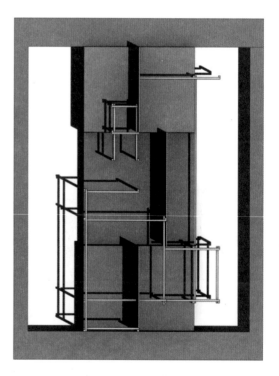

Coded color

In contrast, the images to the left and below use an abstract color scheme to underscore the nature of the constructional procedure. The three-axes rendered in red, yellow and blue (19) remind us that the x·y·z construction of the intersection derives from the work of the De Stijl group mentioned previously. The principle that material should align to an axis rather than occupying the center is at its heart a diagrammatic proposition rather than an easy means of construction.

Once introduced, the color scheme shows itself congenial to further use in analysis. In the section diagram shown, black and white play their usual roles of outline, *poché* and surface (20). The superimposition of transparent colors – red, yellow and blue – clarifies the relative position of the three originating forms, including the form bypassed by the section – the long blue rectangle. Following the general palette, red lines mark horizontal and vertical axes while dashed blue lines identify the boundary lines of the three forms. The use of related rhetorical color allows a diagram to both represent the section and identify the underlying structure that brings it about.

In a similar manner, the transparent model below (21) offers a view into the spatial and constructed logic of the result of PROJECT 3. Here the red, yellow and blue transparencies identify primary, secondary and tertiary deployment of planes within the scheme, representing the hierarchy of the design. The opaque white grid identifies the way that the linear elements support and follow from those decisions.

The colors and transparencies act as overlays to the physical form. They identify and amplify components and array, moving beyond the mere manifestation of form to display design thinking. They propose order to the elements embedded in the design declaring both intent and interpretation. In doing all that, they allow the designer to critique her work from another perspective

In a physical model or its virtual equivalent, material can play the same role. Rather than representing substance – brick, wood etc. – materials can visualize a formal hierarchy such as primary and secondary forms, or grain and cross-grain, as well as amplify distinctions between planar and linear elements. The model of a separated figures composition pictured (22) uses

Figure 19: Diagram model of the three cardinal axes rendered in red, yellow and blue.

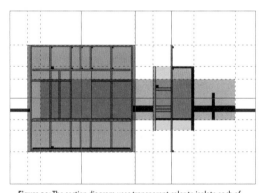

Figure 20: The section diagram uses transparent color to isolate each of three figures and coordinates with the existing palette of line colors.

Figure 21: The model uses a elementary color scheme to identify primary (red), secondary (blue) and tertiary (yellow) planes in a virtual hierarchy, all transparent. Frame structures, in contrast, are achromatic and opaque.

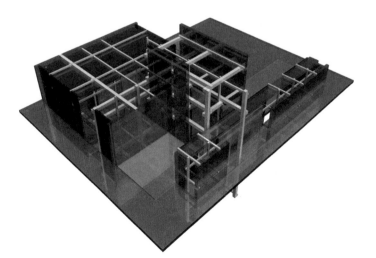

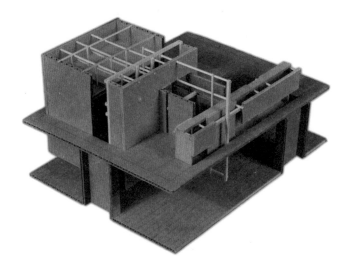

Figure 22: The model uses two planar materials to identify primary grain (chipboard) and cross-grain (cardboard) planes, and frame elements in the composition. The use of cardboard for the presentation base is a rhetorical decision that ties the cross-grain elements to the site plane.

cardboard, chipboard and basswood to identify correspondences among the three figures that rely on grain as an organizer of spatial hierarchy.

In the images below and to the left (23&24), we see a similar material scheme translated to visualize a tectonic scheme, this time in a virtual model from the same project. The colors identify a hierarchy within the spatial forms. Each of the three volumes presents its formal order, making the interrelationships among forms more apparent despite the model's overall complexity.

Unlike a monochromatic set of drawings, a model – with its obvious materiality – readily prompts a discussion about formal intention and execution. The primary vertical planes in (24) demonstrate an obvious formal gesture linking the large cubic volume to the long, narrow tubular form via the connecting vertical form. Other planar elements carry on adding enclosure and subdivision of spaces to the mix. In addition, the linear elements articulate the proportional scheme that underlies and articulates the entire composition.

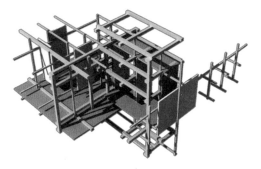

Figure 23: The virtual model fragment above mimics two planar materials to differentiate primary internal planes (chipboard), secondary interior planes (white mat board) within the frame elements of the composition.

Figure 24: The virtual model fragment on the right mimics three planar materials to differentiate primary planes (cardboard), secondary planes (chipboard), tertiary planes (white mat board) and frame elements in the composition.

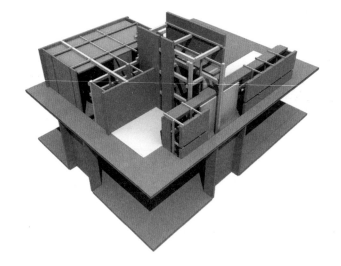

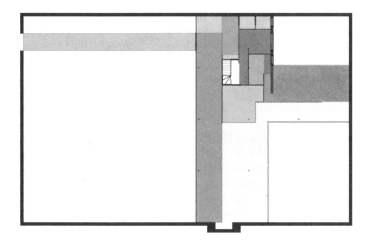

Figure 25: Color allows us to distinguish a more intricate reading of the turned space diagram of Mies' *House with Three Courts.*

Color in analytic drawings

In the same way that material can enhance clarity in a model, color can also enrich the two-dimensional analysis of three-dimensional space and form. Images composed of colored elements open the potential for a richer reading in which each color identifies a distinct theme or category – as materials do in the previous models (23&24). In drawings, however, the potential of color transcends the role of simply identifying material form and offers the possibility of articulating immaterial space as well.

In the diagram above of Mies van der Rohe's *House with Three Courts,* the analysis of turned space seen earlier in CHAPTER 8 (29, p.179) benefits from the addition of color in a number of ways (25). First, we can more readily identify each 'turn' by its color. Second, transparency adds a more precise rendering of overlapping space. In addition, multiple colors allow for a more detailed and numerous depiction of the L-shaped motif as it plays across the design.

When a building includes changes in elevation, layered and volumetric drawings can help sort through spatial relationships within the plan. In our earlier discussion of Terragni's *Danteum,* sequential plans together with a grayscale isometric drawing illustrated the complex series of ever-rising spaces. With the addition of color, the isometric can also better illustrate the narrative idea behind the spatial order (26).

Beginning in the green forest, the poet's journey through Hell (red) and Purgatory (orange) and ending in Paradise (blue) makes more visual sense in color. In addition, the unattainable level uses purple, the Tyrian dye of royalty, as a visual clue to the divine. The vertical arrows also use color to show movement, fading from departure to arrival along the poet's path. Although the drawing in the diagram remains the same as in the grayscale version, color allows details such as the added text, and underscores variation in columns and frames and their roles in the narrative of the building project.

Other color schemes

The *Danteum* is a rare example in architecture in which the building embodies a completely independent narrative – Dante's *Divine Comedy.* In most buildings, program dictates form – either in specific detail, or by general function. However, in those buildings color can also help reveal the diagrammatic

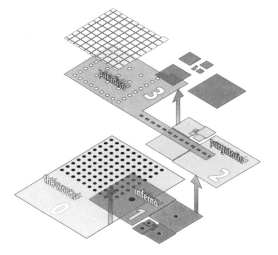

Figure 26: Color clarifies the spatial sequence of floor plates in the interior of Terragni's *Danteum.*

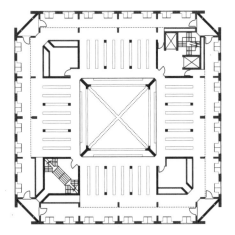

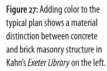

Figure 27: Adding color to the typical plan shows a material distinction between concrete and brick masonry structure in Kahn's *Exeter Library* on the left.

Figure 28: Added color distinguishes the mezzanine (darker ochre) and vertical circulation (lavender) within the typical plan on the right.

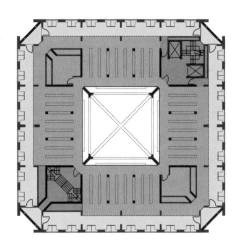

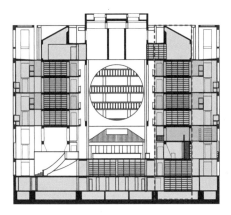

Figure 29: A color scheme similar to Figures 27 & 28 helps link the section to the plans.

relationship of function to form. We have already seen an analysis of Kahn's *Exeter Library* in CHAPTER 9. Our presentation here focuses on simple, judicious use of color and how it can yield diagrammatic insight by highlighting particular design elements.

To a basic plan of the building, we add color to visualize the use of materials. Identifying the brick masonry structure as opaque red and the concrete structure as solid black, displays an important part of the design's spatial character as appropriate visual pattern (27). When we add transparent overlays of ochre – to distinguish the stacks from the study carrels – and lavender – to mark vertical circulation –, we add to our sense of space along the floor plane (28). Observing a similar color scheme in section emphasizes that the mezzanines – which lower the height of the stacks – follow from the same design decisions (29).

Effective color palettes are seldom random. What works in one image may fail in another. Compare the two palettes used in (30) and (31). The red and ochre used in the first illustration allows an easier reading of the plan

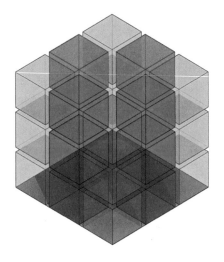

The choice of palette affects the visual outcome of the diagram, often in profound ways.

Figure 30: The red palette makes the nine-square pattern more clearly perceptible on the left.

Figure 31: The blue palette, on the right, shows the formal coherence of the scheme to better effect.

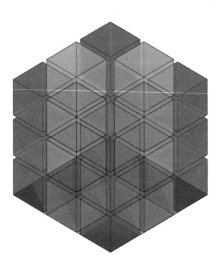

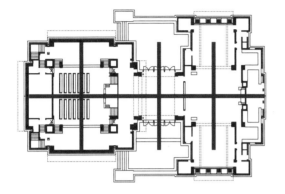

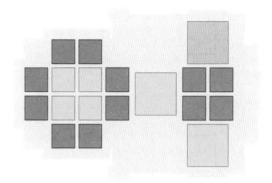

Figure 32: Marking axis and cross-axis with a dominant color, makes a simple diagrammatic declaration within the plan on the left.

Figure 33: A more subtle palette better represents the broader intentions of the diagram of footprint and modular parti of *Unity Temple* shown on the right.

elements. The blue hues in the second illustration, in contrast, create a sense of atmospheric volume rather than structure.

In the end, color is only one component used to structure diagrams. However, it provides subtle and comprehensive choices for visualizing ideas. For example, three diagrams of *Unity Temple* (32–34) document an investigation of the organizing axes of two volumes and their relationship to their connecting space. Unlike the plan and section diagrams of the *Exeter Library*, the sequence attempts an evocative visual analysis without proposing a definitive conclusion.

In the first image (32), the opaque red separates the diagram overlay from the floor plan. The rudimentary color scheme matches the simple intent of calling out the cross-axes. In the next diagram (33), color facilitates a comparison between component spaces and modules along the central axis. Inverting the colors (yellow and blue) at the two cross-axes highlights several differences in deploying modular spaces. Furthermore, reducing the building to its footprint in gray emphasizes the patterned character of the analysis. The final diagram combines the previous two observations, replacing the footprint with a plan overlay and adding a light red cruciform under the modular elements of the sanctuary (34).

Studying the three diagrams should prompt multiple interpretations and that is a reasonable point to conclude an essay on using color in diagrams. Monochromatic diagrams are austere pictures – observations in black and white. Color can underscore that austerity by adding another layer of code to the analysis. However, it can also create nuanced patterns that promote speculation – a boon to insight and the ultimate source of the Big Idea.

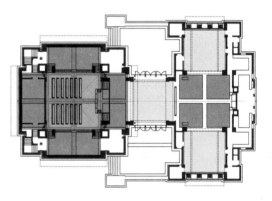

Figure 34: A careful adjustment of the visual structure allows for the plan to act as an overlay of the color fields.

TINT: COLOR + WHITE

SHADE: COLOR + BLACK

TONE: COLOR + GRAY

Figure 35: Illustration of the three color descriptors, tint, shade and tone.

GLOSSARY OF TERMS

CHROMA: Term used to identify the purity or intensity of color – also referred to as SATURATION.

COLOR: An object property producing different sensations in the eye depending on how the object reflects or emits light. The constituents into which light separates in a spectrum. Color includes black and white.

COLOR THEORY: In physics this indicates the prevailing insights into how we describe and account for difference in color.

· In the visual arts, color theory refers to practical understanding that aids color use, as well as general guidelines for mixing and combining color.

DE STJIL: A Dutch artistic movement founded in 1917, also called 'Neo-plasticism', which advocated pure abstraction and universality by a reduction to the essentials of form and color.

HUE: Refers to the attribute of a color that we discern as red, green, etc. Specific hue is a property of its wavelength, and independent of VALUE or CHROMA.

PALETTE: Term that identifies the range of colors used by in a particular image. The word also applies to the fundamental colors used to mix a particular color range.

PSYCHOPHYSICS: The branch of psychology that deals with relationships between physical stimuli and sensory response.

SATURATION: See CHROMA.

SUBTRACTIVE COLOR: The darkening of color as pigment is added, lessening the amount of reflected light.

TINT, SHADE and TONE: Three related terms used primarily in the paint trade but also in general parlance (35).

· Adding white to any base color produces a TINT.

· Adding black to that color creates a SHADE.

· Adding gray – both black and white – results in a TONE.

TRANSPARENCY: Refers to the degree of being transparent – letting light pass through so that you can see objects behind.

VALUE: Indicates the relative light or dark appearance of a color and independent of HUE or CHROMA.

VISIBLE SPECTRUM: The range of the electromagnetic spectrum typically visible to the human eye.

YELLOW TRACE: A range of light-weight translucent drawing paper used in design studio – color range varies from a pale buff to deep canary yellow.

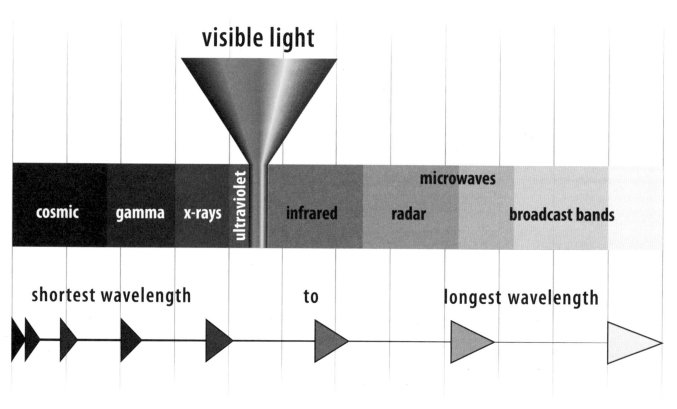

Figure 1: Visible light is a small portion of the electromagnetic spectrum.

DEMONSTRATION 10·1
The language of color

Color as a subject

We observe color throughout our environment. It adds differences and similarities that we sort out for better or worse. Intentional color use can help to structure our experience, while a random confluence – a visual riot – can overwhelm our sense of order and leave us feeling disoriented and lost.

Learning to understand and use color effectively is akin to learning a language. We begin by acquiring a repertoire of discrete experiences, then construct a framework to extrapolate a sense of the whole. This process helps make color simultaneously sensible and knowable. Moreover, while mastery of color can be a life-long pursuit full of nuance and discovery, we can secure reasonable practical knowledge in a relatively short time by understanding something of the language of color.

Color features

Color is a property of light, a perceivable attribute of wavelength. As illustrated in the diagram to the left, we see a limited range of wavelengths of energy (1). We thus distinguish the VISIBLE SPECTRUM from a broader range of wavelengths with other attributes. In the diagram, visible light appears within a continuous sliding scale, from the edge nearest ultraviolet to the infrared. The display mimics the constituent colors of our sun, pure and unmixed.

We encounter light, and therefore color, in three principal modes; as an attribute of surface reflection, as transmission through a medium or as direct emission from a source. Reflective surfaces include both opaque and transparent materials, such as clear glass. Transmissive materials include the same clear glass as well as colored filters and translucent material. Emitted light includes everything from a star to a glowing ember. In all circumstances, however, colors combine by either subtraction or addition.

When white light strikes an object, the color that we perceive reflects from the object's surface while the material absorbs the other wavelengths. This is how paint renders color. As we add one pigment to another, the resultant color represents only the wavelengths not absorbed by the combination. As you add pigment, the colors become darker because there is less light to reflect (2). We refer to this as SUBTRACTIVE COLOR.

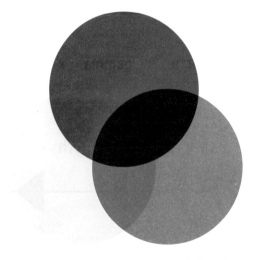

Figure 2: As we mix three pigments – cyan, magenta and yellow – they become darker. This is the principle behind subtractive color.

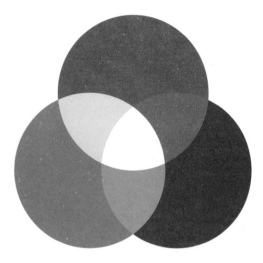

Figure 3: As we mix three lights – red, green and blue – they become lighter. This is the principle behind additive color.

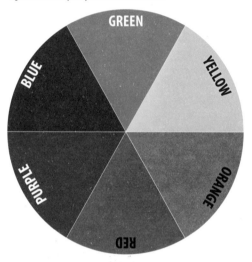

Figure 4: A simple generic color wheel limited to showing hue separated into primary and secondary colors.

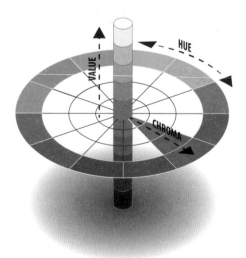

Figure 5: A more advanced color model displaying twelve hues, five chroma and ten degrees of value.

Transparent materials also work by subtraction. They filter light as it passes through, absorbing some wavelengths while transmitting others. However, when transmitted light from three different filters overlaps on a white surface, the colors mix in a distinctly different way – they add rather than subtract. The image to the left illustrates the effect of three lights overlapping (3). The brightness of the color is additive.

Emitted light works additively. It is present in stage lighting, flat screen televisions and the glow of the fireplace. How we respond to our experience of color in the world is the focus of PSYCHOPHYSICS, a subject beyond the scope of this essay.

The reason that we introduce additive and subtractive color – however briefly – is that they play a broad role in understanding color in different media.

Color systems

Estimates of the number of perceptible colors vary from one source to the next, but they all range in the millions – ten million being the number most often given – and none of estimates includes variations of light and dark. So the question arises: where do we start counting?

The image on the left (4) may seem familiar to anyone who attended grade school. It is a simple color wheel representing so-called 'primary' and 'second-ary' colors. The theory behind the wheel holds that mixing the primary colors – red, yellow and blue – yields the secondary colors – purple, green and orange. In a crude fashion, this is true. Colors, when blended, make other colors. How-ever, in this instance, five of the colors correspond to distinct wavelengths of light – purple is the exception. Nevertheless, if all you need to explain is how to blend three crayons, the basic diagram holds.

The six-color color wheel has its roots in another color model, pictured below (5). The illustration shows the inner workings of a color sphere, an ide-alized image of the interaction of color. There are three measurement axes described by the model: HUE, VALUE and CHROMA. The sphere exhibits twelve hues banding it, ten vertical intervals of light and dark values and five radial intervals of chroma – including the gray center. The axes help us to visual-ize a system for defining three variables for every color and the relationships between them.

The geometry of a sphere allows us to view each color property by itself as a logical concept. The sphere's ordering system mirrors our view of the earth with poles, longitude and latitude serving as mapping aids. Although the visi-ble spectrum is linear, the equatorial hues of the model joins its ends. The two colors at the extremes – deep red and violet-blue – blend to create purple. In this way, the model connects the dots.

In a flat array, the extremes remain as ends. Depending on the illustration, purple may appear on either or both ends. In the example on the opposite page, there are two variations – bluish purple and red violet – added as appro-priate conclusions (6). The result is twelve continuous hues.

Directly below the hue spectrum, we find a ten-step chroma display. Seen in the context of continuous movement from neutral gray to pure red, the range of chroma is easier to observe. The third scale in the illustration shows the same red moving from dark to light. While we might probably call the dark red by other names – maroon, brick, etc., – and the lighter colors likely seem to us like pink, to the degree that modern software allows they are all the same hue.

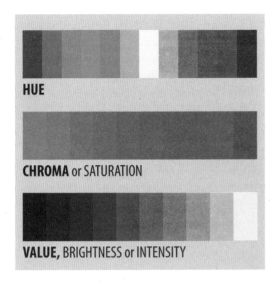

HUE

CHROMA or **SATURATION**

VALUE, BRIGHTNESS or INTENSITY

Figure 6: Linear displays of three variable attributes of color:
- **Hue** changes with relative wavelength.
- **Chroma** identifies the degree of color purity or saturation.
- **Value** names the degree of light and dark exhibited by a sample.

Note that some colors fit the CYMK color space less closely, accounting for minor flaws in color rendition.

Itten's color contrasts

A combined display of hue and value effects produces a color scale such as the one shown to the right (7). Based on the work of Johannes Itten, it depicts twelve hues and twelve values. His book, *The Art of Color,* remains an important treatment. Contemporary reprints may do the original small justice, yet the principles described still serve as practical guidelines.

In his book, Itten describes seven contrasts apparent in color. His contrasts include: hue, light and dark, warm and cool, complementary, simultaneous, saturation and extension. We previously discussed hue, saturation and light and dark as they appear in other models as hue, chroma and value. The contrast of extension concerns responses to specific color groups and, as with psychophysics, is beyond the scope of this essay. The other three contrasts, however, have become part of the common language of color. Each of the three describes a particular quality of hue useful when working with color.

Cool colors, as defined by Itten, tend toward blue, whereas warm colors tend toward red – leftward and rightward respectively in his color scale. As seen in the examples to the right, even red and blue have relative warm and cool manifestations (8). Moreover, in the context of similar colors – or surrounded by gray – the effect of these subtle differences tends to multiply. The gray ground demonstrates simultaneous contrast, illustrating the effects of context on our observation of color.

Complementary contrast describes two phenomena relating hues that sit 180° opposite each other on the color sphere. These colors, when mixed, can form a visible neutral color – a gray without apparent hue (9). In addition, when either of the pair is adjacent to its opposite, the edge of the field proves difficult to focus on. The effect is particularly acute when both colors share the same value and chroma. However, variations of either or both do not completely negate that outcome (10).

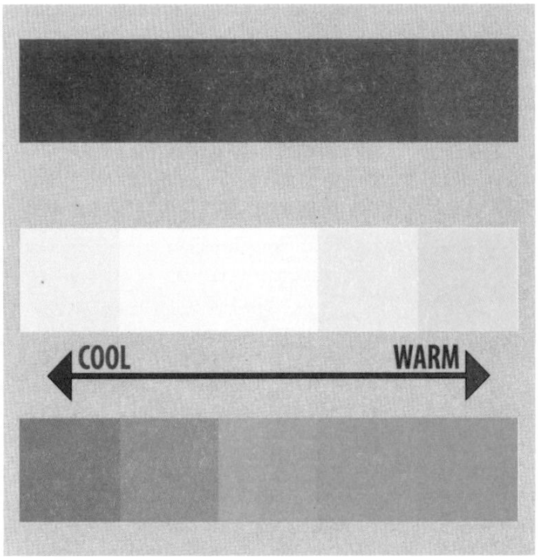

The Munsell color solid

Around 1905, the artist and teacher Alfred Munsell, dissatisfied with available – mostly commercial – systems, began his own color research. In 1924, he published his own treatise on color and from then on was an active color theorist.

Figure 7: Johannes Itten's color scale, displaying twelve hues and twelve degrees of value.

COOL　　　WARM

Figure 8: Thee color groups – red, yellow and blue – showing warm and cool contrast.

BLUE　　　RED-ORANGE

Figure 9: A display of complementary contrast as a scale from blue to red orange.

Figure 10: The red orange complement of the blue field exhibits jarring contrast, even with lessened chroma and value.

*MUNSELL'S HUES, VALUES & CHROMA

Munsell's color wheel identifies ten hues arrayed evenly: red, yellow-red, yellow, green-yellow, green, blue-green, blue, purple-blue, purple, red-purple.

The nomenclature calls out five hues as 'primary':

- Red
- Yellow
- Green
- Blue
- Purple.

The in-between spaces fill with five complementary hues named as combinations:

- Yellow-red
- Green-yellow
- Blue-green
- Purple-blue
- Red-purple.

Munsell's second dimension, value, describes pigment, not light, but corresponds to measurements of lightness in a general way. Similarly his third dimension, chroma, designating the density of colorant, coincides with saturation, the proportion present of the dominant wavelength in light.

His book, *A Grammar of Color,* describes a system of color based on light; using the terms favored at the beginning of this essay – hue, value and chroma.*

Using his own keen eye and test subjects, he proceeded to parse observed color within a 10×10×10 radial grid – a color tree. The result depicts an asymmetric color solid wherein the colors progress in equal visual increments along all three axes, reflecting the color space we perceive rather than imposing an ideal structure without regard to experience. His color solid provides the means for visualizing color relationships that have proven to be remarkably accurate in their structure and logic. Once we are familiar with the fundamental structure, it becomes possible to design or specify specific colors that support practical intention.

In the end, it is the practical dimension of his system that accounts both for its longevity as a reference and its utility as a learning tool. The rational structure demonstrates that the principles for developing useful color palettes need not be arcane or remote.

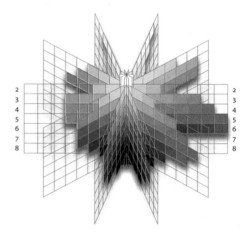

Figure 11: This first view of Munsell's system displays the underlying radial grid and the place of each of ten hues within that framework.

Colors perceived as visually allied in chroma and/or value occupy similar positions on the grid. Certain colors – e.g., the red at 10·5 on the right – are shown to have no visual counterpart amongst the hues.

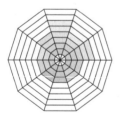

Diagram 12·1: Plan view of colors at values 1 and 2 combined.

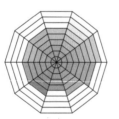

Diagram 12·2: Plan view of colors at value 3.

Diagram 12·3: Plan view of colors at value 4.

Diagram 12·4: Plan view of colors at value 6.

Figure 12: An alternate model of the Munsell color solid, constructed as a series of ten lateral sections. This representation allows easier comparison of colors occupying each value in the color space.

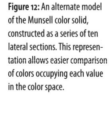

Diagram 12·5: Plan view of colors at values 7 and 8 combined.

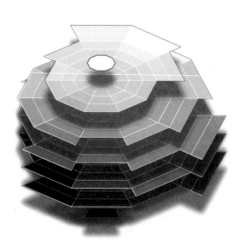

Designing a color palette

Choosing particular colors to mix within a picture creates that image's color palette. We refer to the full range of possible mixtures within as its 'color space'. A video display using red, green and blue phosphors displays in a particular RGB space consisting of additive colors and corresponding to the light-emitting characteristics of the three phosphors. A printed document, such as this page, uses specific cyan, magenta, yellow and black inks to render its contents subtractively within a specific CYMK profile. Both RGB and CYMK generate color spaces capable of complex color rendition within broad spectra.

In painting, color palettes may include mostly muted tones, such as those found in a Rembrandt, or the kinds of vivid hues favored by the Impressionists like Monet and Renoir. The choice ultimately reflects availability – Rembrandt painted before the advent of modern pigments – and intention – Monet's palette in his late career tended to reflect his subject matter.

The construction of a simple palette generally follows four basic descriptions of color harmony, as seen in the illustration to the right (13). The four basic harmonies are: complementary, triad, split triad and tetrad.* These describe the selection of colors relative to hue as seen in a simplified color chart. Because color mixes in a straight line, a palette of complements occurs along the line connecting the two colors. Where three or more colors describe a figure the palette consists of the colors within the perimeter.

Designing a working color space for an image consists of deciding which and how many lines to follow within the field of possibilities. It also allows for electing to use a color outside the general palette as a means of visual emphasis – placing a blue object within a split triad of red-violet, red-orange and green singles out that object.

In the example to the right (15), the chosen colors are imperfect complements and yet their mixtures result in a coherent palette. This is a common strategy for simple color in diagrams and illustrations, as well as in graphic design. The limitation of color to black, white and grays follows the same general structure as complements, resulting in a visually coherent palette. For that reason it is a perfectly reasonable start from which to explore three-color palettes.

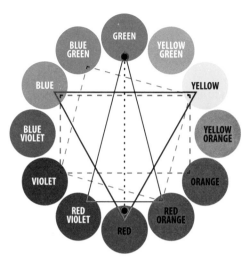

Figure 13: A diagram of harmonic color relationships used to describe color palettes.

*HARMONIC COLOR RELATIONSHIPS.

· Complementary harmony relates any pair of colors directly across from one another on the color wheel, such as red to green – the dotted line.

· A triad defines any three colors separated by 120° such as red, yellow and blue – the black equilateral triangle.

· A split triad or complementary harmony expands a complement to the warm/cool – the gray isosceles triangle.

· Tetrad harmonies are either pairs of expanded complements – the dashed rectangle – or four colors located 90° from one another – the dashed rotated square.

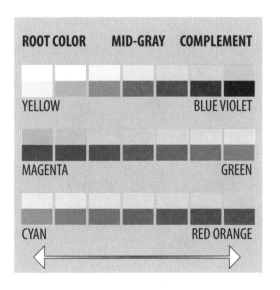

Figure 14: The example shows the three complementary harmonies based on root CYM inks – cyan, magenta and yellow. The complements are mixed equivalents, not separate inks. Note that the absence of black in the mixtures renders the mid-grays not quite perfectly.

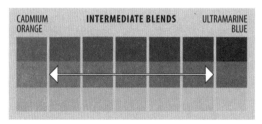

Figure 15: A complementary harmony using pigments that are not exact complements produces visually related tones without a true mid-gray.

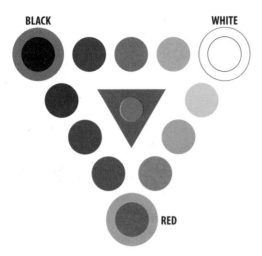

Figure 16: This simple triad of black, white and red shows a surprising range of variation involving tint, shade and tone.

*HIGH AND LOW VALUES

It is important to recall that value works independently from hue or chroma. We tend to think of yellow as light and blues as dark like they appear in the rainbow. In fact, the value of colors found in a prism reflect the amount of the wavelength found in the light source.

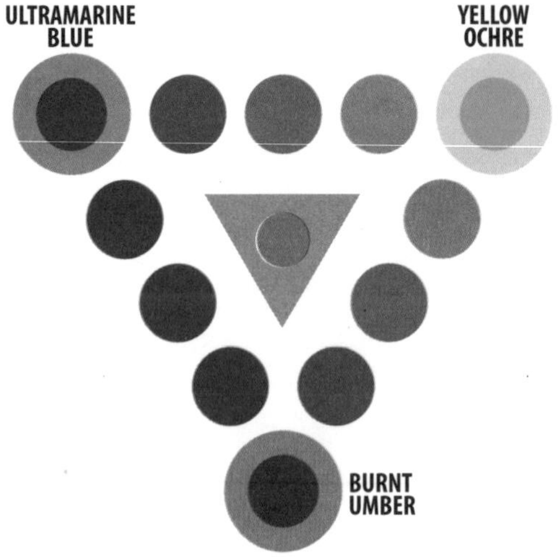

Practical palettes

The first palette to the left adds red to black and white to construe a simple triad (16). The result is a color space with tints, shades, and tones in addition to a complete range of grays. Even this simple structure offers a great degree of subtlety, as demonstrated in the center triangle of the diagram. There, a true gray circle sits surrounded by a tonal red of equal value and, following the principles of simultaneous contrast, appears as a low-chroma complementary blue-green.

The one-hue palette best lends itself to more abstract diagrams. Our second triad replaces the black and white with light and dark yellow hues and the near complement of a warm blue (17). Yellow ochre is a higher-value color of similar hue to burnt umber – itself a dark value of pure yellow. Ultramarine is considered a warm blue by virtue of its reddish cast. The resulting admixtures create a congenial range of natural tints, tones and shades, making this palette a good choice for images presenting light and dark with hints at warm and cool color temperature. The center triangle, in this instance, is a true gray surrounding an admixture of the three colors which exhibits a distinct greenish cast.

Adding a red hue, crimson, changes the palette to a related natural tetrad. In our example, we also exchange the previous blue hue for cerulean – a cooler hue in relationship to the previous ultramarine (18). Versions of this limited palette abound in the oil sketches of the nineteenth century. One of its principle benefits is its congenial admixtures of blended or 'broken' colors capable of yielding subtle shades that mimic natural scenes. These colors make use of the chroma reduction gained by adding burnt umber to their mixture. This makes it an ideal learning palette for quick studies of locale and lighting effects. Adding to this benefit, the presence of variants of three primary colors – a red, a yellow and a blue – allows for a full range of hues albeit somewhat muted.

The fourth palette presented here includes modern versions of the three simple primaries of the generic color wheel – high chroma hues of red, yellow and blue (19). These colors mimic the palette of the De Stijl movement and the common colors of modernist practice. The intent is that they all seem bright and deep, even in their printed versions. The structure of the original palette was symbolic, intent on archetypal pure color rather than in creating useful

Figure 17: (Left) A simple triad of yellow ochre, burnt umber and ultramarine blue shows a nuanced range of warm and cool hue contrast.

Figure 18: (Right) Four colors produce a related tetrad of yellow ochre, burnt umber, cerulean blue and crimson red. Its spectrum includes subtle, blended colors and intermediate, lower chroma mixtures.

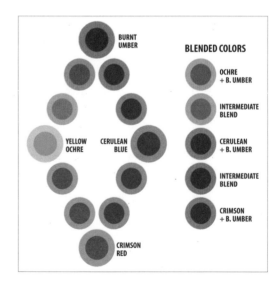

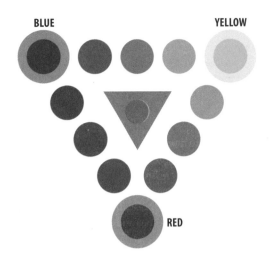

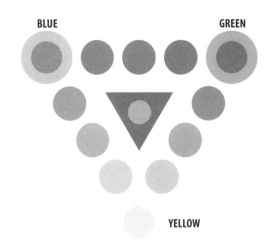

Figure 19: (Left) A modernist variation of the standard printer's triad of blue, yellow and red.

Figure 20: (Right) A close triad of blue, green and yellow allows for a broad exposition of warm and cool related colors.

admixtures. The closest single pigment to the red is naphthol red a modern replacement for cadmium red medium pigments. In the illustration, the color is a mixture of magenta and yellow – 100+50. The yellow of Modernism was most often cadmium yellow medium, here displayed as yellow with magenta added – 100+15. The usual blue in this palette is cobalt blue, warm and nearer to ultramarine than to cerulean. The color shown affects its visual demeanor mixing cyan with magenta – 100+60. When compared to the gray triangle, the central mixed sample demonstrates the dominance of red throughout this palette.

The final palette demonstration shows a triad composed of closely related colors a blue, a green and a yellow (20). Although greenish colors result from mixtures of yellow and blue, greens are also independent wavelengths found in multiple distinct pigments. A comparison of the intermediate colors shown between the yellow and blue with the 'pure' green shows that difference clearly.

The choice of simple palettes ultimately should reflect intention for the task. Stark contrast between components of a diagram calls for similar austerity in color. Figure-ground images display well in black and white. Extending the range to include grays can introduce a lot of subtlety. Adding a single other color as in the first palette can open dramatic possibilities.

Each of the four examples to the right uses one of the four palettes discussed (21–24). The kinds and degrees of contrast remain constant throughout, as much as possible given the rages of the palettes. They hint at the effects possible within the four color palettes discussed.

This demonstration ends with a set of specific color contrasts applied to the same figure-ground strategies shown earlier in black, white and gray (DEMONSTRATION 3·2, pp. 49–52). The examples (25–40) exhibit a range of contrasts and color, some subtle, others less so. Although simple in the extreme, they illustrate the idea that in diagrams, color affects the outcome.

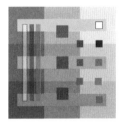

Figure 21: The black, white and red triad remain distinct and separable – a diagrammatic color space.

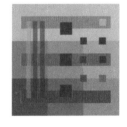

Figure 22: In comparison, the earth-tone colors blend into a unified composition – a pictorial color space that befits images.

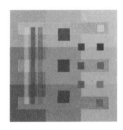

Figure 23: The blue, yellow and red palette slip easily Into a pattern that seems harmonizes and yet yields distinct elements – a graphical color space.

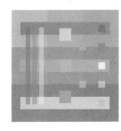

Figure 24: The blue, green and yellow palette of continuous and closely related hues is capable of great subtlety but little contrast – a thematic color space.

USING COLOR

Color affects contrast and can profoundly affect figure-ground perception, even though the composition remains unchanged.

As the composition acquires more elements than a single figure, the importance of the color scheme grows.

Figure 25: Saturation contrast: yellow hues.

Figure 26: Simultaneous contrast: blue-green hue and gray.

Figure 27: Warm-cool contrast: red hues.

Figure 28: Light-dark contrast: orange hues.

Figure 29: Warm-cool contrast: blue hues.

Figure 30: Complementary contrast: blue and orange.

Figure 31: Warm-cool contrast: red hues.

Figure 32: Light-dark contrast: muted yellow hues.

Figure 33: Warm-cool and light-dark contrasts: blue hues.

Figure 34: Complimentary and simultaneous contrasts.

Figure 35: Light-dark complements: red and blue-green.

Figure 36: Warm-cool contrast: green hues.

Figure 37: Light-dark complements: blue and orange.

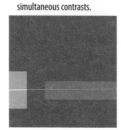

Figure 38: Light-dark complements: blues and orange.

Figure 39: Warm-cool contrast: green tones.

Figure 40: Light-dark contrast: blue hues.

GLOSSARY OF TERMS

ADJACENT: Describes anything – particularly a figure or field – next to or adjoining something else.

ALIGNMENT: Arrangement along a straight line, or in visible relative positions.

ANALYSIS: A detailed examination of the parts or structure of something, the process of separating something into its constituent elements. Derived from the Greek for 'unbundling', it is often contrasted with synthesis.

ARCHETYPE: An ideal form that existing things approach but never duplicate.

ASSEMBLAGE: A number of things gathered together; a collection, group, cluster.

ATTRIBUTES: Qualities or characteristics inherent in any composition.

AXIS: An imaginary straight line that divides any space or figure into two portions. Axes in diagrams take a cue from their mathematical use as reference line for coordinate hierarchies of cause and effect. Thus, in diagrams, multiple axes can identify the interrelationships of movement, SPATIAL HIERARCHY and grain.

AXONOMETRIC: A type of paraline drawing; an orthographic projection of an object – such as a building – on a plane inclined all three principal axes. Alludes to the three-dimensional but without perspective. Architects often use the term in referring to the PLAN OBLIQUE convention.

BALANCE: A distribution of elements visually equals to each other. Balance may be symmetrical or asymmetrical.

· SYMMETRICAL balance is equal in weight and tone on both sides of a composition.

· ASYMMETRICAL balance is unequal in position or intensity using the tension between positive elements and negative space to achieve parity.

BEAMS: Linear elements, positioned horizontally.

BIG IDEA: The primary idea or conceit governing the development of a particular design. Architects often call this the PARTI or main concept of a project.

BIM: Acronym for Building Information Modeling, a term that defines processes of generating and managing building data, generally achieved with the use of parametric modeling software.

BOUNDARY: Any line that marks the limits of an area, a boundary divides a figure from its ground.

· In diagrams, BOUNDING LINES (or BOUNDARY LINES) extend a figure's boundary past the figure and across the ground to provide visual evidence of formal influence – most often alignment.

BRIDGED: A composition in which two or more elements are joined together by a single, linking element.

CANON: In the sense in which we use it here, a list of literary or artistic works established by long-standing practice as being of the highest quality. More generally, the term describes a general law, rule, principle, or criterion by which something is judged.

CARTESIAN GRID: Also called a universal grid, it represents infinite lines that cross one another at right angles at regular – sometimes numbered – intervals to precisely locate and measure objects and space.

CENTER: A point equally distant from all sides, the middle point.

CHROMA: Term used to identify the purity or intensity of color – also referred to as SATURATION.

COFFERED CEILING: A ceiling defined by an articulated relief pattern, usually conforming to an orthogonal grid determined by the spacing of primary and secondary spanning members.

COLOR: An object property producing different sensations in the eye depending on how the object reflects or emits light. The constituents into which light separates in a spectrum. Color includes black and white.

COLOR THEORY: In physics this indicates the prevailing insights into how we describe and account for difference in color.

· In the visual arts, color theory refers to practical understanding that aids color use, as well as general guidelines for mixing and combining color.

COLUMNS: Linear elements, positioned vertically.

COMPOSITION: The elements that comprise any intentional arrangement, form or shape. The formal configuration of parts within a whole.

CONCEPT: An abstract idea or mental picture of a group or class of objects, formed by combining all their aspects.

CONTRAST: An abrupt shift in weight and/or intensity.*

CONTEXT: In architecture, the circumstances of a form or design, may include environment, setting or formal composition.

CROSS-SECTION: The surface or shape exposed by making a straight cut through something, occurring usually at right angles to an axis. Also refers to any diagram or drawing illustrating what the cut would reveal. See also SECTION.

DATUM: A reference point or plane against which all relative positions in a composition are measured and regarded.

DE STJIL: A Dutch artistic movement founded in 1917, also called 'Neo-plasticism', which advocated pure abstraction and universality by a reduction to the essentials of form and color.

DEFINED and IMPLIED FIELDS: Terms used to distinguish kinds of related boundaries and corners found within compositions.

· Defined fields directly correspond to an existing edges.

· Implied fields correspond to locations inferred by existing pattern and measure either through interpolation or extrapolation.

DESIGN THINKING: A practice for discerning, analyzing and composing systems of order, wherein critical assessment is balanced with generative and iterative creation.

DOMINANT and SUBORDINATE: Terms used to describe elements as if within a perceived visual hierarchy.

· A dominant figure appears as the most influential field in a composition.

· A subordinate figure acts seems as less influential or dependant on another figure or field in the configuration.

DUCK and DECORATED SHED: Terms used by Robert Venturi and Denise Scott-Brown in *Learning from Las Vegas*. One of two strategic categories for architectural form. The term 'duck' identifies any building whose function manifests in a particular form. In contrast, a unified volume that denotes function through ornament or tectonic expression results in a 'decorated shed'.

*THE LANGUAGE OF CONTRAST

In describing contrast of objects and their context, we encounter several terms that overlap in meaning.

· The term FIGURE-GROUND denotes the perception of an intelligible picture or pattern of organization by distinguishing objects from the background in an image. Architectural plans often borrow from mapping convention the particular use of figure-ground to depict buildings within a setting.

· Designers refer to NEGATIVE SPACE to identify compositional balance particularly when the space, not the object, presents itself as the more dominant shape. In that context, POSITIVE SPACE distinguishes the role of the object shape or form.

ÉCOLE DES BEAUX-ARTS: Generally considered the first 'school' of architecture, it developed many of the formal rituals and terminology of architectural education. Responsible for a corresponding 'style' of public works of architecture, which held sway in Northern Europe and America throughout much of the nineteenth and early twentieth centuries.

EDGE: The outside limit of an object, area, or surface farthest away from the center. Often synonymous with BORDER.*

ELEMENTS: The major components of a composition: color, value, line, shape, form, texture, and space.   .

ENCLOSURE: That which is contained within defined boundaries.

ENFILADE: A suite of adjacent rooms with aligned doorways or other openings.

ESQUISSE: From the Italian *schizzo*, for sketch, the initial sketch or thought of a design. Used in conjunction with PARTI.

EXPRESSION: Manner or means of representation. The process of manifesting qualities by appearance or other forms of evidence.

EXTERNAL ASSEMBLAGE: One of two general expressions of the design process, the other being INTERNAL DIVISION; also defined as complexity without or outward accretion.

FIBONACCI SEQUENCE: A sequence of whole numbers in which each number is the sum of the two preceding numbers: 1, 1, 2, 3, 5, 8, etc. As the sequence continuos, the ratio of each Fibonacci number to the previous one tends toward the GOLDEN RATIO.

FIELD: In visual composition, any area observed as an independent region. In gestalt, both figures and ground are potential fields for other elements.

FIGURE: Descriptive shape or form that appears in contrast to a visual ground – as in FIGURE-GROUND. Also used to refer to any distinct element in a composition.

FIGURE–GROUND: The perception of images via distinguishing objects from background by contrast.
  · Also refers to contexts wherein the distinction is ambiguous.

FOOTPRINT: In architectural convention, the reduction of buildings to the plan outline of the entire building without interior detail.

FORMAL: Of and relating to form and composition.

FREE PLAN: A floor plan with non load-bearing interior partitions. A product and conceit of Modernist architecture, wherein a structural frame relieves the exterior envelope and interior walls from supporting a building's mass.

GESTALT: In psychology, an ordered whole that we perceive as greater than the sum of its parts. The overall form that we perceive rather than the components that we assess.

GOLDEN RATIO: An irrational mathematical constant, approximately 1.618, its geometric expression – the golden rectangle – has traditionally been considered aesthetically pleasing since Greek mathematicians first described it. Other names and symbols frequently used for the golden ratio are the golden section, golden mean and the Greek letter PHI.

GRAIN: Term used in design to describe apparent formal direction or orientation of objects and space.
  · CROSS-GRAIN: Describes the orientation or implied movement of figure, field or element that runs counter to its context's apparent direction.

GRID: A network of lines crossing each other to form a series of similar units, usually squares or rectangles.
  · A RELATIONAL GRID results from the geometric subdivision of space relative to an initial field.

*ABOUT EDGE
  · A BORDER is that part of a surface nearest to its boundary. It may also refer to the boundary line itself.
  · A MARGIN is a border of a definite width usually distinct in appearance from what it encloses. Distinct from border, it commonly refers to a void around a shape or form such as the margin on a page.
  · Both terms refer to something circumscribed, while EDGE refers to only a part of a *perimeter,* or the line where two planes converge.

· A UNIVERSAL GRID represents infinite lines that cross one another at right angles at regular – sometimes numbered – intervals to precisely locate and measure objects and space.

GROUND: In composition, the largest field in which figures may interact.

HALF-WALL: A wall roughly half as high as a full-height partition.

HIERARCHY: The order of dominance, or priority, of the various elements within the composition.

HUE: Refers to the attribute of a color that we discern as red, green, etc. Specific hue is a property of its wavelength, and independent of VALUE or CHROMA.

HYBRID: A thing made by combining two distinct or different elements.

IDEA: A mental event about a possible course of action, often synonymous with the aim or purpose of that action. In its broadest sense, an idea can reflect concepts, opinions or feelings about something as probable, desirable or possible.*

INHABIT: To dwell in, occupy as an abode. To permanently or habitually live in, to reside in.

INTENTION: Reference to a plan or aim. Intentions may directly reflect the central idea or may serve to define an element's relationship to that end, including being distinct in method or form.

INTERNAL DIVISION: One of two general expressions of the design process, the other being EXTERNAL ASSEMBLAGE; also defined as complexity within or inward articulation.

ISO 216: International standard for paper sizes derived from the ROOT 2 or LICHTENBERG RATIO.

ISOMETRIC: A technical or architectural drawing that incorporates a visual projection representing the three principal dimensions along three axes set at 120° to one another. Isometric drawings display consistent scale for all linear measurements.

LINE: A long narrow mark that divides, penetrates, encloses, or defines form or space.

MASS: The visual or physical weight of an element or the collective weight of a group of elements.

MEASURE: Comprises the dimensional attributes of form and space.

MATTER: The 'stuff' of the physical world, material.

MODEL: A translation of an idea or object into another medium of particular characteristic for the purposes of study and analysis. For those purposes models place select properties into an appropriate framework.

MODULE: Standard unit of measure or proportion used in the design of a particular project. The module can be a unit of length, area, or volume.

MOTIF: A distinct group of simple elements that creates a single impression. Motifs most often accrue in larger, more complex compositions. Thus, two walls abut to create a corner and four corner motifs aggregate to form a square composition. The term also describes thematic variations perceived among formal sequences, for example a closed corner, a folded corner and an open corner.

· MOTIVIC: Of or relating to a motif.

NINE-SQUARE A square array, three squares to each side; a common figure used in architectural composition.

OCCUPATION: The action or fact of living in or using a building or other space.

ORDER: The organizational principle of any composition.

ORGANIZATION: The structure or arrangement of objects in a group or system. Related to COMPOSITION.

*ABOUT IDEAS

The term IDEA generally refers to something either perceived through the senses, visualized or imagined. It is a comprehensive word that includes most aspects of mental activity.

· In contrast, a THOUGHT results from meditation, reasoning or other intellectual activity.

· The term NOTION denotes any vague or capricious or unreasoned idea.

· We define any widely held idea that identifies something particular as a CONCEPT.

· External phenomena often trigger an IMPRESSION, something less mentally rigorous.

ORIENTATION: The particular placement of an element, form or building in relationship to something else. In architecture the something often relates to site constraints including, but not limited to, the sun, topography, adjacencies and boundaries.

ORTHOGRAPHIC PROJECTION: A drawing convention representing three-dimensional objects as two-dimensional; a form of parallel projection wherein projection lines are perpendicular to the picture plane.

OVERLAPPED: A composition of two or more superimposed elements.

PALETTE: Term that identifies the range of colors used by in a particular image. The word also applies to the fundamental colors used to mix a particular color range.

PARALINE DRAWING: A method of representing three-dimensional objects in which all parallel lines remain parallel, vertical lines remain vertical, and all elements stay true to scale.

PARTI: A diagram that delineates the dominant organizational or formal concept governing an architectural scheme. From French, translates roughly as 'option' or 'course of action' – what we might call the Big Idea.

PATH: Any route defined for or made by continual passage fulfils the literal, commonplace meaning. More broadly it describes the course or direction in which something moves or can move.
   · A path axis is an axis aligned with the grain of a path
   · Path surface and path volume are the two- and three-dimensional attributes of a path.

PATTERN: The repetition of any element in sequence or arrangement in a design.

PHI: Greek letter used in modern mathematics to symbolize the GOLDEN RATIO.

PLACEMENT: Putting something in a particular place. In design placement generally reflects particular reasoning and formal logic in combination.

PLAN, SECTION and ELEVATION: Three drawing types commonly used in architecture, see main glossary for more specific definitions.

PLAN OBLIQUE: An axonometric projection on an inclined plane – most often rotated 30°, 45° or 60° – with both true measure and true angle maintained in plan. Vertical edges remain vertical.
   · In cavalier projection, lengths along the vertical axis remain without scale.
   · A cabinet projection scales the receding axis to seem less distorted.

PLANES: Two-dimensional elements within a three-dimensional composition.

POCHÉ: The filled-in areas of a plan or section drawing. The convention reveals the parts of a building cut by an imaginary section plane.
   · Giambattista Nolli's figure-ground drawing of Rome employed contrasting fields of black and white space to represent architectural objects and their context.
   · Beaux-Arts drawings used black poché to distinguish walls and columns from (white) space.

POSITION: The placement of elements in a specific area. Position demands an understanding of space as an organized total to which elements are applied according to the various principles of design.

POSITIVE and NEGATIVE SPACE: Terms used in discussing overall organization of an image or form. Related to FIGURE-GROUND.

PRECEDENT: An example to be followed or copied. In architecture, an exemplary project, usually influential and closely studied, and often emulated.

PRINCIPLE: A proposition that serves as the foundation for a chain of reasoning. Also refers to a theory with multiple applications in a practice. Thus a PRIN-

CIPLE OF ORGANIZATION identifies the basis for a fundamental attribute that determines the arrangement of objects in a collective.

PROCESSION: The action of moving forward in orderly succession in a formal or ceremonial way.

PROGRAM: A project-specific list of spaces and functions created to guide and govern the subsequent design of a building.

PROOF BY INFINITE DESCENT: A type of mathematical proof used to establish the existence of irrational numbers.

PROPORTION: The relationship of one thing to another in terms of quantity, size, or number; the ratio. The comparative measurement of parts to a whole.

PROXIMITY: Nearness in space to another element.

PSYCHOPHYSICS: The branch of psychology that deals with relationships between physical stimuli and sensory response.

PURPOSE: The identification of ends reflecting a sense of final state or goals.

REGULATING LINES: In drawing, this indicates any guide line that aids in determining placement or dimension of an element or figure in a defined area. Typically attributed to the diagonal lines drawn across any geometric field and used to determine proportion or dimension within a relational grid.

RELATIONSHIP: The connecting principle shared between or among elements.

REPETITION: The recurring use of the same element or theme.

REPETITIVE UNIT: Module or some other component defined by its multiple iterations.

REPRESENTATION: A description or portrayal of something in a particular way.
- A depiction in a in a picture or model in a visual medium.
- A likeness or reproduction of something.

RHYTHM: The moving force, or flow, which connects elements within a composition.

ROOT 2 or LICHTENBERG RATIO: The positive algebraic number which, when multiplied by itself, equals the number 2; an irrational number approximately equal to 1.414. The length of a diagonal across a square with sides one unit in length.

SATURATION: See CHROMA.

SCHEMA: The representation of a plan or concept in the form of an outline or model. The plural form is SCHEMATA.

SECTION: A general term used in architecture to refer to viewing the CROSS-SECTION of a building or object in the context of parallel surfaces behind the section cut. Plan drawings are usually devised to include horizontal surfaces such as floors, doors and windowsills that are below the cut line.

SEPARATE: Non-contiguous elements within a composition.

SHAPE: The outline of an area or figure (compare to FORM).*

SOLID: Any unbroken area that has a definite shape.

SPACE: The area in which all elements act and occur.

SPATIAL HIERARCHY: Term used to identify the formal pattern in architecture wherein constructed space manifests a sequence of importance.

STRATEGY: A plan of action designed to achieve a major or overall end.

SUBTRACTIVE COLOR: The darkening of color as pigment is added, lessening the amount of reflected light.

SYMMETRY: Exactly similar parts facing each other or around an axis.

SYNERGY: An interaction of two or more substances that yields a combined effect greater than the sum of the parts. The term has a shady life in the language of corporate aspirations, but in design it succinctly describes gestalt laws at work.

*ABOUT SHAPE
- SHAPE and FORM, commonly used interchangeably, usually refer to two- and three-dimensional objects respectively.
- AREA refers to the defined interior of a shape, whereas VOLUME refers to the spatial content found in a three-dimensional form.
- MASS, in contrast, refers to the solid content of a form.

TACTIC: An action or strategy carefully planned to achieve a specific end, a component of an overall STRATEGY.

TECTONIC: Short-form for architectonic, describing a clearly articulated structure, or relationships among structural and material systems.

TEXTURE: Interwoven patterns of tones or surfaces.

TINT, SHADE and TONE: Three related terms used primarily in the paint trade but also in general parlance.
- · Adding white to any base color produces a TINT.
- · Adding black to that color creates a SHADE.
- · Adding gray – both black and white – results in a TONE.

TRANSPARENCY: Refers to the degree of being transparent – letting light pass through so that you can see objects behind.

TURNED PATH: A common MOTIF of Modernist architecture, in opposition to traditional linear axiality.

TURNED SPACE: A common MOTIF of Modernist architecture, characterized by an iterative, peripatetic, yet fluid unfolding of a building's spaces.

TYPE: The general form, structure, or character distinguishing a particular kind, group, or class. In architecture, a taxonomy of buildings, using PROGRAM and function as primary criteria for classification.

VALUE: An element of art that refers to the lightness or darkness of a color or tone. Value is an especially important element in works of art when color is absent, as with gray scale images.

VISIBLE SPECTRUM: The range of the electromagnetic spectrum typically visible to the human eye.

X·Y·Z GRID AXIS: The three-dimensional network of intersections established by a universal or Cartesian grid.

YELLOW TRACE: A range of light-weight translucent drawing paper used in design studio – color range varies from a pale buff to deep canary yellow.

TINT: COLOR + WHITE

SHADE: COLOR + BLACK

TONE: COLOR + GRAY

INDEX